FROM
PAIN *to*
PARADISE
MY LIFE

Antonia Wasielewski

WESTBOW
PRESS®
A DIVISION OF THOMAS NELSON
& ZONDERVAN

WestBow Press books may be ordered through booksellers or by contacting:

WestBow Press
A Division of Thomas Nelson & Zondervan
1663 Liberty Drive
Bloomington, IN 47403
www.westbowpress.com
844-714-3454

ISBN: 979-8-3850-0921-3 (sc)
ISBN: 979-8-3850-0922-0 (e)

Library of Congress Control Number: 2023918970

Print information available on the last page.

WestBow Press rev. date: 10/25/2023

GLOSSARY

Cast of Characters

Yuzia Agurzynski
Anastasia
Aniela
Antony
Bakers
Mrs. Bates
Bella
John Blazeski
W. Bliss Foundry
Bogusz
Mr. Beigert
Mr. Brigers
Brzuska
Mick Burczynski
(Buszki)
Mrs. Chase
Dilia
Aniela Firgolski
Jadwiga
Aniela Marunoski

Mrs. Cirzinski
Pani Cizeski (Mrs.)
Pan Cizeski (Mr.)
Constancia
Fagon Foundry
Felix
Dr. Finke
Wladek Firgolski
Flinta
Mrs. Flynn
Frana (Frania)
Mr. Gaintshimer
Frank Gawronski
Geneveve
Goldsmith
Detinning Co.
Graboska
Greligh
Stanley Gryczeski
Wladek Gurtaloski

Dr. Holloway
Ignate
Jadwiga
Jan
Janicki
Jankoski
Uncle Julius
Mrs. Just
Kaminski
Wladek Kempcinski
Mr. Kizer
Jozef Kowaleski
Jasiek Kowalski
Kostusia
John Kwiatkowski
Priest Kwiatkowski
Tilly Lada
Lazaroski
Dr. Mahoney
Mr. Malone

Marion
Aunt Mary (Maryanna)
Mr. McCormick
Mr. McFadden
Mrs. Michalski
Mr. Micik
Motileski
Mrs. Nathy
Mudrzicki
Rozia Mutkowska
Navaroski
Pan Navatkowski
Nawrocki
Priest Nowak
Miss O'Donnol
Miss O'Gara
Mrs. Locke
Uncle Palinski
Mrs. Parks
Pani Piekaski
Adam Petrowski
Pickarski
Dr. Piskorski

Jozef Pivnicki
Lady Pivnicki
Pukarski
Mrs. Roberts
Rosalia Stella (Rosalie)
Mr. Ross (the gardener)
Sabo
Dr. Sexsmith
John Smidt
Smolinski
Mrs. Sprague
Stas
Stash
Adam Stawski
Stella
Sulinski
Joe Sullivan
Mrs. Sullivan
Reverend Swider
Mrs. Szeleski
Uncle Symon
Mrs. Szymanski

Teofil
Tonia (Tosia)
Toshulma
Maris Tyburski
Ursula
Victoria (Victa) (Vicky)
Wagner
Antonia Wasielewski
John Wasielewski
Stanislaus Wasielewski
Wawroski
Charles Winowiecki
Jozef Wisniewski
Wladka
Wladek (Willy)
Priest Wrzeciono
Wladek Zdanoski
Mrs. Zdrojeski
Stanley Zegler
Mr. Zloty

DEDICATION

To my dear mom, Rosalie Wasielewski Golonka, for her care, patience, and dedication to grandma her whole life - and now in death, mom's desire to see grandma's life story in book as grandma always said she wanted it to be.

Antonia S. Golonka
Granddaughter

Contents

ACKNOWLEDGEMENT

People who listened to my grandma relate her life to them always told her she should write a book. Grandma often agreed and said she should. We never thought much of it because grandma was always writing something - poetry and songs she made up as she went along. In 1998, Nearly nine years after my grandma died, my mother, Rosalie Golonka, decided to go through the songs, poems and stories grandma had left with her. Sentimentally digging through the boxes she was astounded to find that grandma had indeed written much of her life story. As mother leafed through the old, handwritten manuscript pages she realized no one would be able to understand the broken Polish/English and misspelled words. So mom began to type them into a readable form.

One day while visiting my mother, now 82 years old herself, I found her typing and asked what the project was. She told me how amazed she was to find over 458 handwritten pages of grandma's life on 8 ½ x 11" lined notebook paper, among the other original writings by my grandmother. I was even more amazed than she was, especially since mother told me she had been typing these handwritten memoirs for over a month.

It struck me that here Rosalie Golonka, my mother, who is Antonia Wasielewski's eldest daughter was taking the time to type from Grandma's original, handwritten manuscript on that same little, old manual portable typewriter that Grandma often used to type her songs and poems. This was no small task for my mother, since Grandma wrote as she spoke, in broken, ungrammatical English mixed in with a little mother-tongue Polish!

I told mom the document really should be typed into computer, put on diskette, put into book form and copyrighted to preserve the history and original story. Mom agreed, and here is that story. In my liberty to faithfully recreate the document, I have tried very hard to keep the flavor of the story so the broken English could still come through, yet revising the spelling and grammar so it would be readable, creating a book.

This story is the story of a woman who was born into adversity and overcame with the most positive attitude and loving personality of anyone I have ever heard of outside of Mother Theresa.

Since my grandmother lived with our family as we three girls were growing up on the farm, she was a second mother to us, and was the greatest influence on my life. To this day I find myself quoting her wisdom and quaint peasant philosophies which still work for me.

I only hope that along with her name, some of her persona rubs off on me throughout my life. Her easy-going, yet firm nature and unwavering faith in God her Savior were solid. In spite of her "misery" that followed her there was never a doubt that in the end everything will turn out the way it is meant to be. This should be a gift everyone is blessed with.

Thank you mother for giving me this privilege of sharing and compiling this life story of the woman we both loved, your mother and my grandmother, Antonia Wasielewski, and blessing me with ownership of the story.

In spite of the hardship in her life, Grandma lived to nearly 104 and died in March 1990, just six weeks before her 104th birthday. If grandma were alive today I think she would be pleased to know that finally her life story has been told in written format.

Antonia S. Golonka
Granddaughter

PREFACE

1950 - My Desire to Write My Story

(by Antonia Wasielewski)

When I was thirty years old I wanted to write a story, but I was laughed at and called all kinds of names, so I didn't write one then, but it was gnawing at my mind, and I wished I could.

At that time I was buying *True Story* magazines, and the more I read them the more I wished I could write a story too. Once I picked up the nerve to write to Mr. McFadden[1], asking him how I could write my own "true story". I received a reply from him telling me to write everything that has happened in my life, and the way I wrote it would be the way it would be printed and nothing would be changed. Instead of encouraging me, this scared me more. I thought if I wrote everything and it would be printed as I wrote it, then all who were my enemies would see their names in the story, and I had better move to the South Pole. I wouldn't mind if my friends were mentioned, but not my enemies.

Then I just bowed my head down and sighed. To write stories you have to be educated. You have to pass the grade in schools to know the right words and where to put them. My husband John was

---

[1] Mr. McFadden apparently was an editor at *"True Story"* magazine.

right. I am just a dummy. I never went to any school, never had a chance to get any kind of education. Anyway, if I wanted to write a true story some people may not like it as I might not like it if they wrote a true story and included parts about me in the story. People may say this or that shouldn't be brought out into the open, but what is the use of writing a true story if you hide the most horrible things that make you suffer the greatest in that story? I wouldn't knock anybody or revenge against anyone to hurt them. I would just write true facts and happenings in my life as I was growing day by day and year by year.

So I would ask my dear readers if you find some words misplaced or misspelled or even missing, to please overlook it, as I have no formal education and no chance to get one. As my husband said, all I was good for was to wash the diapers all day and wash the dishes all night.

Now I am 64[2] years old and have been sick in bed for over six months with ulcers in my ankles and rheumatism in my arms and no income of any kind. So I am taking courage to write my story in hope that it will be accepted.

---

[2]   This would have been the year 1950.

Chapter 1

1886 - The Beginning

Misery was born the day I was born, and followed me throughout life – or it did at first. It followed my grandmother and my mother before I was born from as much as I could remember from what mother told me. I was the youngest one of seven children and had the chance to stay with her the longest.

I don't know much about my father's side of the family, but mother's parents were well-to-do people. While her mother lived they had a nice home, plenty of land, a power flour mill and two wind mills. My grandfather thought he was rich enough to spend his life taking it easy and having lot of fun, leaving grandma to take care of the mills and the fields. Grandma worked hard and as long as she could stand it, but grandma was failing in health. When the workers didn't see grandpa around for weeks at a time, they didn't work either.

Grandpa lost the two mills and that woke him up a little. There were two girls, not big enough to help around. When little brother came, grandma died at his birth. Grandpa couldn't get along by himself and got another wife and then lost the power mill. The other woman took control of the land *AND* grandpa, and so he signed what was left to her.

At that time my aunt was sixteen, my mother was ten and their little brother was two years old. The stepmother told grandpa to put the children out somewhere or get out with them. Grandpa knew he couldn't take care of the children, so he crawled to his wife.

He let my Aunt Mary marry a man twice her age, and the man let my aunt take my mother and the baby brother with her and raise them until they were old enough to work for themselves. My uncle wasn't a rich man, but he had a life-long position with rich land owners because he was raised by them. My uncle's family's land was confiscated by the Russian government and all the strong men folks were sent to Siberia. This left the women and children to live as they could, in God's care. As my uncle was left without parents, the rich landowners in a place called Sosnova took my uncle as a companion for their baby boy (named Sir Pivnicki). The boys were about the same age, and they grew up inseparable. As my uncle grew up he was always given work according to his age, and he lived to eighty.

During my uncle's life he had a chance to help others who were in need. When my mother was old enough to work for herself she was working as a cook in Lady Pivnicki's home and met a boy two years younger than herself who was working there also. They fell in love and got married.

After they married, Russia took him into the army, since at that time every man had to put in eight years of service in the army. My father was lucky that he wasn't sent out on the Turkish border for 25 years where his sister's husband was serving. When his sister's husband came home from the army he didn't enjoy his life long afterwards. He took sick and laid in bed for 17 years before he died.

My father served in the army just a couple miles away in a city name Sierpc and he was allowed to spend furloughs with mother. He was in the army band and played a flute. When father was released from the service he was shifting from place to place looking for work. Mother said that father was a good man when he was home, but easily influenced by other people.

Russians and Poles never liked each other then as they don't like each other now-a-days. Poles weren't allowed to have their own schools, so the villagers there wanted to organize a committee to demand a Polish school in our biggest village, Sosnovo. Before they had a chance to go any further with the committee some of them had a chance to skip out of the country before the Russians got them. My father had a sister living in Germany and an older brother in America. He skipped away to Germany and wrote to his brother Symon. Uncle Symon sent my father a ship card and got him over to this country (America). That was in the year 1887.

When my father left us to go to America (as I was told by my dear mother) I was then not quite one year old. Four children had died when father was home and mother had three of us left to raise. The oldest one, Maryanna, ten years old; Victoria, three years; and I (Antonia) was one year old. I thank God as I am writing this story, that both my sisters are living and look fine[3].

In Europe, as in America, when you are poor you work hard and struggle and you are still poor. Thank God, that now-a-days in our beloved America I'm proud to be a citizen. People here get more from Social Security and different organizations, and children get free schooling. In Poland, under the Russian rulers, the poorer the Poles were the better Russia liked it. The less education the Poles had the better. Russia didn't want smart people because they might find out what was going on in the country.

But going back to where I came from, the place where I was born was called Zamosc. It was over the bridge from Sosnova, and my mother was working hard to keep us alive after father went to America. Years after father left, mother got a letter from him. Father was asking if he would be allowed to return to Poland, but mother was told by the higher officials that father had no chance and as soon as he put a foot on Polish land he would be nabbed and jailed. From then on mother never saw or heard from father. Later on mother wrote to Uncle Symon inquiring if he knew where father was. Uncle Symon wrote to mother reminding her that she knew Frank was shifting from place to place when he was dragging her around, and he was still doing the same thing here. Uncle Symon

---

[3]   Maryanna and Victoria predeceased Antonia at the ages of 94 and 96.

said he couldn't keep track of father and told her not to waste her tears for him because he wasn't worth it.

Mother was doing the best she could to keep us together, but it was hard work. One day Aunt Mary came to visit us and asked mother if she wanted to give Maryanna to her. Mother knew that Aunt Mary and her husband had brought mother up so she was sure that Maryanna would be all right in their hands. So Aunt Mary took Maryanna and raised her as her own. Aunt Mary and her husband never had children, but they were always raising somebody else's children.

Next went Victoria (who was like my second mommy). When mother went to work she locked the door on the outside for the whole day, and Victa, as I called her, was taking care of me. She did this until she was six years old.

Then one of my father's distant nephews (Peter) who was running his small piece of land with his sister Frana, was called to serve in the Russian army. Peter asked mother to let Victa stay with Frana for the years he would be in the army. The service in the Russian army was shortened to five years (instead of eight) so Victa had a home for five years while helping Frana with housework and taking care of geese in the summer.

With only one of us left (me) mother couldn't always leave me home. So she was taking me with her as she worked until one day my grandpa was thrown out of his home by his second wife and his second set of three children. He was ashamed to go to Aunt Mary, and came to my poor mother. Mother now had one more mouth to feed, but then grandpa was now watching me.

One day he was watching me outdoors when Gypsies came to our village. We had a lot of Gypsies who came around the villages and we had to watch everything from a needle to a cow and mostly chickens, so they wouldn't steal them. We owned only one pet hen. Mrs. Cirzinski sold it to me for one groszy (penny). Grandpa was watching the Gypsies and a Gypsy woman was watching my only pet hen and my best and last dress on the clothesline. When the Gypsies went away, my hen and my dress went with them. Grandpa was sorry. I cried more for the hen than for the dress because the hen laid an egg every day and proudly called out "kto, kto, totak!" Another hen Mrs. Cirzinski gave me for nothing didn't want to go in grandpa's bed and lay eggs.

In the winters mother couldn't go out to work much, so she was taking in spinning and knitting for the villagers. Then I was with mother and we both were glad to be near each other. Winters were very cold with a lot of snow. So much that the forest animals were coming to the villages looking for something to eat. If it was only a fox, it sometimes ate sheep or a pig, chickens or geese. But if it was a wolf, it looked for bigger game. There was so much snow and cold that wild rabbits were eating from small boy's hands to get food.

It was one of that kind of winter my grandpa got sick and my mother got sick. It was just three days before Christmas. Everybody was busy working hard so they could enjoy the holidays. No one noticed us.

Mother was getting worse and she worried that we didn't have enough turf in our little hall. We kept the turf up in the attic. Turf burns like coal, but it is dug out from a swampy field and cut like the size of bricks and dried for fuel. Mother wanted to get some more down from the attic, but she couldn't make it. She was half way up on the ladder and fainted and fell down. How long she laid there I don't know. When I opened the door I saw her gathering herself up. Mother didn't remember how she got up and how she got to bed with my little help, but she got to bed and until the New Year she didn't know, nor care, I suppose, that the world existed.

Grandpa and I were all right until what was in the pot on the stove was finished. I fed grandpa and myself. Mother didn't want to even answer when I wanted to feed her, but when the pot was empty, neither grandpa nor I could fix anything for ourselves. When the fire went out, grandpa was too weak to make a fire and I didn't know how, so we just stayed in beds, the three of us. Grandpa was praying, I was crying. We were cold and hungry.

Then came the day before Christmas. In the part of the country where I came from we observed tradition. On Christmas Eve people had a big supper, men went to church and the organist played. They baked very thin oplatek (waffles) and people gathered their families and guests to break the waffles and wish each other good health, while they were eating the waffles.

When the Cirzinski family gathered by the table to wish themselves health, Mr. Cirzinski asked his wife if she had seen Rozia Mutkowska these days. His wife said that she had not, since they were so busy all week and never gave a thought to anybody else. They said our path was covered with snow up to the doors and the door and windows were covered with snow so you couldn't see at all. The Cirzinskis wondered if we went to mother's sister in Brzystek. Mrs. Cirzinski didn't know, but said Rozia always told her when we were going to her sisters, but what about her father, they wondered? They thought he might be sick, unless Frania took them to spend Christmas with her and Victa. Then Pani Cirzinski's father recalled that when they were both out and everything was quiet last night he thought he heard something like a cat meowing, or a child crying, and then he thought maybe it was the wind in the chimney.

"Oh, my God," Pani Cirzinski screamed. "Maybe Rozia Mutkowska did go out and got caught in the storm somewhere and Tonia (Antonia) and old grandpa are home alone!"

"I'll run to Frania," said Pan Cirzinski, "and ask Frania and Victa. Maybe they know something about it. I will go there, and if Victa thinks her mother is home, you better gather some men to clean the snow off the path and get to the house. It might be too late already."

As Pani Cirzinski went to Frania's, Pan couldn't wait until he came home to tell her what he had found out. She took a ladder from her side of the house and put it up to the attic over to our side and climbed down. Pani had to push the door hard, the lock was frozen. She pounded and kicked until she loosened the lock. When she got inside, she stood for a while, afraid to move until she saw me sticking my head from under the covers to see who was there. When she came near the beds and looked at mother and grandpa, she knew all she wanted to know. She covered me again and told me not to cry, she would give me supper.

She gathered some wood and turf in a hurry, made a fire, and wanted to cook some water for the herb tea. She found the water was frozen in the barrel, so she went back up the attic again to her side of the house. She got a pail of water and carried it down to fix some herbs as a medicine.

The doctor was in the city, and it took a man on horse and carriage two hours to the city and two hours back, and in heavy winter it took longer, so every woman in our village picked all kinds of flowers and herbs and made their own medicine to help themselves and their families. When Pani Cirzinski took a look at my mother, she knew that mother was fighting pneumonia. While Pani Cirzinski was busy inside, she heard her husband busy with other men shoveling the snow away from the door.

Mr. Cirzinski didn't wait long when Victa told him mother should be home. Grandpa was very sick and he wouldn't be able to walk to Brzystek, one hour's walk in the snow.

Mr. Cirzinski called on the men of the village to come with shovels, which they willingly did. While the men were shoveling the snow the women folks came cautiously and followed the men shortly after. Each one brought some food or herbs.

When they all got into the house and found out from Pani Cirzinski what had happened, the people cried and prayed and blamed themselves that they were so busy thinking of themselves and the joy of Christmas that they would have had three souls on their conscience (if we had died). They were promising themselves that this will never happen again in their village.

When midnight came that night, everybody was singing everywhere *Bog sie Rodzi*, (God is Born), and I knew that that dear God, that dear baby Jesus was born in that shabby little room of ours and the people were bringing their gifts of food to us.

I have thought of God often through life. I might have stepped off the right path sometimes, but I didn't fall off all together because my God was with me. All I had to do was call to him. "Please don't let me fall, O God, let me gather the strength and patience from your cross, O dear Jesus," and I felt I was getting out of the wrong path. Coming back to that day of the Christmas night, the good villagers kept their promise. We were kept in bed and warm. After ten days mother recognized things around her, but when she got up on her feet she wasn't able to use them on her spinning wheel, because when she fell off the ladder she had injured her spine. She never was herself again. She couldn't lift in hard work.

Mother stuck to her knitting throughout that winter, and Pani Cirzinski took me to her house to mind her little Stanley, who was one year younger than I was (four and a half) and Stash (Stanley) was three and a half. Pani Cirzinski was a dressmaker the whole year around, but in the winter nights she taught the villager's children to read.

The villagers were taking chances watching out nights for thieves and Russian spies, because Russia didn't want smart people. So people covered windows with blankets, locked the doors and educated their children the best they knew how. Pani Cirzinski was teaching them to read. She didn't know how to write, herself, so other village men were teaching the writing. Anyone could afford to send his children to get that much education when they were young. When they grew up they had to fight for more education for themselves and for their children.

Of course my mother could not afford it, so I was glad when Pani Cirzinski took me in to mind Stash. Then I could watch the other children read their books. I couldn't even afford a book or a pencil, so I just listened to what they were reading. To my good luck, Pani Cirzinski's nephew was a thick head, and got nothing straight into his head. Pani had to repeat and repeat the words to him. I stood behind him and swallowed the words. Before school was closed for the summer, I knew by heart every word of the two books that were taught. That fellow who let me swallow his words was named Jozef Kowaleski, and when I was 14 years old he asked me to marry him.

When Easter came my Aunt Mary and my sister Maryanna came to visit us. My sister had a book my aunt taught her to read and she was proud of it. I stood up before her and told her all of what was in her book by heart. Then she was ashamed and hid her book. My aunt asked my mother where I had learned the book. Mother told my aunt how I learned and what had happened to her. Mother said that she would like to buy me a book, but she wouldn't be able to do much hard work that summer.

When Aunt Mary went home she took grandpa with her so mother wouldn't have to take care of him, and on my birthday, May 8th, Aunt Mary sent me a prayer book and a holy song book. Was I proud of it! People who knew my age didn't believe me that I could read. I had to read to them to prove it.

That month of May, the whole village was putting their geese out on the pastures. My Godfather Lazowski gave me a job to mind his geese. There were boys and girls aged five to 19 years from every house that were minding geese or cows or horses at the same fields. Victa was there with Frania's geese too.

In late August buyers came and bought the young geese. They were mostly Jewish people that were in the business of buying geese from Poland and sending them to Germany every year that I remember. My Godfather sold his one hundred and fifty geese and just left a few of the old layers. So he added a few young calves for me to mind for the rest of the summer. He kept me for the winter, but as they had a house maid and a boy to help with work, I helped around where I could with dishes and minding their baby boy.

CHAPTER 2

Six Years Old – Mother Goes to Work in Sosnovo

Next year in May I was six years old. Mother felt a little better and decided to go to work in Sosnovo. She felt lonesome being left all alone all winter and last summer, as grandpa was with Aunt Mary.

Once I remember my father ran out, grabbed Victa and was beating her with a strap. That happened to be on a Sunday and people were coming from church. Pan Navatkowski was coming in his carriage and he saw my father beating Victa. He jumped out of his carriage, pushed my father from Victa so my mother had a chance to pick Victa up. He asked what the child was getting a beating for? Father told him Victa killed a gosling and he would teach her not to do it anymore. Pan Navatkowski turned to the woman who owned the gosling and asked how much she wanted for the gosling. The woman told him a price like for a grown goose. He paid it and told my father if he didn't want that child he would take her. He would raise her and she would have more with him than father could give her and she wouldn't be beaten.

But mother just thanked him for his kindness and didn't let

Victa go. I think that maybe poor Victa would have had a better life with Pan Navatkowski than she had all her life afterwards.

So people always came to my mother with their troubles. Tyburski's had a stepmother who didn't always agree with them, and they came to mother. Also my Godfather's son had a stepmother and their help were orphans when they came to work for Lazowski, and so my mother was like a mother to them.

When the orphans knew that mother wasn't able to do things for herself when she was sick they tried to do what they could do for her, but they always seemed to do it in the wrong way.

Once I told mother that it was nice of Pan Navatkowski not to arrest mother for taking some wood. She said so quietly,

"Daughter that man once asked me to marry him before I met your father".

Mother told me that was the second time he had done a good deed for her. When Victa was one year old mother and dad lived near his village. Mother put Victa outdoors to play. She put her on the ground and the neighbor's goose came out with her little goslings by Victa. Victa reached for one and started to kiss the gosling so much she bit the head off it, and the neighbor was hollering for that was her gosling.

Mother was loved by our neighbors, old and young. One Sunday afternoon the neighbors gathered around our home. While the older ones were talking to mother, the young played games. Mother mentioned that she didn't have any wood for the next winter. The older neighbors promised that they would throw a few bricks of turf for her. The young boys and girls heard and looked at mother but didn't say anything. When the time came to do their chores they all left.

Later that week mother looked out the window one morning, gasped and then said, "How could this happen?"

She saw a nice pile of wood right by our door. She didn't know where it came from and she didn't know who to thank for it. She met the neighbors, but nobody mentioned anything about the wood.

When mother told them and showed them the pile nobody knew anything.

Mother said, "I don't believe in fairies. That wood wasn't here last night. I can pay whoever brought that wood here."

Two days later it was Sunday. Some men and women went to look over their fields of rye and wheat to see if it was time to cut for harvest. Mother walked with them. As they came near the pasture where we minded our geese and horses, they all came to talk with us awhile.

While they stood there we saw a man riding in a carriage on a road near us. The man stopped his horse, got out of the carriage and started across the fields toward us. Everyone knew the man. He was a forester for a company who bought some acres of forest in the next village to cut and to sell to saw mills and some to cut in cords and sell for firewood. Everybody knew the man was a good, respectful man with his own piece of land. He was honest and reasonable with everybody and he was coming right straight to my mother.

The first words that he said were, "Mutkowska, if you weren't Mutkowska you would be in the jail tomorrow. I know you were always a good woman and I know you would never get the two cords of wood to your house over in one night, and I know you are not able to pay for it. If you came and told me you needed it I would have loaded a wagon full and brought it to you."

Mother stood there so embarrassed and tears were in her eyes. She said not a word.

My uncle and my Godfather said to the man, "We didn't hear of what this is about."

They offered to pay for the wood, but he looked at the group, then at the boys and girls and said, "If they love you that much, I'll stand for the rest."

Then he said goodbye to all of us and went away. When he looked the people in their faces he figured out that the older men couldn't have done it, and the boys looked scared. He didn't know if mother had asked the boys to do it, or if the boys did it without asking. He didn't want to cause any trouble for mother, so I guess he paid for the wood himself, and mother never did know who brought that wood.

After mother died, Maris Tyburski told me who brought that wood. She had kept the secret. Her sister and brother, young Lazowski and their boys and the girls helped, and the Navatkowski boy and girl. They loved my mother because Wawroskis had no mother, just a father, and she was like a mother to them.

When I was seven years old my mother went to work for Pivnicki in Sosnova. She got herself and me a job, hoping for around $18 a year. I was there at the right time to take care of Pivnicki's geese.

I took care of geese all summer. In winter I was helping the cook's chambermaid who cooked for Pivnickis and their guests, or I helped the cook that cooked for the working people. I helped the girls around there as there were several girls, young boys and men who worked there.

In that place I saw good things and bad things I shouldn't have seen. I heard lots of things good and bad and didn't understand them until I grew older. I had to figure those things out for myself, and to find out that no matter where you go you will find the same thing and you have to pick you own path, and watch your step on the path so you won't stumble.

I heard there that Sir Pivnicki was insane because he lived all by himself in one room on the second floor and didn't want to meet people. I heard people were talking on the quiet that Sir Pivnicki was smarter than the Russian government and he had outsmarted the Russian government. He was a great patriot and had been helping Poland a lot, and the people who fought Russia's spies. The spies came to Poland and were weeding out the patriots, sending them to Siberia and taking their land. Pivnicki went insane and the government thought it was no use to punish those people. They were looking for the smart ones.

Pivnicki was the best man around. He got along with people and paid everyone as he deserved. If someone worked for him and did something wrong, Pivnicki told him not to do it next time. When someone stole something off Pivnicki's property, he came and admitted it. Pivnicki asked him if he remembered the Ten Commandments, told him to go home, say his prayers and respect the Ten Commandments. He told him not to steal and when he needed something and Pivnicki could afford it he would give it to him.

Pivnicki didn't have much trouble with anyone, but if anyone was squealing on someone the squealer got a cane over his back and was told that was his pay for squealing.

Pivnicki liked children. The time I was there Pivnicki was starting to come out from his second floor room where he was supposed to have stayed for twenty years. He was taking long walks and every walk he took, he took with him candy or a lump of sugar. As he went through the village the children were watching him. He told them to close their eyes and open their mouths and was dropping candy in their mouths.

Sometimes Pivnicki came to me where I was watching the geese and when I was alone he sat on his cane and was telling me to watch out for spies and don't tell anyone anything. Some words I couldn't understand then until I went further in the world and met people who knew Poland's history. Then I knew what Pivnicki's words meant. I did like him even though I didn't understand his words and he would sooner have me doing something for him than the others. Then the big girls and I liked to work for him and I liked to work with the girls too.

The girls taught me singing and dancing. They taught me to dance on waxed brushes. The girls had to wax floors with waxed brushes. The floors had to shine like a mirror. I was light on my feet and I strapped the brushes to them and danced, rubbing the wax into the boards. Then the girls were taking me to a real dance with them. At first my mother didn't want to let me go, but the girls pleaded with mother and promised they would bring me home at 12 o'clock sharp. The borrowed me as sort of a chaperone. When the girls went to dance alone the boys kept the musicians playing longer to keep the girls longer a the dance. When they were taking me with them the boys couldn't keep them at the dance longer. The boys pleaded with the girls to stay longer, but the girls said,

"Uh, uh, we promised Aunty to bring Tonia home at 12 o'clock." All the girls and boys called my mother Aunty.

I must say here that the dance was held in anybody's place who had a big room for dancing. The village was of forty families and most every one of the men could play some kind of music. So they were changing off, playing and dancing, and the boys made up between themselves which home the dance would be in the next Saturday.

At first the boys didn't like the girls' idea of bringing me with them, but they got used to me, so they were dancing with me too. The boys and girls taught me to dance so well that when I was eight years old I knew all the dances. I might not give the boys the thrill like when they were with the big girls but they had one more to dance with and I had my fun. That's the only fun I remember that I had between my seven and twelve years of age because a few years after, misery joined me.

The elders learned to like me, the younger ones and my age liked me. When I was going through the village with my geese, singing, all the small children would leave their homes and follow me to the fields. Many times mothers were looking for their young ones and I was called down for taking them away from their homes. They told me I should chase the children home. I asked the mothers if they wanted me to beat them up and chase them away from me. I told them I didn't call the children, they followed me. Some days when the women saw me coming or heard me singing they called to one another to close the children indoors because the singing piper was coming with the geese, but they couldn't keep the children indoors.

The Pivnickis had their own private field for their geese, so I was alone when I was minding the geese and I was glad to have the other children with me. I taught them to sing and dance and I showed them how to sew doll's dresses. I also showed them how to make braids from rye and wheat straw, and when the braids were

long enough we sewed hats that men wore in summer. I had learned
that when I was minding geese with the bigger girls.

When I was eight years old I was made to work more around
the kitchen. I had to get up with the older girls at 3:00 a.m. to help
milk the cows. I had three cows to milk. One of the cows was a
beauty - shiny black with a white star between her eyes, but she was
a kicker. Nobody wanted to milk her because she kicked, but she
was the easiest milker. So I tried her. I went to her easy and gave
her an apple and patted her, scratched her all over her head, feet and
belly until I came to her milk bag. I tried standing a little ways away
from her. I pulled her teats and she kicked. I went back to petting,
scratching, singing to her and gave her another apple, then pulled
again. She lifted her foot up but this time didn't kick. I didn't beat
her or kick her like some of the others did. From then on I milked
the kicker, starting with an apple or a carrot, singing and scratching.
I milked her for a year.

One morning I got up sick and was not in the mood for singing
and scratching and forgot the apple. I just went and sat under my
cow. All of a sudden I felt myself flying high. The girls who finished
milking their cows were looking for me and they found me across
the barn with the young calves around me, unconscious. My cow
mistook me for somebody else and just whizzed me with the tip of
her hoof, and up to this day I can't breathe on one side of my nose.

It just happened that the next night somebody stole the cow.
Pivnicki sent out men to look for the cow but the girls wished the
thief good luck. The cow was never found, though.

When I was ten, mother thought that I was doing too much for
nothing in return. That winter they had a big hunting party for two
weeks. The place was crowded with people and dogs. Some dogs
were six feet high when they stood on their hind legs, some long
with short legs, some so small a man could put it in the palm of his
hand and cover it with the other hand and you couldn't see the dog.
I was selected to nurse the dogs for the two weeks; feed them, let
them out and let them in. The little ones slept on my lap and the big
ones jumped over me knocking me down when they saw their master

going out. I made enough tips at this job. Then mother bought me a dress and pair of shoes for Easter and I found out that there were good dogs and bad dogs too.

Young Pivnicki, the son, who lived six hour's ride in a wagon with two team of horses, bought a new place and needed a lot of lumber. He didn't have enough on his land so he had been sending his men to our place where there were acres and acres of timber. There were twenty to twenty-five extra men for mother to feed for years. One group went out while the other one was coming in. I had plenty of potatoes to peel and dishes to wash.

Mother took a day off and went to the next village to get a job for her and me. When she came back, young Jozef Pivnicki (a cousin) who was supervisor over the workers in our place spied mother and said to her,

"Mutkowska, where the devil were you, with Tonia?"

Mother said, "Looking for more money. Here we are both getting eighteen dollars a year."

He asked mother how much she was offered there. Mother told him thirty dollars a year for both of us. He said he would pay the same but Tonia would have to do some work outside if needed to, so mother canceled the other job and we stayed on until I was nearly twelve years old.

I was tall for my age, and slim, but I was pretty strong. I thought I could go to work daily and make more money. Lady Pivnicki changed the whole system around for the next year. Some of the girls went and got married, some went to other places. The men that were eating there got more in salary and a home and went on their own, but were compelled to keep one hired help, a girl or boy. That's when I decided to go hire myself to one of them.

One family's man was a night watchman at night and during the day was taking care of the fireplaces so there was enough wood for the new girls that came in to work at the place. One new chambermaid came and two to work in the kitchen. My mother started to complain that her back was bothering her badly. I persuaded mother to take a room with someone and rest and I would talk to Victa to come and the two of us would work to give mother a rest.

Since Peter came from the army and got married and Frania left Europe and went to America, Victa was working for my Godfather's brother Lazaroski, whose wife was very sick. Victa was working there for over a year and had been doing so well that Lazaroski promised her a cow and a hundred dollars as a wedding present if she worked for him until she got married.

CHAPTER 3

Twelve Years Old – To Work in the Fields

But Victa didn't get married in Europe, although she almost did. Victa was a good girl of fifteen years old and I was twelve. Victa always loved me and I loved her as I loved my mother. Victa was with me more than my mother was, before she was six years old and when mother went to work. So Victa and I were working out and mother had time to rest, so she would feel better.

I found out that work was harder than I thought. Frosty winters, heavy snow, slosh, cold, having to be out working from six in the morning to six at night. We worked around machinery that was thrashing rye and wheat. We worked with oats in the granary, fanning the grain, cleaning and filling bags a hundred pounds each. We helped pack the bags onto the trucks that were sent out to Germany.

In my time, Germany was buying a lot of wheat, rye, geese and cattle. We workers - girls and boys, were working and treated alike, and got paid eighteen cents a day. Of course our bosses got a little more themselves and their families. In the summertime we got six cents a day more or we worked piece work and made thirty cents a day if we were quick and strong enough.

On this earth everyone has his or her friends and enemies, and so did I. There were fellow workers from the age of fourteen to thirty; single, of course. There were lots of married men also, and there were girls from the age of fifteen to about thirty, so I was one of the youngest. I was twelve, but I looked older, so I put my age as fifteen also. Some of the older girls were against me, especially when I couldn't lift a bag of grain as they did. They told me I was getting paid as much as they were and I should do my share. Of course they were right.

Some of them were good to me and treated me like a grown up girl, but when I was stuck on some work they chipped in and helped me out. So I tried to please them in some other way. I sewed bags for the boys to put their tobacco in. I went to my sister Maryanna who was a big lady by then, and a good dressmaker. I picked all the scraps of material that she didn't need and cut them out in triangles and made them into squares like for a quilt. Then I made them into bags with nice strings and tassels to tie the bags. I had learned in Zamosc from big girls.

And they all liked my singing! I had to sing for them. I knew a lot of songs they didn't know, and they wanted to learn them. A lot of the songs I made my own words and my own melody to. They asked me where I learned such nice songs. I was afraid they wouldn't believe that I made them up. I told them my mother taught me, though I didn't hear mother sing often while I was with her and don't know if she knew any songs or felt like singing. I wanted the girls and boys to like me so I was glad to sing for them. None of us knew how to write so we had to memorize the words and as most boys played some kind of instrument they picked the melody out quickly. Many of them knew me as I was chaperoning the girls last year. Some were newcomers. I tried to please them all and get along with them.

There I again met Jozef Kowalski, the one whose reading I swallowed when he couldn't grasp the learning. He was a big boy now, and once he and I were in a haymow filling the platform for the thrashing machine with bundles of rye. He came to me and wanted to kiss me. I slapped his face and told him I would rather kiss a dog's hind end than his face. I thought surely he would be mad at me forever after, but he wasn't.

He said, "Oh child, what are you saying?" and never asked for another kiss.

But whenever my shoes needed fixing, he took them and fixed them without charging anything for it. I have to mention that almost every man played music and was just as good as a shoemaker because they had to be. The cities were far from us and there were plenty of children in every home.

Jozef's mother was a widow with six children, five boys and one girl. Jozef was the oldest. They had three acres of land of their own, but that wasn't enough to raise six children on.

Came spring, then summer, day in and day out rain or shine, work was harder and harder. In the spring the yards had to be cleaned out and all the manure taken out to the fields. In we go, men and girls, cleaning out the cow barns, sheep barns, horse stalls, pig pens, chicken coups. One was filling the wagons. The drivers brought it to the fields, and the others were out there spreading it around. The next day we changed off. The ones who had been filling were now out spreading and the ones who were spreading were now in filling wagons. It lasted about two months. Since it happened that I was always among friends, they told me not to take too much manure on the fork so it wouldn't be heavy to lift up on the wagon. I minded them too.

When that was finished with the manure, then came the plowing and planting. Five or six plows went out. The first plow made the first row. After the first plow made the first row, four people went with pails or baskets of potatoes and were throwing them in the rows. After the first row you had to be quick about it as the next plow was right on your heels followed by more girls with potatoes until the last plow came covering the last row.

The work went fast planting potatoes. Other planting like peas and oats were broadcast. Rye and wheat were fall broadcasting. All other vegetables were planted and transplanted by hand. Then came weeding. Potatoes were cultivated. All others were done by hand. Hoeing, pulling weeds. Everyone including me had two rows to do. My shame was that I would always be in the rear if it were not for good friends who helped me in distress. They told me to always stay with them wherever the work was hard, so I did.

One day the boys said, "Tonia, lent is over and it's after Easter. We will have dances again if you will be good and help us."

"Sure, I said, my cousins Jozef Wisniewski and Wladek Kempcinski and Adam Petrowski explained to me how to be a leader in their dance."

Here in America I think they called them Hostesses.

The boys told me what I was supped to do. It was a habit of the boys on Saturday night or Sundays, that they took a walk from village to village. When they heard music they walked in and stood for a while in the dance room. If no one asked them to dance they walked out and went to another place, but where they were asked to dance by the girls they stayed all evening and chipped in for the musicians.

So the boys picked me to lead the dances with the strangers. The older girls didn't want to approach the strangers first and ask them to dance. Well I took the job. I knew if I didn't dance as I was told, misery would dance with me all week at work, so I danced. I walked to the boy and asked if he would dance with me. He of course said yes, and I danced with him a while and brought him and set him by one of our girls. That meant he could sit there or take her and dance. Then I asked the next stranger, until they all were introduced to our girls. Then they could dance with whom they liked.

Some of them were good dancers and I enjoyed dancing with them but some of them didn't know a step. Hop-hop, ouch my toes! I lost my toenail because of it, but that was my job to dance with them throughout the evening. If they wanted me, they paid the musicians and I had it easy at work through the week. I danced and sang then. The boys always came to ask mother first before the dance started.

Mother said, "All right, 12 o'clock sharp."

So it was twelve – unless the men from Kuchazy came for the timber on the weekend. Then we would dance all night. Then they would come to visit mother and ask special permission. Mother knew all of them. They took me and Victa and brought us back after the dance.

Then I found out I had an enemy who was jealous of me and Victa. There were two sisters and a brother whose mother was a widow. The younger, Aniela Firgolski, with blue eyes and blonde, was Victa's age, and tall and slim like me. We both wore the same size clothes. Her brother was blonde, blue eyes, and lisped when he talked, but he was good natured fellow like their father was. Aniela told me Wladek Firgolski loved his sister Aniela, and so did I love Aniela.

But their sister Constancia, who was 21, had black hair, black eyes, dents all over her face left after small pox, and crossed eyes like her mother. "Costa" didn't like her sister Aniela, because she was pretty. Costa had all kinds of clothes and dresses. Aniela had not any. They all worked the same place where Victa and I worked and Aniela was my best friend. Costa wanted to part us in the worst way, but Aniela wouldn't part with me. Costa was going to dances and wouldn't let Aniela go. She didn't want Aniela to come to my house, but Aniela did. I taught Aniela to dance and sew some handwork, and if I was going to the city or to make a pilgrimage to some shrine or other church, I lent her my clothes and we went. Costa was dripping mad at me.

One day we gathered at my cousin Aniela Marunoski's, the one whose father served in the Russian Army twenty-five years and was bedridden for seventeen years before he died. Aniela worked as we all did to support herself and her mother, my aunt. My cousin Aniela, who had a nice voice herself, asked me to sing, and I good-naturedly said,

"Let Costa sing."

I meant nothing to hurt her or anything, just more like inviting her, and she jumped at me.

"Who do you think you are?" she said. "You are so proud of

yourself because the boys asked you to be a dance leader. If somebody dressed my sister in a silk dress, nice shoes, nice hat with flowers and a parasol in her gloved hand, and dressed you the same way, you would see who would be the lucky one."

Everyone was silent for a while. I got off the chair, stood before Costa and said,

"Yes, Costa, God didn't give me beauty when he created me. I know Aniela is pretty, even with the dresses you hand down to her, and I like her, and I like her to be my friend if she wants to be my friend. If someone dressed my sister Victa in silk dresses, nice shoes, nice hat, and a parasol in her hand and dressed you the same and even put a gold crown on your head, I know whom the boys would bow to first."

The girls put their heads down without a word. Some of the boys smiled, some naughty ones laughed out loud. Costa jumped up and ran to the door, slammed it behind her, and she didn't talk to me for a long time. Her sister was my friend as ever.

Well, whomever eats must work for his living, and so did we. Summer days, harvest time, rye, wheat, oats, then haying. We got up 5:00 a.m. At 6:00 we had to be at work on the fields. We didn't eat our breakfast at home. Mothers and wives had to bring the breakfast to the fields wherever we were working at 8:00 a.m. The pots, pottery made of clay, were two pots together. One compartment for potatoes, the other for zacierki.

Zacierki was made of flour and water. Hot water was poured in a dish of flour and made into small bits of crumbs with the tips of your fingers and put into boiling water, stirring so the bits wouldn't stick in one lump. It tastes like Cream of Wheat. You eat it with milk or salt pork. You can use whole cooked potatoes or mashed potatoes, or without potatoes. Sometimes women cooked a pumpkin, mashed it and put it in the zacierki with milk. That was generally the workers' breakfast, only some were more flavored than the others, with salt pork and milk.

The pots were called dvoyaki, dva, meaning two. Dvoyaki means like a twosome.

As we didn't have a cow, so we didn't have milk. We couldn't buy salt pork often if we wanted to save a few dollars for shoes and clothes, so mother put a tablespoon full of vinegar in to flavor the zacierki. One breakfast time, Wladek Kempcinski, passing where Victa and I were eating, noticed that our food wasn't as richly flavored as his. He went, making believe he was having fun, and was going from one to another tasting their food until he came and tasted ours with vinegar. He grabbed our dvoyaki, went to the woods and left his in my lap. Victa and I didn't know what to do. We called him to bring our breakfast back. So his mother told us to finish his breakfast. Of course his was better than ours and we enjoyed and didn't guess at that time that he did that on purpose. He had his idea that we didn't know yet what he was doing.

After that, Wladek's mother sent my mother, every so often, some milk or pork or something. Then the other women did every once in a while. And often the other boys and girls, now making a game of it, shared breakfast and dinners when we were eating in the fields where it was too far to go home for dinner and we had our dinner brought to us.

Cutting the rye or wheat, men were cutting with a scythe and girls followed right behind them, picking arms full tied in a bundle, then left them there and kept on doing it. The next group followed the girls gathering the bundles and were making them in two rows for the wagon to go through between the rows, and a man on each side of the wagon was throwing the bundles on the wagon. One man on the wagon was packing on while the driver brought it to the mounds for thrashing in the winter.

Thank God for the inventions now-a-days. They have easier methods of harvesting and people don't have to work so hard as the machines do it quicker and easier. But in my young years that is how the work was done at harvest time.

Then came fall, digging out the beets and potatoes. The beets were first pulled, loaded onto big trucks and were sent out to a sugar factory, and some were used for the animals in winter. Cabbage and carrots were the last to pick out of the ground. Pivnicki didn't have enough people in the village to dig the acres of potatoes. He called on the Russian Army headquarters, and the army sent some of their soldiers. The soldiers were spread around the bigger homes if there was only one or so. If there were a hundred or more they made a barracks for them.

The soldiers were doing their own cooking and made their own pumpernickel bread - fifteen pound loaves. Each soldier carried his own spoon in his boot. The spoons were made of wood, and if anyone lost his spoon he had to make another for himself. When the soldiers were in the village, mothers kept their girls home evenings. They didn't trust the Russians.

Fields were cleared, food was stored indoors, Christmas and the New Year were nearing, and people were planning where they were going to work and for whom. Some said they would stay longer, some were going to look for better work or maybe they would find worse, but people liked to travel.

In December, Costa went to America. Somebody sent for her, so she said goodbye and went. Some new girls came to work. Victa got tired of working out by day and got herself a job in Pivnicki's kitchen where mother was, for the next year.

CHAPTER 4

Thirteen Years Old - Runaways

At Christmas, my Aunt Mary came visiting. Aunt Mary told mother that in the village where we were going to church two hours walk one way, there was a school where teaching goes on, but in Russian. The teacher, Brzuska, needed a servant. Aunt Mary said she didn't know how the work was there, but I could try it. I didn't know what to do. I knew I would be lonesome without Victa, and Aniela and I never was far away from mother. I was afraid, but I went and got the job for $14 a year. Pani Brzuska said the work was very easy. There were the teacher, his wife, three boys from three to ten years old and another ten year old boy who was boarding with them, and me. That's seven people, and a dozen chickens, three pigs, a calf, a milking cow, a horse and a colt, three rooms and a schoolroom to take care of. Easy work for a girl thirteen years old. The animals had to be fed supper, some twice a day, some three times a day. The cow had to be milked morning and evening.

Every Saturday when the teacher wasn't teaching, he made me help him to cut straw, like rice, to feed the cow and the horse. When he was sharpening the knives, I was turning the wheels with the knives. His wife used to come to watch us working. She was afraid that we might fool around. She was homely and jealous, about forty-eight years old, while he was nice looking and thirty-four years old.

He never bothered me and never gave me a bad word for the time I was there, but her, my God, we all had enough of her – him, the children and I. I knew when I got the job that my misery moved right with me, but I tried my best to stick it out that year. I was afraid to admit that I couldn't take it, but I was sweating blood throughout that winter. If I sang, she called me all kinds of a fool for it. If I felt lonely and she caught me crying in a corner, she called me all kinds of silly sissy fool names because I was crying. When the boys came to the kitchen laughing, I laughed with them to be sociable and I was called silly fool and told not to teach the children silly laughing.

On Sundays we went to church, just for the Mass. When she heard the Mass she came home, told me to get dressed and go to church. I got dressed, went to church, and when I got there the church was closed. I tried the main door, I tried the side door, all closed until the evening services. Well, I didn't know what to do. I thought, what is she kidding me, or what? I came home, didn't say anything, and went to my usual work.

The next Sunday came and she went to church. I thought maybe she would tell me to go again. When she came back I wanted to go to church for once. I liked to sing and hoped maybe I would meet someone from my village, or since it was a nice day my mother might come, so I was ready when she came.

She said, "Get ready and go to church."

I went right out. I got there just in time when the church taker was closing the doors.

"Too late, girly", he said, "church is over."

I knelt down on the step outside, said "Our Father Who Art in Heaven", and started home.

Then the church taker said, "You are working for Brzuska."

"Yes," I said.

He said, "I thought so. All her girls say their prayers on that step."

I told him I didn't know what her idea was sending girls to church when church was over.

"You know," he said, "she thinks that she's so good, that she only hears the Mass, and for the rest the Priest says, she doesn't have to listen, it's only for the poor farmers and poor workers."

One Sunday as I was going into the church door the Priest just came out to go home. The Priest knew me well because he saw me in Pivnicki's when I was there. He used to come to suppers and play cards two or three times a week, so he said to me,

"What are you doing here? I think all your villagers went home already."

I told him, "But I am here. I work for Brzuska. Every time I get here the church is closed."

That Priest was rough and nasty at times and people at the Parish didn't like him very much – not all of them anyway. But he gave me a good lesson I remember until today.

He said, "Well, when you are working you have to do what you are told to do if you like it or not, but if you can't go to the church, you go to the barn and kneel on top of the manure. If your prayer is right from your heart, God will listen to you. God is everywhere."

I told him thank you and went home to my work. Sometimes when it was a nice Sunday, I expected my mother to come to see me, so that day was nice. When I expected mother I didn't eat breakfast. All I got for my breakfast was one cup of coffee and one slice of dry bread without butter or anything. I put my slice of bread under my pillow in my bed and diluted my coffee with hot water and I had two cups of coffee. I drank one, even though it wasn't strong, but I had a cup and left the other for mother. One day Brzuska walked into the kitchen and mother was eating the slice of bread and the cup of coffee before her. Brzuska said nothing, turned around quick and walked back to her room. Brzuska didn't mention anything through the week, but she watched me the next Sunday. I didn't see her standing in the door when I put the slice of bread under my pillow and poured water into my coffee and hid one cup in the oven we baked bread in. Then she knew that I didn't steal anything from her, just shared mine.

That day after mother left, Brzuska asked me if I ate my breakfast. I told her I wasn't feeling hungry. She let it go at that and the next Sunday she left two smaller slices of bread and two cups of coffee. Believe me, I could eat the two slices of bread and two cups of coffee myself every breakfast. When I was home with mother I ate zacierki flavored with vinegar, but I wasn't hungry. In Brzuska's, I cooked fancy meals and was always hungry. Brzuska put on a plate not as much as I could fill my stomach, but as much as she felt like leaving for me in the kitchen, and took the pots into their room to feed themselves up, and the rest went for two dogs that they had. The two little dogs were getting fatter, while I was getting skinnier the longer I was there. Many a time I felt like running away, but I didn't know how to start, until a girl next door to me started to leave.

The girl named Ursula, and I didn't know one another much, were strangers and didn't have much time to talk to each other as she had still harder work than I. She was over twenty years old. Her boss was like an acting Mayor here in America. There were five small children and they had a lot of young men as clerks. Ursula was there a little longer than I was at Brzuska's. The only chance we had to talk to one another was when we were carrying water, thirty pails each day from the well. The well was on a road, so half of the villages could get water. People kept big barrels in their houses and filled them up once or twice a day for home use and for animals.

One day Ursula said to me when we were carrying water, "I am going to run away from here, and I advise you to do the same, because if I go you will have to do some of my work. When a girl ran away from Brzuska's before you came here, I had to go and help Brzuskas. That is the way they help each other, and the girls have to do the work."

I asked her where she would go if she left here and she told me she would go home to her parents. Her father was working, taking care of cattle in Sniezawy. Also, Ursula said it was dangerous for a girl to be in this place. Even the Priest told her that this place is no good for girls to work here.

At that time I was only thirteen years old. I didn't know what she meant by that, but I got scared, and the next time mother came to visit me I told mother. For the first time I complained about my hard work to her and mother said that she noticed herself how thin I was getting. She asked if it was the work or not enough food, and I told her both. I told mother even the Priest said this place is no good to work at. I did the wrong thing to mother when I told her that, because if I knew then what I know now, I would have told mother that it was Ursula who told me that the Priest had told her, but I kept the rest and didn't give the girl away, not even to save myself from punishment.

Mother saw Brzuska and asked her to relieve me from her service and let me go home. Mother pointed out to her that I was getting thinner every time she came around and I complained of hard work.

Brzuska jumped at mother and hollered loud that mother raised a sissy. She said that I would never be a good worker because all I liked to do is sing and cry. She said she was trying to be good to me and that I hired myself to her for one year and she wouldn't let me go. I started to cry, and something gripped me around my heart and I passed out.

I don't know how long I was lying in that state, but when I woke up it was dark in the evening and my poor mother was gone. It had been afternoon when we were talking. I found myself in bed with a fever, and the little ten year old boarder was sitting by me silently and sympathetically, asking me if I wanted water or something.

He looked around and didn't see anyone coming, and asked quietly, "What did she do to you? I know what she is like. I have been here three years and she always makes my mother cry by complaining about me. I have to stay here because this is the nearest school where mother can come to see me more often. You see, she doesn't like my mother because she says my mother was a poor servant and my dad was a rich old bachelor. Dad died when I was six years old and asked mother to send me to school, and this is the nearest one. Girls don't stay here long. Some stay here but a week."

I was sick in bed three days and didn't care if I lived or not, and neither did anybody else. Mother couldn't get to me because such a heavy snow storm came down that no one could go far from the house. So just my little friend sat by me whenever he was free from his lessons, and Ursula was helping around.

When I was stronger and took to my work, Brzuska asked me when did the Priest tell me that her place was no good for girls. I told her the Priest didn't tell me.

She said, "Well, your mother said that he did."

My poor mother didn't know the rest of Ursula's story and with the sorrow in her that Brzuska didn't let me go home with her, she told Brzuska that the Priest told me that.

Spring came and I was forced not only to do the regular housework and the outside chores, but the garden work too.

Several days later at the water well, Ursula said to me, "Tonia, be ready for Saturday night, twelve o'clock, when your boss and my boss are going to play cards with the keeper."

I told her I didn't know about this because it might make trouble for me and my mother. She told me I saw what had happened several weeks ago that she had been forced by my boss to do my work, and asked if I wanted to work their garden and my garden too.

I finally agreed, and off we went that Saturday night. Not through the road, so we wouldn't meet someone who knew us, but out through the field and pasture far behind the village. We were running away. I was running from hard work and starvation, and Ursula was running away with shame. I found out later she was going to have a baby by one of the clerks.

We got to Ursula's house and her mother opened the door for us, but her father showed like he wasn't glad she was coming home at all. As it was after 2 a.m. I didn't sleep there long. I had another two hours to walk and I wanted to get home before daylight. I walked from Sniezawy and didn't meet anybody on the road.

When I was near my door I heard something running behind

me. I looked around and saw Brzuska's two little dogs. My God, I know they were in Brzuska's room. When I left their house the dogs must have run out the first thing in the morning and found my trail and caught up with me just as I was by my door. I knocked on the door and mother came out. She was surprised to see me there so early.

I told her I ran away from Brzuskas and said I wouldn't go there anymore.

Mother said, "They will trouble us, child, but I can't stand it anymore."

Then mother spied the dogs.

She said, "Why did you bring the dogs with you? Now it will be double trouble."

I told her I didn't bring them, they must have found my trail and followed me. Now how was I going to chase them away from here? They were so glad to see me and wagged their tails and jumped all over me.

While we were standing there, the door of the next house opened and my friend Aniela and her brother came out. They saw me coming from their window as it was looking over that road. They were glad to see me. I told them what I had done and about the dogs, so Aniela, Wladek, my mother and I spent an hour and a half to chase the dogs through the forest over the border until they saw their village where they came from. The dogs didn't want to go away from me. We threw stones at them. Not to hit them, just to scare them.

I was home that week to rest and recuperate, and the girls and boys were glad to see me home again. The neighbors saw how thin I was and were bringing milk to feed me and fill me up.

Sunday when the villagers were coming from church, one of them came to mother and told us that the Priest had called out our names. If we were in church to come to his office, if not, someone should tell us to come to him Monday, and some girl from Sniezawy told us. Oh, oh, I just knew what was going to be, but didn't know how bad. When I didn't show up to work the whole week, Brzuskas went to fight with the Priest on the word my mother said the day I fainted.

Let come what may, we went to church early. We met Ursula there after church and we went to the Priest's office. He came out to us mad, and asked Ursula first if he ever told her at any time not to work at the Mayor's place. Ursula said he never did, and never heard anything about it. She said she would sooner have thought of death then of him telling her any such thing not to work there.

I looked at her and my mouth dropped open. I was shocked. How could she lie like that! But the Priest didn't give me a chance to say anything. He turned to me and asked if he ever told me not to work for Brzuskas. I said he did not. Then the Priest asked mother if he ever told her anything like that. Mother said he did not. The Priest then asked what right did she have to tell Brzuskas that he said such a thing. Mother said that I told her, but the Priest was raving that he would hold me and get the church taker with the rope from the bell and beat me up. Ursula went out smiling and I stood in for her lie. The Priest wouldn't let me explain how the thing started.

When he finished raving he said, "Now I excommunicate you from the church and from the holy communion forever!"

I didn't understand the meaning of that and I didn't care what he said anymore. My poor, dear mother. She was so good, so religious and innocent of Ursula's guilty lie.

We came home and my mother was always sad. I didn't know how to cheer her up.

CHAPTER 5

Fourteen Years Old – Two Days in Jail

On May 8th I was fourteen years old. Mother didn't care about anything.

Then I got to thinking, and told mother about Ursula - how she coaxed me and I didn't want to listen to her at first. But she was scaring me and telling me that if she ran away I would have to do her work as she was doing mine when I was sick. She told me that she met the Priest by the church and the Priest asked her where she was working. She said when she told him where she was working the Priest told her it was a dangerous place for a girl there. Why didn't she explain herself in the Priest's office? Why did she say no, the Priest did not tell her that?

Mother said, "Tomorrow we'll go to Ursula and ask her to explain herself, and go to the Priest with Ursula to correct the wrong she has done us. But when we got there the next day Ursula wasn't there. She left her baby with her mother and went to Germany to work (as a group of boys and men did every summer, because they were paid more there than in Poland under the Russian rulers. That is why Polish village landowners had a shortage of workers.)

"So Ursula went to Germany," mother said. "No use to go to the Priest and try to explain to him without Ursula to prove it. He would not believe us."

We went home to live our life of drudgery. I went to work by day again. I missed a couple boys and girls and found new faces that moved in from other villages and other Parishes. I made new friends. Another widow woman moved to Sosnova with a daughter Frania and son Antony. Frania was working to help Victa in the kitchen. Antony worked by day. Some of the newcomers were traveling on Sundays to the churches they left or to visit their old friends. I started to go with them. We were traveling to different cities, to different churches. I felt happy and gay for a while.

One night I had a dream. I dreamed that I was digging potatoes with Aniela and down came a big storm with rain and thundering and lightning. It scared us so we both knelt down and prayed, and as we were praying, the big black cloud opened up and God stood in the cloud and spoke to me.

"Don't be afraid of the thunder. It loosens the earth and rain softens the ground to bear better fruit."

And the cloud closed again. I woke up. I went to a very religious woman (who never got married) and sacrificed her life praying for her brother who lost his mind when their father died.

I told her of the dream I had, and she said, "Child, heavy sorrow is coming to you soon, but pray and be brave. God will be with you."

I met Frania and she told me she felt like going to her old church on Sunday, but she didn't want to be alone. I told her I would go with her. She said it would be all right, but she would have to have her mother take her place for the day at work, and we would go. I told her to wait a minute and I would ask my mother if she would take Victa's place for that day and Victa could go too. That was fine, so that Sunday our mothers let us go.

We started early in the morning to be there for a noon mass. I don't know if Frania told her brother where we were going, or her mother. Coming out of the church there was waiting for us her brother Antony, and Wladek Kempcinski, and Wladek Gurtaloski.

When Antony found out where we were going he called the other two and came after us. Frania was glad to see Gurtaloski. She had her eyes on him, but he didn't care for her. As we didn't take anything to eat, we were hurrying home for supper, but the boys took us to a store and bought some rolls and soda. Antony wanted me to be his girl there, but Gurtaloski got in first, and paid for his and mine. Kempcinski paid for his sister and Victa.

Antony looked at his sister and said, "Here, Frania, you too."

That embarrassed Victa and me, but of course we couldn't help it. We didn't invite the boys, they invited us.

When we got home Frania said to her mother, "If not for Antony, I would have come home hungry."

She didn't ask us to her church any more, but she was a good girl.

About a week after that I received a note to come to court. I went. I knew what it was. Brzuskas were suing me for running away from them. The judge asked me why I ran away. I told him. Too much work, not enough to eat, and the Mrs. was nasty.

The judge said to me, "A quiet calf can suck two mother's teats. Two days in jail for running away and go back to work. They promised they will give you more to eat and more work."

I thought, but I couldn't argue with the judge. So the next morning I started for the jail. I got there by noon and reported to the jail caretaker. He asked my name.

"Antonia Mutkoska," I told him, "From Sosnova."

He looked at me and said, "Say I know your father in the army. He played a flute. I played a drum. And what are you here for?"

"For running away from Brzuskas."

"Oh," he said, "They sued girls left and right, but none ever go back to them. I would let you stay here with my wife for three days, but if I don't lock you in there, I would lose my job."

I told him to do his duty, and he told me tonight I would have company, because there was another girl there that ran away too.

When he opened the door, the girl and I gasped together, "Kostusia?" "Tonia?"

The caretaker said, "Oh, you knew each other?"

"Sure," I told him, "Kostusia had a stepmother who never treated Kostusia any too good."

Kostusia was Wladek Gurtaloski's cousin. When I went to work for Brzuskas I didn't know that Kostusia got herself a job in Vilno and couldn't take it either, so there we met in jail.

Kostusia didn't bring anything to eat with her, and her stepmother didn't give her any money. The poor girl was there without food since the day before. I asked the caretaker to get us some milk, cheese and bread, enough for two of us. Kostusia was so appreciative she cried. She always had a habit to say, "I will do the same to you some day." So she promised to do the same to me some day.

The next morning the caretaker called for Kostusia to take her back to Vilno and he wouldn't be back for me until the next day. So I sent him for some more milk and bread and kielbasa to feed Kostusia because she wouldn't be eating until she got home that night, and I had enough for myself until the next day.

Kostusia asked the caretaker if she had to stay at work the whole year. He told her it was his duty to take her to the place, but if she didn't want to stay there she could go right out and go home as soon as they saw her there with him. He had done his duty. So Kostusia went with him.

The next morning he came to bring me to Brzuskas. It was early and Mr. Brzuska wasn't in school yet, so they went in the kitchen. The caretaker told them he brought their servant back.

"Oh good, they both said." "Plenty of work is waiting for her."

I said to them, "I came here, but for my four month's pay, not to work."

"Then you go to jail again."

I said, "I will go to jail again, but I won't work for you."

Mr. Brzuska said, "Money? You workers are looking for money and easy work. We have to suffer for you, but a day will come that you workers are going to work for a whip."

I turned to him and said, "Someday that whip will turn on rich people", and walked out.

I waited out on the road for the caretaker and told him that meant him too. He was only a poor worker also. The caretaker said, "I don't think he will live that long to see it."

I said so long to the caretaker, I might be back soon again. But they didn't bother me anymore.

I went home. Aniela came and told me that her cousin Stash and his cousin Kostusia and she were going to make a pilgrimage to Obory, to the Monastery and the shrine there. I said I would go too, to pray to God for better days.

Mrs. Zdrojeski went with us. We started with daylight and got to Obory on time for the high mass. After the mass we prayed before the shrine and before the stations. Then we ate lunch and went in for the afternoon service. At four o'clock we were ready for home.

Coming out from church my company met a relative of theirs who lived nearby, one hour's walk. The woman was Stash's sister, and the woman's husband was Mrs. Zdrojeski's husband's nephew. All the relatives were asked in for the night. They all went in, shut the door behind them, and nobody thought of me, not even Aniela. I stood by the gate for a while, swallowed something hard that came to my throat and said to myself,

"Well, keep on, Tonia, you have four hour's walk before you."

So I walked slow at first, in hope that they may think of me after the excitement was over, but no. So I started faster and faster. I didn't want to admit that I was scared to travel by myself over strange places, but I was on my way, so I kept going. I passed the village, came to the open, but I would soon come to the forest and I didn't know if I would meet any Gypsies there. I wasn't afraid of the gypsies in our forest because they used to come to dances in our village, but in a strange place, strange stories were going around about them.

But I was near the forest, so I had to go through. Just as I was nearing the first woods I heard a voice.

"I followed you all the way from the village and was wondering if you really had the spunk in you to go through it."

I turned to see who he was. There was Wladek Kempcinski. Victa told him that I went to Obory, and with whom, so he followed us but couldn't catch up with us and couldn't see us in the crowd at

Obory. He was walking home and saw me standing by the gate and then went on. He was too far behind me to call to me, so when I walked slow he caught up to me.

Then he said, "We might walk together to go home now. Would you be afraid of me?"

I told him I was not afraid of him – he was not a wolf and I was not a sheep, and he wouldn't eat me up. I told him I was glad he was here because I was afraid that maybe there were gypsies in this forest.

Wladek said, "All right! Good Girl! We are going home."

We were home nine o'clock in the evening.

The next day Zdrojeski came to my mother and put the blame on me that I walked out on the company. They had enough room for me, she told my mother, but I didn't come in. Mother looked at me sadly.

I said, "Mother, what would you do if you were in my place" They are relatives. Naturally, they are walking all in a group. You are a stranger and you walk behind them so you won't interfere. They open the door and say, "come in", but shut the door before you, and the last one closes the gate. So I walked on home."

Mother said, "So would I."

I told mother I even waited a few minutes by the gate, thinking maybe someone will open the door and say "come in". Nobody did, so I went on.

"Oh, no," said Zdrojeski, you kept on walking because of Wladek Kempcinski. You came home with him. People are already talking that you and Wladek are running around too much and that you are going to have a baby."

I looked at Zdrojeski and felt like spitting at somebody, but I said, "Just wait until I get that Wladek and ask him what did he do to me that I am going to have a baby."

I went to see Aniela and she was sorry about what happened to me. She said she did tell her cousin that her friend was left outside and asked the woman to bring me in, but when she came out looking for me I was gone.

I told her to forget it and we would be friends just like we were.

The next day I met Wladek at work. I asked him if he heard the story about him and me going to have a baby. He ran over to me and grabbed me and hugged me and said we were going to raise it! I said, "Don't be silly. You think it's nice to hear people talk about you that way?"

Wladek said, "Tonia, you can't stop a dog from wagging his tail. No matter how short you cut it he will still wag. You know that you did nothing to be ashamed of and I know I didn't either, so let their tongues wag."

I told Wladek, "I think I know who made up that story."

One day as we had been coming in from the fields we were riding in Adam Petrowski's wagon. Adam let Jasiek Kowalski drive his horses and he came into the wagon and said he was going to kiss all the girls. I told Adam he had better not come near me because I would smash his face for him. Adam didn't believe that I would do that to him. He always thought too much of himself. He was too sure of himself, and before he got hold of me I swung my hand and smacked him across his face. He shook his head, cursed at me and went back to his horses. He was grumbling to Jasiek that he kissed better girls than me and no one smacked his face. He said he should have thrown me out of his wagon. Jasiek told me Adam let him kiss the better girls.

I said, "If they were better girls they would not have let Adam kiss them."

I remembered two years back when the two pretty Wagner sisters both had babies in one year. Their mother was chasing the men who were supposed to be the fathers of the babies, with rakes and throwing stones at them. I promised myself to pray to God to give me strength enough to keep men away from me. Dance with them, sing for them – that's different. Kissing is out!

The harvest was over, the fields were clear and there were only a few days left to finish haying, and it was the first of September. The whole village got lively and excited in getting ready for September 8th. On that day, every year, hundreds and even thousands of people were making a pilgrimage to a place called Skepe. To Skepe would go people from churches from all places. They gathered their parishes into big groups call companies. Of those companies some lived far and it took them two and three days to walk. They were carrying flags and big statues from their churches. Every company had its music band. Drummers, music playing and people singing church songs all the way to the shrine. They would stop for lunches and rest a while as there were old men and women and women with young children and babies. They all were walking, and wagons were following behind them with food. In case someone got sick or too tired, then they were put on the wagon. All that could walk walked on.

As the companies were from different directions, they met on the roads. Sometimes three, four or five, then the flags bowed to each other in gladness. All bands played, all people sang God's praise. Whoever couldn't sing prayed in silence. When the company was near the shrine, maybe some other company was there already that came earlier or the day before to the church. They would come out with their flags and statues and their bands to greet the new coming companies and bring them in the church.

Going back home was the same way. The first company that came there was the first company to leave, and later companies were brought to a certain distance and then turned back to church. It was that way all day, and the masses went on. Priests were at all altars as the company was coming and going. Then every Priest had a mass. All you had all day was music, singing, flags, bowing, greetings and sending off. It was beautiful to watch it and you just felt in your heart that you had to mix in that crowd and pray. People held each other's hands in six or ten together so they wouldn't get lost from one another.

The church is very big. If you go there on other days when there are no people, you need a guide to get you through the church from all directions.

It was the harvest time. Some poor beggars came. Sick ones on crutches or on wheels. Some tricky ones too. Healthy in body – men and women too lazy to work for a living making themselves look like beggars. They were spreading themselves around the church and on the roads going to church saying their prayers. Some of them were silent, some of them praying aloud so the people would be sure to hear them. You dropped a coin in their hats with the request to pray for you. Some of them picked up enough money to go get drunk on and come to beg for more, and sometimes they said worse things than a prayer if the money didn't drop fast enough in their hats. Sometimes the ones with the crutches got mad at each other because one picked up more money than the other, or had picked a better seat. They would start to beat one another with their crutches, then the gendarmes pulled them in to cool off and say their prayer in the coup instead of by the church.

Our village was excited too. People talking, planning where they were going to go with the church company or in groups. From our village it was only about three hours walk to Skepe. We workers generally gathered ourselves after work, had our supper and started near midnight and marched on all the way with songs and prayers and got to Skepe about three in the morning. We then had time to wash ourselves in the big river by the church and shake our road dust off our clothes and shoes.

We had our hot breakfast, or just hot tea, and ate our own food that we brought with us. We rested a little and were ready for church to pray and watch the companies coming and going on with their processions.

But Victa and I didn't go to Skepe that year and never after.

CHAPTER 6

Death of My Dear Mother

I had bought some material a few weeks before for new dresses for Victa and me. On the first of September before I went to work I asked mother to go to Bristol to see if sister Maryanna would make the dresses for us so we would have them for September 7th. Mother promised to go, but after I went to work at six in the morning, the foreman went to mother asking her if she could come for two or three days to help with the rest of the haying. They were short of steady workers so he was gathering extra hands. He needed more help from the housewives to finish the hay because after September 8th it was beets and potatoes digging time.

So mother forgot the dresses. She thought for two or three days she would try to make a few dollars for herself as the extra hands got more pay per day, from eight in the morning to four in the afternoon than the regular daily workers. The daily workers were also getting the use of some land to do their planting, whatever they wanted to raise.

Mother thought she would be home before me and I wouldn't know that she was working. So she went to work.

A driver brought the workers on wagons to work and brought them home for lunch. The drivers started to race one another, who was going to be home first. The ones that kept to the road got home first, but Adam Petrowski thought himself smart and told his people to hold on tight and he would give them some ride. Before the people had a chance to protect themselves, Adam turned onto a side road - a shorter road home. But that was a forgotten and forbidden road to drivers.

That part of the forest had new trees planted there and strangers going through with their wagons were stealing the young trees, so the foresters were told to dig ditches across the road every few feet so the wagons wouldn't be able to go through there.

But Adam wanted to have fun, so as he came to the first ditch the four horses were jumping over it and the first wheels of the wagon fell into the ditch. The hay ladder the people were sitting on broke. The younger folks came jumping out with twisted arms, broken ankles or some bruises and scratches, but my poor mother was forty-nine years old with her stiff spine from when she was hurt as a younger woman. She was in the middle where the ladder broke into the ditch and the back wheels rolled over her and crushed her ribs and her intestines. She was brought home unconscious.

When I came home at 6:00 p.m., I found the house full of villagers. When I was told what had happened and how it happened, I said,

"Oh, mother, why didn't you listen to me this morning and go to Maryanna's. You wouldn't be suffering here now."

I was told that the doctor was there. Pivnickis sent their horses to the city, Rypkin, for him. But the doctor said that there was no hope. If that was done in America, Adam would be punished for his murder. Here nobody questioned him for it. May God have mercy on his soul.

The next day Pivnicki sent for the Priest of our parish. The Priest wasn't home from his vacation yet. He was away for a month. There was no other Priest around during the week days, so Pivnicki sent for one to the city Rypkin. There were three Priests in Rypkin, but everyone was out on duty. The dopey driver didn't know enough to wait for one, and came home without a Priest.

On September 4th at 1 a.m. mother died. Aunt Mary, Grandpa and Maryanna came to help. Maryanna and Victa made a dress for mother. Grandpa went to notify the church taker to ring the bell for mother at her funeral and see if the Priest was there to have a mass for her.

Grandpa found out that our Priest just came back home, so Grandpa went to see him and asked the Priest to have a mass. We wanted mother's body in church through the mass as people always have. The Priest asked if she had confessed. Grandpa told him she was killed, and the Priest wasn't here and we couldn't get a Priest from Rypkin. The Priest looked at Grandpa and said,

"Your daughter can't be let into the church and can't have a mass because she wasn't confessed."

The people were mad at the Priest. He wasn't liked much before and they didn't like him any better after that, and held it against him in their hearts. Was mother supposed to wait for him until he came back from his rest and good times so she could confess?

The people didn't know, but I did, that the Priest had his last revenge, and poisoned my mind against Priests for all time. He had his revenge because he didn't give us a chance to explain to him before, and later we couldn't get Ursula so we could clear ourselves from the words she had put in my mouth to say, and afterwards she denied them.

So September 8th Victa and I didn't go with the Pilgrims to Skepe. I was sick. Aunt Mary took me with her for a few days until I got better. Aunt Mary wanted me to stay with them. Uncle Julius was the kind of man who would take anybody and keep them, but the house was crowded already. There was Uncle Julius's sister, an old maid, and another sister's children whose land was confiscated by the Russians when their parents were sent to Siberia. The young men were old enough to take care of themselves but were hanging around Uncle Julius.

And there was Grandpa who came home sad, and never told us what he heard from the Priest. The people dressed mother up and put her in a plain coffin that my Uncle made. It cost two dollars. Then my Aunt had her hands full with me as I got very sick.

On September 6th, people came from all the villages around to pay their last respects to mother. All who knew her and the ones who heard of her loved her and respected her. They all followed her body. There the people would follow a funeral just a way out of the villages and just the relatives and nearest friends went on. With mother's body, all who could go went to the cemetery. They wanted to be in church at her mass.

When we came by the church bells were ringing to tell that a body was going to be put to rest. We stopped to bring the body to church, but the church was shut tight. People were standing there wondering why the Priest was not in so they started on again for the cemetery, and then the Priest came out of the church gate with a dish of water and sprinkled it over the coffin.

"In the name of God, of the Son, of the Holy Ghost, Amen."

That is all that was done for my mother. And she was laid to her rest.

Afterward Grandpa told the people that the Priest didn't let mother go to church for mass.

My sister Maryanna now had a two year old baby daughter. Maryanna had married a young man who wanted to save himself from going to the Russian army. He cooked tobacco and vinegar and drank that for a couple of weeks. He saved himself five years from the Russian army, but shortened his life. Maryanna didn't know he had tuberculosis. They lived together one year. The baby was born a week after the father died.

Maryanna had moved back home and Aunt Mary was taking care of the baby as she had taken care of Maryanna. Maryanna was a good dressmaker and she was making a nice living.

Aunt Mary asked me what I was going to do when I got back home.

First I had to dig my potatoes, then I would see what I will do.

So I went home and started to dig my potatoes. Maryanna came to help me a few days. Then the neighbor asked me if I wanted to sell my potatoes. I told her I would sell them as I could do without them anyway. So I sold them.

I thanked my sister for her help as she wouldn't accept any pay. I helped the neighbor then when that was done, I went back to day work. When the superintendent came to me he said, "Tonia, my wife needs a girl. The one who came with us has gone back to her village. You can go right now to see my wife if you want to."

I thought, Janickis haven't been here long in our place, but he is a good old man. I will take a chance on his wife. Anyway, I'll be near Victa.

I went to Pani Janicki. She told me my pay will be 20 dollars a year. Well, I thought that was as much as my uncle gives, and there is more work there than I will have here.

Janicki had thirty chickens and two pigs. Just for their own use they killed two pigs a year. There was one cow to milk, and you didn't have to take care of the cow. Pivnicki's men were taking care of all the people's cows who worked there as long as they could afford to buy one. I thought I would be starting pretty and I took the job.

I was getting along and I was never hungry there.

Then came the New Year again. People were coming and going, changing their jobs. Wladek Kempcinski's father moved out with his family, the Pivnicki's sold out their sheep and left just a few that a boy could take care of, and didn't need two men any more. Kempcinski and his son Felix got a job near the village to care for sheep, as that was their trade and they always made good money at it.

Kempcinski moved out but Wladek was coming often to visit us. Then one day Wladek asked Victa to marry him. He wanted to make it just a quiet marriage as it was so soon after mother's death. Victa didn't love him, but people tried to talk her into it by saying that Kempcinski men folk never let their woman folk work out. They make enough money to keep their women home. So Victa got herself engaged to Wladek.

Wladek got the rings and Victa washed and pressed her Sunday dress to get ready for her wedding. They were going to get married in the next two weeks before lent started. That week Victa got engaged a letter came from America in mother's name. Who was it from? We went to the carpenter uncle who made the coffin for mother. He read the letter and said,

"Where was that man all those years. If he had written at least sooner, that wouldn't have happened to your poor mother and you girls. The letter is from your father. He's not mentioning any of you here, only asking mother if she cares to go to America he will send her a ship card and money to get to him."

I looked at Victa and she looked sad. I felt something glad in me. Maybe if I had known what was in my future I would not have been so glad, but then I was glad and didn't care who talked bad about my father.

I said, "Well, God took mother from us and is returning our father to us. Anyway, I will get somebody to write a nice letter to father. If he finds out that we are left alone here, maybe he will take us to America."

Victa said she wouldn't go. I said I would go. She said she wouldn't let me go alone, so I told her to come with me, and the two of us were arguing before we got somebody to write the letter to father for us.

I went to Zamosc. Uncle Palinski's new son-in-law Sulinski knew how to write well. He wrote the letter to our father explaining to him what happened to mother and how we were working for ourselves, and if he had a heart for his children to help us some way.

After that letter was sent out, Victa and I had a lot of arguing and talking, but we were waiting for what the answer was going to be.

In the meantime we had so many advisers, so many buyers for our things that we owned. So many sellers to sell us such and such things we may need on our way to America. Our heads were dizzy from all that advice from friends and different people.

Wladek heard about it and he wanted to take Victa to the church right the next Sunday. Victa postponed her wedding to wait to hear from father.

Uncle Palinski came one day to me and said, "You know Wladek

Zdanoski. His father used to pull your teeth when you were small. Well, Wladek saw you and he wants to marry you."

"You marry him, uncle!" I was sorry for the old man after I said it, but it was too late. But I said, "Wladek is twenty-eight years old and I'll be fifteen in May, and I don't want Wladek."

Then fellows were coming from near and far to marry us. I told our bosses to tell everyone who asked for us that we were not home. Wladek got mad at me because on account of me Victa was postponing her wedding. Victa hired a woman, paid her a dollar and sent her to bring the wedding rings to Wladek, and the wedding plans were over.

One early morning before breakfast, Jozef Kowaleski's mother parked herself in my kitchen. I thought something had happened in her family. I was just going to milk the cow. I asked her if anything had happened. She said nothing had happened, she had just come to help me to do something.

"You came to help me? Oh, no," I said. "You sit down by the stove while I go milk the cow. Pani Janicki will be up soon, then you tell her what you want."

I didn't understand her meaning and I left her in the kitchen.

When I got through with the cow and came in with the milk, Pani Janicki said to me, "Jozef Kowaleski sent his mother to ask you for him, would you want to marry him? She said Jozef works in the brick place and makes good money, but he is afraid to ask you himself."

I looked at Pani Janicki and then at Kowaleski and thought of the day I had told Jozef I'd sooner kiss a dog's behind than to kiss him in the face, and he had said, "Oh child, what are you saying!"

I felt sorry for the poor woman, she had her hard luck raising her six children, so I said to her, "Kowaleski, everybody takes me for much older than I am. I'll be only fifteen in May, and I don't think I will ever marry in this country, as I will be going to America as soon as my father sends for me."

She didn't say anything, just looked at me and walked out.

Pani Janicki took a man in to board. My Uncle Julius was getting old and wasn't able to do much walking. Pivnicki pensioned him for life and got a new superintendent over the forest. He was waiting until the home for him would be fixed to move into, so he was staying at Janicki's. He was single, a man about thirty. He asked me if I knew of a good housekeeper for him, but I didn't know of any.

I was so anxious and nervous waiting for the letter from my father that I lost my appetite and ambition to work. Days just dragged for me. Victa just ignored everything. A new fellow came into her eyes and got into her heart better than Wladek. So she just waited to see what would come of it. Victa was always easy going, while I was always on fire.

CHAPTER 7

Letter from Father

Then the first of April we got our answer from father, and it said, *"Get ready, both of you. The ship card is on the way. Wait for word from your agent."* Another wait, but we knew we were going. *"Just wait for the word from your agent."*

Then I asked Pani Janicki to relieve me from my work. I wanted to rest a while, get things ready for myself for the trip. Pani Janicki said to me that I would have to get her somebody to take my place. That's the way the rules were if you wanted to get your pay for the time you worked there. Get somebody or finish the year. I had ten dollars coming to me for the six months I worked there and I needed it very much, so I asked if she wanted a young girl or an older woman, as there were more of the older than the young.

I heard of a widow about forty-five or so. I told Janicki of her. Janicki thought it over and said that might be better than a young girl. Maybe she would stay longer. So I went after the woman, brought her over and got myself cleared out.

I went to Aunt Mary. I found her somehow sad, and Uncle Julian was staying more in the woods than home. Once I caught him sitting in the garden crying. Maryanna was trying to avoid everybody, so I gathered up some courage and asked Aunt Mary why it was everyone was acting that way.

Aunt Mary said Maryanna was leaving them. She said, "You know how Uncle Julius loved her. He would give his life for her. Now since she heard that you and Victa are going to America, she is preparing herself to go too. Besides, there are two boys and another girl from this village that are going and they are leaving from here the first of May."

I felt sorry for Aunt Mary and Uncle Julian, and thought, why is Maryanna doing this to the old people now? They raised her from a child. They gave her everything. She has love, money. She was married, had her own place and sold her place. She has plenty of money. Victa and I were lacking all of that. Why was Maryanna always acting like she was jealous of us, especially of Victa. She gave me once in a while a dress, or a shawl, but never to Victa. And her things fit Victa better than me – they were too big for me. When I passed them on to Victa, then Maryanna threatened me that she would never give me anything now. I bet she is jealous that we are going to America. She wants to show us she's going to be there and wouldn't even wait for us or tell us she is going. She wanted to be there first.

I asked Aunt Mary what she was going to do with her baby. Was she taking it with her?

She wanted to at first, but Uncle told her she would take it over his dead body, so she changed her mind and was leaving the baby with them.

I said, "At least she could wait for us. She knows we are going alone."

"That's what Uncle Julian told her, but she said she is going with those going from here."

I was there a few days and I was restless. Then I saw the forest foreman coming. He said he was looking for anybody who wanted to work planting trees. I thought, well, since I'm not doing anything I'll go put in a few days. He said that was swell and went to get a few more workers.

Maryanna closed up her dressmaking business. She didn't take any more sewing. She was restless too, so she said she was coming also.

The forest foreman got a couple more girls and older workers from the village. The next day there were about a hundred workers from the nearest villages. We were going in pairs. You stuck a digger in the ground, made a hole, the next worker stuck the tree plant in that hole. You stuck the digger next to the plant and tightened the plant, and so on. That's the way we planted trees in those days.

We had been planting one week and we put in a couple thousand trees.

The next week one day was cloudy and cold. We from Bristek came, but very few of the others showed up. We worked half the day, then we sat to eat our lunch. Two fellows were there and ate their lunch faster and made a fire to warm themselves up. Then they got funny with the girls. They put the green pine brush and twigs on the fire and that made a lot of smoke. So they were catching the girls, one by the arms, and one by the feet, and holding them over the smoke. Even my sister. I sat there grinding my teeth in disgust. The girls were screaming. Their clothes could catch on fire!

When they smoked all the other girls, one of them was coming where I was sitting, saying, "We didn't smoke this one yet!"

"And you won't!", I said.

"Oh," he said. "I will take you myself!"

He came from behind me and put his hands under my arms, but before he had a chance to pick me up, he hollered for help. He didn't expect it. I grabbed him by his head and twisted his neck and held it. The other fellow wanted to pick my feet up but I was watching him, and from a sitting position to laying down pulling the fellow down with me and putting one of my feet between the other fellow's feet and twisting the other foot around when he was bending down he fell and couldn't untwist my feet from his. Then laying on my chest he couldn't get my hands off his neck.

The forester who was showing us how to plant the trees was eating his lunch and was laughing at the boys, that they smoked the older girls and they couldn't take me, so he came to help them. He bent down and wanted to loosen my hands from the fellow's neck. He did. He loosened my hand and I grabbed him by his vest and ripped all the buttons off it.

He cursed, and then they all let me go.

The boy with the twisted neck gave me another curse, and called me a wild tigress.

The forester was really mad, because he had a much older wife than himself and she was a very jealous one. He was afraid she might ask him to explain himself, how come he lost all his buttons off his vest. I told him to tell her he got caught on a Christmas tree. We got up to start the work. The foreman came around on his white horse. He told us we could go home because it started to rain and was getting colder. The boys and girls went in the group ahead. I followed far behind them.

The foreman turned on his horse and came to me, laughing. "Where did you learn jujitsu?"

He said he saw the whole circus. He was standing in the brushes watching what was going to turn out and what happened that they let me alone all at once.

I told him I tore the buttons off the forester's vest.

He laughed, bent down off his horse and picked me up and sat me in front of him. He covered me with his rain cape and galloped past the group quickly and brought me to Aunt Mary and went home.

I took a pail and went to the well to get water because I wanted a drink. A woman was taking water also, so we were talking for a while. Then the girls came and passed by.

My sister said, "How in the world did you get here before us? You were so far behind us?"

I told her an angel brought me on his wings.

The next day was Sunday, and I went to see Victa. Victa told me she had news for me. Ignate and Wladka were going to America and they would wait for us.

"Oh, thank God," I said. "We won't be all alone on the way."

Ignate, our distant cousin had two brothers in America, Antony and Jan. Antony sent for Wladka so they would be going to get married. Jan sent for Ignate to keep Wladka company on the trip. They lived in Pennsylvania. I went to see Wladka and Ignate to plan our trip.

Ignate, Sulinski's brother-in-law asked me, "Have you seen the pass over the border?"

I told him no, Sulinski and I had to go with Victa and get our pass from the acting mayor.

He said if we couldn't get our passes from him not to argue with them in the office, it wouldn't help us any. We should come back and tell him. Wladka and Ignate didn't get their passes there either. Wladka couldn't get her pass because she wasn't born in this district and she couldn't get it from her district where she was born, because she moved out from there ten years ago to live here. Ignate couldn't get his pass because they wanted him in the army next year. Sulinski said if we all kept our mouths shut tight he would bring us all to a place where we could get our passes.

The only thing was that here we could get them without charge. There we would have to pay five dollars each. There was an acting mayor in Skudzawy who would give any pass to anybody for money. He had been doing this for years and wasn't caught yet.

I stayed with Sulinski overnight. Monday I called on Victa and told Victa to ask the head lady if she would let her go for a half day. She did, so we went for our passes.

They all knew me there. They all got their passes. Victa got her pass too, but I couldn't get mine. Ignate asked them why. They laughed at me. One said I had to finish my year for Brzuskas. The next one said I was old enough to get married, but not old enough to get a pass. They told me I had to be eighteen to get a pass.

So I came back to Sulinski's and Victa went back to her work. She was worried that I might not get a pass, but Sulinski took the three of us and we went to Skudzawy. We got our passes for five dollars each. I was put on the pass as eighteen years old with my right name, but from Skudzawy, not Sosnova. The man told us not to say anything and not to show the pass to anyone around. He told us just as soon as we pass the Russian side to the Germany side to tear the pass down and throw it away. But when we were out of the man's office Sulinski told us not to destroy the pass right away on the Germany side. He said something might happen that we would have to come back and we would have to have this pass.

I took Sulinski's word for it and brought my pass to America.

I showed Victa my pass so she wouldn't worry anymore. I met Uncle Julian in the place. Uncle gave me a letter that came in the morning. I thanked him, opened it and told Victa it was our ship cards.

Uncle said, "Shhhh." Then in a low voice he said, "Pivnicki is here. He came a while ago and he is complaining that everybody is leaving Sosnova. He is getting short of people. He asked me to try to stop you girls going away, somehow. I know I have no right to do that. I told him that you were going to your father, so he says he will ask you to show the ship cards to him. He will destroy your cards and give you each a hundred dollars and raise your pay, or marry you to any of the boys you want."

I thanked Uncle for warning us and turned to Victa. "Victa," I said, "Gurtaloski said if you have a hundred dollars and a cow you can become his daughter-in-law. Here is your chance!"

Victa said, "I gave Wladek up because I won't let you go alone to America, and I'm not marrying anybody else even if I do love someone."

I asked Victa if she got anyone to take her place now that we got our ship card and our passes and are sure of going. Victa said she thought Suska would take her place until they get somebody else, but she wouldn't quit until we heard from the agent to tell us when to start from here. We were told not to start out until he told us when.

I went back to Wladka and Ignate to show them the ship cards. They had everything ready. They could start any time, but they would wait for us.

Maryanna Tyburski asked me to stay until Saturday. She asked her father if she could make a farewell party for us. She was sad because she would be the only growing girl left in Zamosc when Wladka left. There were only small girls in the village, so Saturday was a big party with music, songs and tears. Boys and girls that knew us and loved us were ashamed to show their tears and wished us good luck on our trip.

The next day as I was going to Aunt Mary's, I met the forester's foreman talking with Janicki. I greeted them and Pukarski said he was asking for me. I told him I was here and he asked when we were going to know about the trip. I told him we had everything except the word when to start. He asked me if I would be his housekeeper until then, and maybe he would be able to get somebody by the time I left.

I agreed to be his housekeeper until I got the word to start out for America, but not for the whole year, although that was one place I wouldn't have minded to work forever. The old bachelor needed someone to milk one cow and keep his room clean. The two of us didn't know what to do with all the milk, butter, buttermilk and pot cheese. We both could have nice meals made of it if I only knew how to cook.

With my housecleaning and animal serving and milking cows I had no chance to learn to cook fancy meals. I knew how to cook potatoes, sauerkraut and zacierki. Zacierki was made just mixing flour with water with your fingertips until it came up crumbs like cereal and dropping and stirring it into hot water so it wouldn't stick in one lump. When it came to the top it was set. It was a good meal in a hurry, or when there was nothing else in the house to cook. It didn't take much flour and you can eat it with milk, sweet or sour, or salt pork or sauerkraut and potatoes, or if no other flavor, vinegar. I knew how to make coffee and tea. I had asked Brzuska to teach me how to make bread, but she told me she paid for her schooling and she wouldn't eat bread made with my hands. So I was only good to care for pigs and cows. Oh, yes, and I could make good egg noodles. Pani Janicki taught me how to make it.

So I took a job for Pukarski for a while and almost starved him with the noodles. He got his coffee for breakfast and noodles for dinner every day for a week until he bought a rabbit one day and showed me how to cook it. So he had a change from noodles.

Then I heard of an old woman, about fifty-eight. She was a woman with money. She and her husband owned Karczma. It was called a "saloon" in English. Well, her husband died and she lost her business and was idle for some time. I told Pukarski of the woman.

He said, "Tonia, you are a brick to my wealth. That's the kind of a woman I would like to have. Then I know she won't chase after young boys. You know why I threw out the woman with that little boy three years old? When you left Janicki she was all right for a couple of weeks and then the boy started to cry at night. I thought maybe the boy is sick or something. She's the mother, I thought. She should know what to do. But that was going on night after night. I got tired of it. First I didn't want to go in her room, but the boy seemed like he was screaming more that night than before, so I walked in and she wasn't there. I wanted to open the door outside. I thought she went out to the back room. What would she be doing there so long? I turned the knob but couldn't open it. I tried to quiet the boy. He went to sleep and I sat to watch for her. She came in at 3:00 a.m. I didn't say anything happened, just watched her the next night. She went out at 1:00 a.m. and returned at 3:00 a.m., and between those hours the boy was screaming, but I didn't mind the boy. When she shut the door I went through my window and followed behind the fences to see where she was going. You know where she went? To the stable."

In protection against any fire or thieves in Pivnicki's place, besides a watchman with two dogs, one or two men slept nights in every cow barn, sheep barn and horse stables, changing off. Pukarski said he didn't want the girl to get herself in trouble in a stable and then put the blame on him, so he asked Pan Janicki to witness the show, and they caught her. Pukarski threw her out and she couldn't sue him for the whole year's pay. He paid her just for the weeks she worked.

I brought the old woman Graboska to him the next week. I was helping Victa to get her things ready to sell out. I met Graboska and asked her how she liked her place, and she said it was so good she didn't want to go to heaven.

At last we received the word from the agent to start on our way, so we sold whatever we had to sell and gathered our money together. We had a little over one hundred and fifty dollars for both of us to make the trip. Maryanna and her group had left already the first of May, so we had our last day May 15.

That morning Victa and I visited our dear mother's grave for the last time, planted some flowers and watered them with our tears. As we prayed, we said goodbye to her.

We then said goodbye to Aunt Mary and all our friends who were there. Uncle Julian was somewhere in the woods praying for us girls. He didn't want to part with any of us, so he went out to the woods so he wouldn't have to see us leaving.

CHAPTER 8

The Russian Border Crossing to Germany

We rushed to Zamosc so as not to keep Wladka and Ignate waiting too long. Sulinski told us we would start at 11 o'clock in the evening so we would get to pass the Russian boundaries at six or seven in the morning.

So we were waiting. Sulinski fixed two nice seats on his wagon covered with blankets. One for us girls, one for him and Ignate. At eleven we bid Zamosc goodbye and were on our way. *gnat* had passed the border many times as he had relatives on the Germany side and had been going to work and on business. He knew the Russians and told us to be careful what to say to them because even if they didn't like your walk they would make lots of trouble for you.

So when we were about one mile from the boundaries Sulinski told us to get off the wagon and walk by ourselves like we didn't know him - go into the building, be as calm as possible and get our passes signed. It was early yet and they might not have eaten their breakfast before the new force came in. They may not ask you too many questions. Just get out quick and don't stop. Sulinski would catch up with us.

He left behind us and we kept on. We came into the building as calm as we could. We were in luck. They must have been hungry. The new crew hadn't come yet, so they didn't ask many questions, only looked at me and at Victa and asked where we were from. I told them Skudzawy. They asked Victa where she was from. She told them Sosnovo, and quickly she added that we were cousins. They said everything was all right and let us go.

Phew! Was I glad that she didn't say that we were sisters! I love her always, but I didn't mind her denying me being her sister. We were so glad and excited we forgot the warning to keep going. We stood outside looking at Sulinski coming. He was some distance and didn't want us to wait for him. He didn't know how to signal us to keep going, but he took his horse whip, made believe he waved over his horse, and in the meantime he hoped we understood what he meant. I knew he never whipped his horse. I grabbed Victa by the arm, and without words, pushed Ignate and kept going to the bridge and kept going fast – over the bridge to the Germany side where we would be safe. We kept on going until the building was out of our sight.

Then Sulinski caught up with us and said, "You fools! Good thing Tonia wised up soon enough to keep you going, otherwise we would be paying nice fines and I'd be on the way to jail. They saw you waiting and I had to use my head to talk myself out of it. I told them that you might be just curious as to who was coming behind them, and I never saw you before."

So we sat on the wagon and drove on past. We came into Brodnica and looked around where we could buy something for our breakfast. Victa saw the first butcher shop open and walked in and bought some kielbasa. I went with the others. We got some bread, milk and cookies and found a bench in a little triangle park right across from the stores. We sat on the bench and began eating our breakfast. I started on my kielbasa first. I liked kielbasa – all Polish people do. Victa had a fit with hers. She chewed for a while, and twisted her face up and phooh! Into the ground she spit it. She looked at me the way I was eating the kielbasa, looked back at her kielbasa, took another bite, then flew like lightning before my eyes and bong! Into the gutter! I looked at my empty hand and the direction where my kielbasa flew. Then I saw a dog carrying my kielbasa away just as if he was waiting there and knew it was coming to him.

"What?" I said to Victa. "Just because you don't like something I should go hungry?"

"Well," she said, "I won't let you eat things that taste bad."

"It tasted good to me! You must have no appetite", I told her.

Wladka and Ignate were eating their bread and ham and looking at us surprisingly. They didn't know what to say, but Sulinski had tears in his eyes from laughing.

Then he asked, "What butcher shop did you buy your kielbasa from, Victa?"

She pointed her finger.

"Do you see what hangs above that door?"

"A horse head", we all said.

Sulinski said, "If you had gone with us you wouldn't have bought yourself horse baloney. Some people in Germany like horse meat. It's the cleanest. That's why they have a sign like that one with a horse head above their shops. Look at butcher shops that sell pigs and other meat. They have pig's heads or some other animal. Isn't it so that pigs or chicken are the dirtiest animals and people eat them?"

Well, Sulinski, Wladka and Ignate finished what they had and I had to be satisfied with bread, milk and cookies, and went back to the wagon.

Sulinski drove us to the station where we were supposed to go. Our tickets were to Julowo, but this was our first agency mill where everybody who was taking long trips had to go through, I was told. The station was crowded with pushing and shoving. Everybody wanted to be first at the ticket window. Wladka and Ignate went in there first and got their tickets. I stood in the line behind a little old gentleman no taller than I, all in gray. A gray suit, gray hair and a little gray beard. He carried a cane and saw me being pushed away from the line. He grabbed me by the sleeve and led me tight to him.

He got his ticket and said to me, "We geisto" or something like that.

It sounded to me like Jewish. He was asking where I was going. I understood a little Jewish from the time I was eight years old. There were three Jewish families living in Sosnovo and on Yom Kippur they always went to Lipno for a couple of days. They took me to play with their children while they were in the synagogue. Sperling's children and Sperling's relative's children from Lipno couldn't talk Polish, so I picked up some of their Jewish words.

I did appreciate our trip through Germany. I said to the little gentleman, "to Julowo" and he saw that I was holding onto Victa.

He called out loud, "Zwei tickets to Julowo."

I handed him the money, he paid for the tickets and handed them to me with the change.

I told him "Dankasha" and ran out after Wladka and Ignate just as the train was starting.

Sulinski wasn't there anymore. He went back to Brodnica and was going to stay until the next day with his relatives. We got to Julowo late in the afternoon. I never had seen as busy a place as I saw there. The place was crowded with men, women and children. Men were put in one room, single women in another room, mothers with children in another. Working girls there were like Amazons. They took us in one room, took our baskets and bundles and money from us. Doctors came and looked in our eyes, in our ears, told us to stick out our tongues and let us go and wait in a big hall.

In the hall we met Ignate. He was sad. He was rejected because of his eyes so he had to go back home. Wladka and Victa rushed Ignate to the station and helped him on the train in hopes that Ignate might get to Brodnica to meet Sulinski there. So it's only three of us girls now.

In the meantime while Wladka and Victa were bringing Ignate to the train, the Amazons were hollering at me,

"Where are the other two? We have no time to wait for them. They are taking our time."

I tried to explain that the two brought our cousin to the train, but they were still mad.

When Wladka and Victa came back, they fed us supper, and after that gave us a room with lots of beds, where girls slept two and three in the beds.

The next day after breakfast they took us in one room and told us to undress ourselves. They left us bare without clothes, shoes or stockings, and pushed us in another room in booths. While we stood there, a pail of water came from somewhere on our heads and got us wet. I found out later in life that it was called a shower. They gave us each a bed sheet to wrap ourselves in and sent us to the next room.

Victa's sheet stuck somehow and she couldn't get it quick enough to spread it around herself, so she just wrapped the top part.

The Amazons hollered, "You long legged one, drop that sheet down."

I had mine on so I helped to pull Victa's down. Then more doctors came in, looked at us front and back and checked our hearts. Our clothes were brought to us red hot, and then we were chased from room to room with papers. Then with papers to the bank they returned our money. Victa and I found that our money purse was much lighter then.

After dinner two men called in line and told us to follow them. We all were put on a train. What a train! Just a narrow board on each side of the car. Not even wide enough to sit on and not enough to go around. People were sitting on their own bundles on the car floor, and just like in every other place when people are not satisfied complaints were going around, but no one could do anything about it. We were on the train and the train was moving.

Some years later I heard that system and conditions got better there but just then when I came there people weren't treated much better than cattle. So we were in a box car.

Wladka had started to sing a church song (she and I had sung in the church choir when the regular singers got mad at the organist and left him flat right on Easter holiday, just before we got our ship cards). So we were singing and everything was quiet in our car. All of a sudden we heard we had competition.

Voices came from the next car behind us, "oh, mee, baa".

That's whose company we were in!

We were on all night and all day. Victa and I finished our food that Aunt Mary had put in the basket for us. Black bread, dry cheese and fruit.

The next day we got hungry. The train stopped at some station where I saw a stand. I got out, bought some bread, fruit, candy and a big bottle of soda.

Victa said, "How did you get this stuff? Do they talk Polish?"

"No" I said. "I put the things in the bag, the man handed it to me and I asked the cost. He showed me a coin in German money and I gave him that much from my purse." (They had changed our Russian rubles into German marks in Julowo.) So we weren't hungry.

Then we came to a big station and two men got on the train. When the train stopped he kept calling, "Who has a ticket to Amsterdam?"

We all looked at our tickets. Those who had tickets to Amsterdam got off and changed trains. Victa and my tickets said Bremen. People were getting off and others came on.

When people sat themselves down, we missed Wladka. We thought that we would be on one ship and it turned out to be that our tickets were to a different part of this country. It was kind of lonesome without Wladka. But we were going on. At that stop where Wladka got off a young Jewish couple got on with a baby. I introduced myself to the little fellow and played with him all the way to Bremen, much to his mother's contentment.

Friday night when we got to Bremen, getting off the train the Jewish couple were coaxing us to go with them. Victa and I were scared. We didn't know which way or where to turn, but were afraid to trust the young people we didn't know, as the man was holding me by my sleeve on one side and another man got hold of my hand from the other side.

This other new comer was an elderly man about fifty or

more – short, stout, and dressed nicely. He asked the young man where he was going. The young man told him he was going to London. The older man gave the young man a mad look, pushed him away and motioned to Victa and told us to follow him. We did.

It couldn't have been far, because Wednesday evening he let us in to a back room the first thing. Then he took us upstairs into a nice room with two beds and spoke to us for the first time in Polish with a great German accent. He told us to sleep separate or sleep together, it didn't make any difference. He asked us to give him our money and we did. He took over our basket and locked us in from the outside and took the key.

Victa and I went right off to sleep and we were left alone. Victa was good. She could sleep on a barbed wire fence, I thought. Well, they took all I had so I slept too. It must have been late because everything was quiet.

The next morning a girl had opened our door to wake us up, but we were already up and washed, as we found water in a pitcher and a basin like at Pivnicki's, and we got dressed. The girl saw that we were ready and called us to follow her downstairs and showed us where to sit down by the table. There sat the old man, his wife and two young growing girls and the one that had called us downstairs. That was the agent and his family.

After breakfast the man told us we were going with him somewhere, so we went in the hallway to wait for him. When we stood in the hallway we heard a lot of noise. Men, women and children were right across the hall, like a big barracks, with two big, long rooms. In one of them were all kinds of beds and the other room was where people eat. I don't know if those people all slept in that one room, but it looked to me that way, as there were a lot of them in both rooms. At the long table right near the door I noticed two nice looking girls and a tall lanky fellow, eating and talking together. I was watching them when the agent called to go.

The agent took us to a big building with a lot of windows and desks where men sat with a crowd of people around them throughout the whole building. A lot of questions were asked and the agent signed papers for us. We got injections against smallpox. Mine didn't take, but Victa was very sick with hers for a few days.

We came for dinner and again we ate with the agent and his family. After dinner the agent told us not to go away from his house so we wouldn't get lost, but that's just what we did without realizing what we were doing. As we stood by the agent's door, Victa and I saw a music band marching on the street coming past the agent's house. A lot of people followed the band, and Victa and I followed them too. When we came to the corner we didn't go any farther. We stood there for a while in the excitement, watching the parade. We turned our heads so we forgot what direction we came from. As we stood looking around I spied the three I saw at the big dinner room.

I said to Victa, "Look, these girls and that fellow! I saw them this morning at the big dinner room. I'll ask them to tell us which way it is to the agent's house."

I went to the girls and asked them to please tell me which way it was to the agent's house. I'm sorry that I don't remember his name today, and he was good to me. Even though I disgraced myself there, he didn't throw me out to the other crowd. The two girls looked at me and sized me up from top to bottom and turned away from me. I got red in the face and didn't know what to say. I didn't offend them, I'm sure, by asking them just to show me the direction to the agent's. I repeated my question, shyly.

Then the man turned and he said, "Oh, yes. We are from the same agent. If you two girls go with us here for a while then when we go back we will bring you there."

I thanked him for that.

Two more men joined the three. They seemed to know one another. They all started for the place where they were going. The lanky man waved to me and Victa to come along. I thought, "That's what they were waiting for, for the other two men. Now they are going to the agent."

We followed them where they went to karczma (a saloon). The lanky man pushed first Victa, then me, then the other girls. It was crowded behind the table. The girl next to me sat herself in sideways and put her arm and elbow on the table so she didn't have to look at me, and just kept talking to the two men in front of her.

The lanky one was busy putting glasses on the table and pouring whiskey and beer in them. Victa and I protested and pled, "Please, no. We never drank. We don't want to drink."

Lanky pleaded, "Oh, just one. We have been staying here for a week, and some of us two weeks, and don't know when the ship will come. Just one. Go ahead, it'll make you feel good."

We said all right, and drank the first glass of whiskey. I felt numb all over. I felt like a wet rag pulled out from a wash tub that you could twist around and wring out. I drank the beer. I thought that might make me feel better, but it didn't make me feel any better. I felt like crying, laughing, or doing something. I looked at Victa. I don't know how she felt, but from the look of her I thought she didn't feel any better than I.

As we were sitting there ignored by the others, just the lanky one was filling our glasses as soon as they were empty. He insisted that we finish them if we left a little in them, so we were emptying them for him. I kicked something hard under the table and looked down to see what I kicked. I knocked Victa and she caught the idea quickly. There under the table were plenty of spittoons and two of them convenient right by our feet. So we were watching for a chance when no eyes were on us from all around. We didn't mind the ones at our table because they didn't watch us. So we were filling the spittoons until they overflowed. We sat there and didn't know what to say to one another.

I said quietly to Victa, "Do you remember the old gypsy woman that came to Sosnova last December before we received the letter from father? The gypsy took your hand and mine, looked in our palms and told us that, *"Soon you two will go far across a big water. You will have an exciting trip."*

We asked her what we would find on the other side of the water, and she just looked at us sadly awhile and said, "God will be with you there too. Good luck."

We gave her fifty cents apiece and she went away.

Victa didn't answer me. I didn't say anymore. I was sick and didn't know how to leave the table. The day was getting darker. I turned my head to the door. "Who is that?" I thought.

The girl who served on us at the table in the agent's house was talking. She was saying something like, *"Anyone from the agent's house come for supper. If they come late, supper won't be served to them!"*

I didn't understand all and I didn't hear all. Victa told me the rest the next day. I didn't see anybody but that girl from the agent. I don't know how I got out from behind that table. How I kept up behind her. I felt I walked on rubber feet, or was flying, but I kept my eyes on that girl. I saw her open a side door from the place across the yard and right into the agent's big hall. That's how far it was, but how could I know? I was half conscious when I got there.

If I had not touched anything to eat, it might not have happened, but I sat by the table and drank a glass of hot tea. I walked away from the table into the hall. How? I don't know. Then whoops! The whole day's good meals were wasted. I saw something like big ants running all around me, heard noises, voices from afar.

"Now hold that broom and the shovel. Now pick it up."

I tried to bend down to do something. Whoops! Came some more right on the shovel. More noise. I don't know if I did what I was told to do, or somebody took the broom and shovel away from me. Something is in my rubber hands.

"Here, now, wipe it up!"

I didn't know any more for a good while until I came back to the world again.

I was sitting in the agent's room. Victa stood by me. No one said a word. Nice comfortable chair. I rested my head on it and feel asleep until we were told to go up to bed.

Upstairs the girl warned us that anyone who would soil the bed clothes or the carpets would have to pay for its cleaning, so be careful.

Victa and I were afraid to fall asleep. Victa was as sick as I, but her luck was that she was half unconscious sitting in that saloon, and that she didn't know how I got out from there. The lanky man did bring her back, and as she was too sick to eat, she didn't eat. She had just that one glass of whisky and a glass of beer and she held hers and didn't throw up. She saw what happened to me and she finished my job there. I had fainted away while the crowd from the barracks were watching me disgustedly and laughing at me (for which I can't blame them).

The agent himself had pushed the chair to me and he and Victa put me on it until I woke up to find Victa standing by me.

The next day was Sunday. We didn't go anywhere all day, but through the day the agent called Victa and me to his office and said, "Now tell me what happened."

I told him how we disobeyed his warning not to go from his house, and how that parade had tempted us and we got lost. I told him about the two girls and how they acted funny with us when we asked them to show us the direction to his home. And how the tall, lanky man offered to bring us back later, but asked us to go with them first.

I never saw the girls anymore, ever after that, but the poor lanky man got beat up by the agent. I don't know if it was on account of us, or something else. The agent asked the lanky man for a key from his room. He told the agent that he left the key in the door. The agent said it was not in the door and started to slap the man's face left and right. I never saw him after that either. I felt sorry for the man and was wondering why the agent, so gentle and quiet, beat the man up.

Monday after breakfast the agent took Victa and me to his office again. He had our basket ready there, and our money. He asked us how much money we had before he took it, and we told him how many marks, because the Russian rubles were taken by the agency in Julowo and exchanged for German marks. He told us how much he deducted for our food and board, and gave us the rest.

There was very little left in the purse, but we would get our food on the ship without charge. In our basket he put two bottles of wine. He told us to keep it until we got on the ship. He said we might get sick on the ship, so we should drink the wine and it would make us feel better. Then he told us to follow him and he called to the barracks crowd to line up and follow him.

CHAPTER 9

Ship to America

We walked about twenty-five or thirty minutes until we came to the water. Our agent told us all from there we would be taken care of by different people, and then disappeared.

I asked, "Would we be put on a small boat that would take us to America?"

A man laughed and showed me a big "colos" standing farther out on the water.

While we were getting on the small boat a rumor passed around like lightening. People went into an uproar. Women were praying, some crying. Men were cursing. Some of them who had money said they would wait for another ship. Some families said they would go back home. I didn't know what it was all about. Then a man in a blue uniform came from the big ship and he called to the crowd for an interpreter. A man came out from the crowd to the man in the ship's uniform and explained what was being said in a couple of languages.

The people were told that they were not taking chances. The ship was all right, but it had sprung a leak on its way from America to Europe. It was in a dry dock and was all fixed now. The men's life in service on the ship were just as much valued as any of ours, the man in the uniform said. We were told they wouldn't take a risk to go on the ship if it wasn't fixed. That calmed the crowd and all went on. The small boat made three trips back and forth to the ship.

Everybody settled themselves where they belonged for the journey. We were third class, so I think we were on the third deck below with men, women and children all around us. Victa saw a double bunk right at a porthole. We took the bottom bunks. Above us two Czech girls (or Slovak?) were there before us We could understand each other already.

Victa and I were going through our laughs and sorrows in our minds. We were talking over how we waited so long for the word from the agent. I told Victa the agent was good to us all the way through. If he had called us sooner we would be wasting time and money for two or three weeks like some of the other people who were waiting. By keeping us in Sosnovo we worked almost to the last day, and with all the deductions for our trip and board, we still had a few marks left. So, so far was so good.

One day, two days, three days. Victa, with not only her vaccinated arm swollen, got sea sick too. She didn't want to eat or talk, and she wouldn't come up on deck. The sailors said it would make her feel better, but she couldn't get up to go outside. Three days I didn't want to go out without her, just for meals to the kitchen where everybody went and got meals for themselves.

We were given a pail-like dish and we were told to hold onto it through our trip. With that dish we went in line to get our meal and whatever the cooks had, they poured everything in our one pot. We had plenty of food and we didn't have to go hungry unless we didn't like the food. Then we threw it to the fishes and waited in hopes the next meal would taste better. We had plenty soups for dinners and suppers. For breakfast we got, or it was supposed to be, but didn't taste like it – coffee and lumps of dry bread. I heard it was called suchary (I don't know what it is called in English) and butter that tasted worse than the cheapest margarine in America. But sometimes your stomach is your boss, not your tongue.

Victa was different. After three days she asked for something to drink. She didn't want the coffee. Then I thought of the wine the agent gave us, and we had forgotten. It was safe on the bottom of the basket. I took one bottle out and reminded Victa what the agent said, to drink it when we get sick. I opened it for her. She took one sip and whizzed the bottle out the porthole. I saw a hand stretch from the upper bunk, but it was too late.

"Ty glupa diewka" (you foolish girl), the Czech girl said. "If you didn't like it, why didn't you give it to us?"

Victa stuck her hand in the basket, pulled out the other bottle and handed it to the Czech girl. Everything was done in such a quick movement by my sick sister before I could blink my eye. It reminded me of the horse baloney in Brodnica. I got mad. If my sister didn't like something she grabbed it out of my mouth whether I liked it or not.

I went on to the top deck every day after that and just brought her food to her. If she liked it, or if not, she could feed the fish. I ate mine outside and she didn't see what I was eating.

After the sixth day on the ship I got weak all over for three days, but not as bad as Victa. I was on deck every day trying to avoid people so I would be all alone, trying to find an empty spot. The whole deck was covered with people like sardines, sitting, lying, sea sickness or some other sickness. I found a place between a woman with her three children and a bundle of blankets with a head sticking out from it – bald on top and gray side hair hanging behind its ears. I sat there.

The woman started to talk to me. She was sick and her three children were as lively as could be. It seems like the children can take it harder than the older ones. She told me she was going to Baltimore to her husband. She said the children were ages two, three and five, and told me their names. I told her where I was going and my name also. The woman got up and went after her children who got away too far from her.

A voice from the blankets came out. "Antonia, you said you are going to your father?"

"Yes," I said.

I thought he was going to mind his grandchildren someplace,

but he said to me, "Would you be ashamed of me if I went to your father?"

"No," I said. "I was taught to respect old people."

But he said, "If I ask your father, will you marry me?"

I looked at him and jumped up off that spot and didn't stop running until I hit my bunk.

I didn't want to get our supper that evening. Victa didn't feel hungry and she thought I was too sick to eat and we just went to sleep.

The next morning Victa got up and thought she was strong enough to get our breakfast.

After breakfast she went out to wash our dishes and came down and said to me, "Aren't you going out on the deck today? It is nice out."

I told her I was not, unless she was going. She said she thought she would go out, so we did. As we were coming out of that chimney hole I stuck out my head first to see if there was anybody out there I didn't want to see. I turned to Victa and told her to duck. I took one step down and she asked me what the matter with me was. She said I was acting funny that day. I got back out again and told her the coast was clear. When she came out I pointed. I told her to look at that bundle of blankets over there, and whenever she passed by some time to take a good look at him, because he asked me to marry him. He wanted father's address so he could come and marry me. For the rest of our trip we kept out of "grandpa's" way.

CHAPTER 10

Arrival at Baltimore

On the 15th day from the time we left Bremen, our first stop was New York. Three parts of the people got off the ship, and "grandpa" too. The ship got lighter. Boxes, bundles and trunks were hoisted out. Then coal was hoisted out. That happened to be Sunday, but men were working like beavers. Victa and I, with the rest were going to Baltimore, so we weren't allowed to leave the ship. We were watching, standing on the deck.

In the evening with the lights on, the ship started moving on again. Monday and Tuesday were a pleasure ride. We got better food and the sailors were nicer to us. We were put up with the second class. Wednesday, we got into Baltimore by one o'clock. Victa and I were standing on America!

Thank God! We left our enemy, Russia. We left our friends in Poland. We left people we knew and didn't know. We left the ocean behind us and now we are in America, our new home!

I didn't know that my misery had followed me still. God bless America, that many orphans like Victa and I can find home here still!

For our first step in America we were taken in to a big building for questioning. They didn't ask many, just to whom and where we were going and how much money we had. We showed them our marks. They took the marks and gave us American money which we didn't know a dime from a dollar, and it surprised us every time we exchanged the money we had less and less.

Late in the afternoon we were put on the American train. Soft seats, soft carpet on the floor like in Pivnicki's. Pleasant conductors. They looked at everybody's tickets. They looked at our tickets, and we were the longest ones going the farthest to father. Then they looked at all the other people's tickets. So we made ourselves comfortable on the soft seats and on we went.

Everything was going fine for us, only we got hungry and didn't know how to buy our food. Victa, as always, a good sleeper, went off as soon as she sat down.

I loved the scenery. I watched the window as the train was going. I watched when the train stopped every so often. People going off and getting on. As we were farther and farther from Baltimore less people were on the train. Every few hours the conductor was calling out the next city – Pittsburgh! The answer came from some seats. Pittsburgh! Chicago! The answer came at Chicago, and so on. Our ticket was the longest one, and not many people were left on the train. Victa occupied a double seat across from me and went to sleep, as ever.

The conductors got used to us so that they knew us by heart. When they called Traverse City, they answered themselves to their own question without looking at our tickets. I figured we were twenty-four hours on American land and we were hungry. Then a black man in a white coat was passing by me with fruit, candy and soda. I stopped him by grabbing his sleeve. I took some candy, two oranges, two apples, two bottles of soda, and I didn't know how much it cost, and didn't know how to ask. I took one paper bill. It said one on it. I handed it to the man and trusted his honesty. He gave me some change and left.

I woke up Victa and said to her, "Victa, you don't know what you are missing! This is exciting, but much better than through Germany! Even the smell from the engine comes to your nose once in a while, but not as bad as a car full of cows behind you. But maybe it is better for you when you are asleep and don't feel hungry so much. So get up and have something to eat!"

She looked at me and asked, "Where did you get this? What language did you talk here?"

I told her, "I didn't talk. I handed the man a paper bill and trusted to his honesty, so we could get something to hold us over for a while. I even had a conductor holding my hand!"

She said, "No!"

I said, "Yes!"

The girls and boys who answered to "Chicago!" were fooling around, and one of the conductors was fooling around with them too. Then he left them and sat by me and put his hand on mine as I had my hand on my knee. I pulled back quick like something bit me and turned to the window. He smiled, said something, got up and walked to his bench where he and other conductors sat before they get up to call the cities. They said something to one another, looked at me, looked where Victa slept and kept answering to themselves, Traverse City, Traverse City.

Friday, I didn't know if the conductors noted that we only ate candy and fruit, or maybe it was their business, because one of the conductors came around with a basket. There were about ten people left in our car. The conductor passed around and stopped by me. He had sandwiches, milk and fruit. I reached for the milk, took two sandwiches, two apples and handed him my last paper bill. He gave me change and left.

I woke Victa up for the second meal in two days.

After a while the two conductors came to me and asked me something. I shook my head. I didn't know what they were saying. They went out into another car and a few minutes later returned with a man from the other car. The man asked me if I wanted to send a telegram to my father, in what sounded to me like Jewish.

I said, "we fill cos?"

He said, "bufcigh cents."

I knew what it meant, but which was the fifty cents? I took a handful of change and held it out. The conductor who wanted to hold my hand took a big, round silver coin and gave me a smile and went out. Victa asked me what they wanted the money for. I explained to her that they will send a telegram to our father. Maybe father will meet us at the train when we get to the place we are going.

Then through the evening we went and the train stopped at a little one-room station. The conductors came to us. One took Victa and our basket, the other took me, helped us off the train onto the ground and called the little old man from the little station and told him something as they pointed at us. The man nodded his head to the conductors. They smiled, waved, and went on.

It was getting dark, but we could still see a town farther away from the station. We were hungry, but followed the man. The little man waved us into the room, showed us the bench by the window, shut the door, turned the key in the lock and disappeared. That reminded me of the prison room I was locked in for running away from Brzuskas. A little light was hanging at the ceiling, lights here and there outside, everything else was dark. We sat there, I don't know how many hours. We had no watches. Victa went to sleep on the bench and I sat up thinking.

In my mind passed all my life, from the earliest days I could remember. Mother's life, our life, the work we had been doing, the dream I had, the gypsies, the trip, all the way to that little station. I started to think about what our future life would be. I heard a train coming. The little man came from somewhere with a lantern in his hand and opened the door.

I was shaking Victa up, but the man said not to. With a shake of his head he stood outside for a while. Some people got off the train and the train went on its own way. No one came inside. The man went out, shut the door and disappeared again. Victa had a longer sleep. I sat there and thoughts started to crowd my mind. The old lady in Pivnicki's had told me, "Pray, my child, God will be with you."

The gypsy woman told me God would watch over us. I was getting tired and drowsy, just ready to fall asleep when another train – rah, cha, cha, ding, dang, ding, dang. I told Victa it might be our train so we were ready before the train stopped. Again the little man popped out from somewhere, took our basket, went out and handed it to a conductor. We followed our basket into the seats. The conductor said,

"Tickets!"

I had heard that word so many times on the first train, so I gave him the tickets. He took them and pinned a little pink card on the back of the other seat before us and left.

Soon the daylight came and it was Saturday. On that train they had a man in a white coat going around with a basket. He had candy, oranges, and some long things with little greenish and black spots, three in a bunch. I didn't know what to do. My purse was getting weaker as we were getting hungrier, but I took candy and the things, three in a bunch. I gave Victa the candy and I looked at the new fruit. We never had seen that in our city markets in Europe. I tested the window. It was shut tight. I looked around the car full of people. The floor was clean, no papers on the floor. "No," I thought, "she won't do it."

I broke two of the bunch and handed one to Victa. I held one tight in my hand and stuck the third one behind my back. I watched Victa. She stuck the thinner end into her mouth and put her teeth into it. She looked at me. I grabbed her by the arm.

"You can't do that here!" I told her. "The window is shut and the car is full of people. You might hurt somebody."

She gave me a mad look and dropped it into our basket that we had under our feet.

I went to operate on mine. I bent down as to look for something in the basket so Victa wouldn't know what I was doing, and stuck my teeth in mine. Then I felt like throwing it away, but I wouldn't give up. I paid for it.

The man changed my last big silver coin. I don't know how we would eat again tomorrow. If people in America are eating it, I will eat it too. I stuck a fingernail on one side. In the other side I noticed at the end I bit in it got softer and it split a little. I pulled on it and the top started to move. I pulled farther. I got the skin off it. Ay? I looked with surprise. It was so big with the skin and inside it was smaller than a sausage. I bit half of it and gave the rest to Victa. I told her to try it – it was good. She didn't believe me, but put it in her mouth, ate it and said it was good!

"How did you get it out?" Victa asked.

I showed her how to peel the skin off it and we ate the third one too. It seemed like we had more garbage left than food. Now I know the name of the fruit – bananas!

We were going by a lake or big river now. The land looked swampy. I said to Victa that I hoped we didn't have to get off here where there were big swamps and the big water, but before I finished telling her that the train slowed down and started ding, dang, and stopped.

We were let off the train and the train went on. Now what were we going to do? No one to meet us. We stood on the side watching the men pushing, pulling, all kinds of wagons, trucks with all kinds of packages to and fro. No one minded us standing there. No one asked us what we wanted. I told Victa, "Nobody cares if we are here or not. We have to do something."

I took the address out where we were going to – Randolf Street (don't remember the number). A man appeared there, and I spread the paper before him. He looked at the address, looked at me and Victa and waved to a fellow who stood farther at the depot and said something to him and gave him the address. The fellow turned around and went away.

Victa said, "What did you give him the address for? Now how will we find the place?"

I got scared too, believe me, but in a while a small wagon with one horse stood before us and two young fellows were sitting in a front seat with my address. They motioned us onto the back seats and on we went.

The ride lasted no longer than fifteen minutes and we were on the right street and number.

The boys got off and helped us to get down. I didn't know

how much they were going to ask for that ride. I was afraid that we wouldn't have enough money to pay them, so I took my purse and shook out all I had on my hand and handed it to them. The boys looked at me. They must have figured out for themselves that we were not knowing, so the one with my address handed it to me and took out of my hand two silver, smaller coins, went away and left us by the house gate.

We stood there thinking what to do, whether to walk in or wait for somebody to come and tell us to come in. Then the door opened and a girl as tall as I and twice as heavy as Victa and me appeared. She started to kiss and hug us and hollered, "Our aunts are here! Our aunts are here!"

I thought, "My, but the girl is lovable."

Then came out a woman. Short and twice as heavy, and hollered, "Victa, get back into the yard, leave the girls alone!"

The girl turned around and ran back indoors. There was another woman sitting in the house watching us besides the one who was greeting us. She saw us get off the wagon and she saw the girl called Victa kissing us. Her name was Mrs. Szeleski. It was her address we had, and she told us to come in.

We followed her into the dining room. The woman sitting in the house introduced herself to us as Mrs. Michalski, and said it was her daughter, Victa, fourteen years old, who was kissing us. She told us she got our telegram that morning but couldn't get there to meet us. She then said to put our basket down, go outside in the yard and wash ourselves while she would go to the butcher to get something for supper.

We went into the back yard, found a water pump there and a lot of dish pans, basins, and Victa at the washtub washing something. We took a basin and washed our faces. We needed it from not washing our faces since Wednesday morning on the ship. That woman, Mrs. Szeleski came out of her kitchen and asked the other Victa if she was washing her pants again.

"Yes," the other Victa said. "Are you washing yours, Aunty?"

Mrs. Szeleski said that Aunty didn't crap in her pants, and went on. She crossed her yard, opened her gate into the next yard, through the next street and went into the house the yard belonged to.

In that house lived Mrs. Szeleski's brother, Charles Winowiecki, his wife Mary and three adorable daughters, seven, nine and eleven years old.

We refreshed ourselves and changed into a house dress. Mrs. Michalski came back from the butcher store. We had offered to do something to help her, but she said no – it was time yet before Mr. Michalski came from work.

"I got a quick supper. Frankfurters, pickles and bread. Come on in my front room and rest a while."

We followed her into her front room. She washed her hands and we all sat down on rocking chairs.

"You've never seen a rocking chair?" She asked.

"No. It is nice," we admitted.

"Your father is not here now, but he will be here for the Fourth of July. Well, when Frank came to me from Manistee he was here for a couple of years," Mrs. Michalski went on explaining to us. "We had a new house. Frank bought me this carpet. It has four corners, so Frank bought me four rocking chairs, one for each corner. The table in the middle, the lamp on it, Frank bought. The sewing machine Frank bought. The couch and this and that that Frank bought, then he left me. Now he is running all over America and can't find a better place than he had here, but he comes every payday to buy his food. Enough to last until the next payday, or just to drink it away."

Oh, God, I know my misery not only followed me here, but she got here first and greeted me here, I thought.

My sister Victa and I couldn't even lift our heads up to look at each other, our chins dropped down so low. We knew what was in each other's mind. Frank bought the carpet, Frank bought the chairs, Frank bought everything for Mrs. Michalski. And our dear, poor mother, with her broken spine, after fourteen years of hard struggle to support herself and trying to help us scattered children, and not a complaint out of her. And she had to be killed there at work, while this Michalski got fat as a barrel and with all these things my father bought for her she is mad at him because he left her.

Victa and I prayed in our hearts for God to please take us away from this house some way, somehow, but please hurry.

Then I heard further information. "Mrs. Michalski said, "You girls wouldn't be here today in America if I didn't look out for you. Frank once gave himself away when he was drunk, that he had a wife in Poland."

Michalski came from Germany.

"I got out the address from him and wrote to your mother. He thought that I wouldn't do it, but I did. And when you girls wrote that your mother was dead, I watched for Frank when he came here drunk. I picked his pockets and saved enough for one ship card. I couldn't pick enough for both of you. He got wise and hid his money somewhere or drank it away, so I went and bought one ship card for one of you, then I showed him your letter and your ship card. Then he said, when the two of you are here he would have to get both of you, but he had no money, so I told him, Frank, there's plenty old drunkards where you work. Borrow some money from one of them and tell them that when you girls come they can marry you. So one of them gave Frank money on that condition."

Mrs. Michalski was bragging and stood in a waiting-like position, like she expected us to thank her for what she had done. We should thank her for it? Why had she done this to us? We loved our father because we didn't know him. Because our dear mother never said a bad word about him. Even though strangers were saying that he was light-headed and restless when he was in Europe we didn't believe it. Mother said father was good, only bad people spoiled him, and we loved him all the way to America. Can we love him now, hearing this from this woman? She got her revenge, but what of us? We sat there numbed, sick. We didn't know how to get up off the chair.

Mrs. Michalski said now, "Mr. Michalski will be here soon for supper." She went into the kitchen and we dragged ourselves out after her, thinking my father couldn't be that kind of a man, and if he was, maybe when he sees us he will find his heart and change.

Supper was spread on the table. Mr. Michalski came in and sat himself to the table. Mr. Michalski was either a dope, sick or just a man that didn't give a hoot what his wife was doing. He had his supper, sat down on an easy chair and read his paper.

My sister Victa and I were hungry, as we were not eating good meals on the ship. We couldn't. We had just had a bit of the frankfurter and a glass of tea and were wishing we could have been left alone to our thoughts, but no luck that night.

Mrs. Michalski had gone to the butcher that afternoon when we arrived, and I guess, spread the news about us, because as soon as we were away from the supper table the house was full of people. Well, to my and my sister's contentment, we were safe from Victa Michalski's kissing, which we started to hate. She was busy kissing all the other guests.

In no time the table was filled with sandwiches and glasses and a small keg of beer on the side. Well, the people were having a party or some kind of celebration. Everybody was asking Victa and me to drink with them. We thought of Bremen, and refused it. Mrs. Michalski said to us, "Eat and drink plenty, girls. Don't be afraid that you have no money, your father will pay it. Soon you will have a lot of fellows and you'll be rich."

Oh-oh-oh, I thought so. This party was on my father too.

Some of the company was disappointed in us because we were too quiet. We were too tired to talk, after eighteen days on the ship, three days and two nights on the train. All we wanted to do is rest.

In that company was a young couple. I don't know their right name, but everybody called them Bakers. They both worked in a baby shop. They had a baby about seven or eight months old. The woman was sitting on a chair, holding the baby like a rolling pin. The baby was crying, so she was rolling him, or her, on her lap and dropped him on the floor. Mr. Baker picked up the baby and hollered at his wife for dropping the baby.

She said the baby had no right to cry, then said to him, "Julius, why don't you get a girl to mind him. If we could leave him home with a girl I could make five dollars more a week. This way I have to care for him more than I work.

Julius looked at me and said, "Say, it's a good idea! We can take one of Flinta's girls!" (My father was called by that name, because he played a flute instrument.)

"How about it?" Julius asked. "You want a job taking care of the baby? I'll give you one dollar a week," he said to me.

I told him I would take the job.

"Wait," Julius said. "We will fix a room for you and come for you Monday evening."

I said to myself, "Well, if they meant it, then I have a job."

Victa and I were glad to be alone in a little attic room. When the party was over we both fell into a sound sleep and slept late that Sunday. Later we had some more visitors to look us over. Not as many and they didn't stay as long. I guess because of Mr. Michalski going to work on Monday morning.

On Monday we were rested up a little. Victa and I got up early. We were helping Mrs. Michalski with the breakfast dishes when a woman knocked on the door. Mrs. Michalski opened the door for her and said, "Oh, hello, Mary. I didn't expect you."

As I found out later, neither Mary nor her family, nor Mrs. Szeleski came to visit Mrs. Michalski. That was Mary Winowiecki, Mrs. Szeleski's sister-in-law.

Mrs. Winowiecki said Mrs. Szeleski told them that we arrived Saturday and asked us if either of us had anything in mind that we were going to do. Victa told her we thought we would get some work as soon as we could, but we didn't know where to go look for it.

Mrs. Michalski said, "What's your hurry? Mary, they just came in. Let them stay and rest a couple of weeks. Frank will be here on the Fourth of July. He will pay for their board."

She was sort of mad at Mary, but Mary seemed to ignore Michalski and kept talking. "If you want to go with me right now, I'll take you. It's a nice place. The name is Mrs. Roberts. Two growing daughters and one son just came back lately from the army.

Very nice people. Mr. Roberts is a lawyer. Their girl just went and got married and they need another girl."

"Oh, thank you," Victa said. "I'll go right with you and I'm glad Tonia got a job to take care of the Baker's baby."

"Oh, all right," Mrs. Winowiecki said. "I might find her a job too."

Victa said goodbye to me and went to her new job and stuck there as she always did on hard or easy jobs until she was not needed any more or forced out by some unexpected thing that she had to quit, like we were from Traverse City.

The Bakers made their word good. That evening they came after me. I was getting my dollar a week. Mrs. Roberts asked Victa how much I was getting, and Victa got a dollar too. We got Sundays and Thursday afternoons off for ourselves.

The work was much easier than in Europe. In Europe, people do their washing according to how big the place is and how many clothes they have. In Pivnicki's, we did washing twice a year, but when that washday came, five or six women were by the tubs for five or six days. Here they did their washing every Monday and a special woman came and did the job in one day. Mrs. Winowiecki was the special woman, but she had not only Mrs. Roberts, but she was in a different home every day. That was her job, washing and ironing for people.

Charlie, her husband, was working on the docks, and their three little girls were named Anastasia (the youngest) Marion and Geneveve. The oldest was going to school all day. If they came home before their parents, then Grandma Winowiecki or Aunt Szeleski took care of them.

CHAPTER 11

Father

I was taking the baby for a walk every day and I didn't know many people there so I was afraid to walk far from the house. It was two blocks away from Michalski's house and I walked that far one day. Walking by her house I wanted a drink of water. I left the carriage on the porch and went into the yard where the water pump was and Victa Michalski was washing her pants. I had my drink, and coming into the kitchen I heard a man's voice in the dining room. He was cursing and swearing about something and sat on a chair near the door. Mrs. Michalski was sitting on another chair across from him sewing something without saying a word. I stood in the door looking at him for a while, then something squeezed me around my heart. My mother said he was a blond, nice looking man, my father. Without a word I passed the floor across to him. I dropped on my knees, put my head on his and cried.

For a while he was still, then he lifted my head up, looked at my eyes and said, "Who are you?"

"I think I am your daughter, father", and kissed his hand.

"Which one?" he asked.

"I am Antonia, the youngest. Victoria is next and Maryanna is the oldest," I reminded him.

"What are you bawling for?" he asked, smiling. "You are here, make sure to get yourself a job because nobody is going to feed you for nothing."

I got up on my feet and said, "We are already working for our bread, father."

"That's fine, then you've got nothing to bawl about."

That's the kind of greeting I received from my father. The baby started to cry and I went out to bring him home and fix supper for the Bakers, thinking, "Is he my father? If he is not my father, why did my heart prick me and pull me to him. He left when I was eleven months old and I didn't see him for fourteen years. He forgot me, and not a word about mother. Oh mother, dear. I thank God that you are there and that God spared you from the heartache and from the shame, and longer hardship here.

Sunday Victa and I went to Michalski's. Father wasn't there. He had gone to visit some friends so we didn't see him. We went back to our work. Victa didn't believe he was our father.

Two days before the Fourth of July the Bakers took me to town with them to show me the ways and customs they had there. The excitement! Carpenters, building big barns like they were in a hurry. I asked Bakers what the buildings were. They told me they were barn dance halls. They said that once a year all the farmers from everywhere were coming to the city on the Fourth of July to do their square dances. I asked if it was so exciting. In Sosnova we had dances every Saturday. Didn't the people enjoy themselves on days other than the Fourth of July?

The Bakers explained that we have music and dancing in homes sometimes. I wanted to know why such excitement once a year?

They told me because the farmers' wives got a chance to come to the city and have some fun too. The Bakers said they do some dancing, some buying, some drinking, and some of them go back to their farm broke.

"Well," I said. "It seems that the people are alike here as in Europe, good and bad."

On the Fourth of July, Victa and I went to Michalski's. No one of them went to the square dance. They had a party of their own again. Some drank, some played cards, someone brought a violin and played, everybody was happy there. I heard my father played a flute. For the first time Victa and I sat watching. Father offered us some beer, but we refused it.

He said, "Good, it will be more for me."

Then he sat down and talked to the players. "You ought to hear my sister play piano. She is some player. She just has the hands for it. She is so smart," he went on. She's go this and she's got that.

I sat there and listened to it. Not a word of mother. Not a word of his wife, not of his children. We weren't there at all. All was his sister. I couldn't stand it to listen anymore. I got up, went near him and said,

"And how about your wife, father? If you have no praise for my mother, than at least don't tell any lies about your sister in my presence, because from what I have heard from people of your sister, when she was younger, and what I have found out about you here, father, she was just as big a drunkard as you are."

He got red in his face, but he laughed and said, "You are smart, aren't you? In fact I think you are too smart."

Then he turned to his friends and said, "In Montana or in Oklahoma, they don't let smart people live long."

I don't know what he meant. I motioned to Victa and we went out back to our places.

I was with Bakers almost a month. Baker brought a ring and brought it to me. He said,

"Tonia, I got a ring for you."

I said, "Give it to your wife."

He said, "No, she has plenty."

"Then she will have more," I told him.

He said, "You have one plain band on your finger. You look like you are married already."

"The one on my finger I bought as a remembrance when I was at a shrine," I told him.

"But this one has a nice stone in it," he insisted.

His wife came in from outside and he told her that I don't want to take the ring he bought, and she said, "Take it, it's only a cheap one and too small for me."

"Alright," I accepted.

Shortly after that Baker went and bought two undershirts, and gave one to his wife and one to me. I never saw such a small thing for a shirt. I had my European ones all hand made from linen my mother spooled.

When I found out where the church was, I was getting dressed to go to church. Baker came knocking on my door. I asked him what he wanted, and told him I would be out in a moment. He asked if I was all dressed and said he wanted to see how that shirt fit me that he bought me. I told him I had it on me.

"That's what I want, to see it on you. I want to see how long it is on you because on my wife it doesn't reach to her belly button."

What's the matter, I was thinking, is the man not right or what? "Wait a minute," I said.

I took the shirt off me, put on my own, dressed myself, opened the door and threw the shirt at him and said, "Now, look at it! I'm quitting!" and left Bakers.

Two girls next door, about my age, saw me come out from the house with a bundle and asked me where I was going. I told them I quit. They said, "I bet he wanted to kiss you too, and you got mad."

I didn't stop to say anymore, I kept on. Now, I lost my job. Where am I going to go now? I went to Michalski's and asked if my father was there.

She told me, "No. He went to the woods again. He said he'll come again soon and he said some day he is going to make you listen to him, or he will show you. You are too smart for him and believe me," she said, "I wouldn't trust him when he is drunk."

I told Michalski what happened to me in Bakers and I quit my job. She laughed at me and called me silly. "Why did you quit? So what if he would see you in his shirt," she said. "Oh well, you can stay here. I'll make your father pay for you."

My father called me too smart, I thought, and I don't know what to do to get away from here. I'm ashamed to go and knock on Mrs. Szeleski's door because she was avoiding Mrs. Michalski. I didn't see her for days. I looked at Mr. and Mrs. Winowiecki's house across the yard at 611 Bay Street. I would have had to go over the fence, but it was too high and there was no gate. I was too confused to go to the corner of Randolf Street, turn to the left, walk one block, turn again to the left and look for the number. I had so much excitement, so many unhappy things happening to me in the last few months that I was afraid of everything. Afraid to walk anywhere by myself, afraid to talk to anybody. Victa, thinking I was still at the Bakers, didn't come to Michalski's since the Fourth of July. She didn't want to see father, and didn't care to see Michalskis. I didn't know how to get to Victa and Mrs. Michalski was no help in that case, because she didn't want me to go anywhere, because she thought by holding onto me she could get some kind of revenge she was looking to get on my father.

So my confusion and my misery were holding me at Michalski's house, until one night I was sleeping in the little attic room. Victa Michalski came in quietly and fell on top of me with all her heavy body. She was kissing me and hugging me, jumping on me. I got scared of her. I didn't know what she wanted. I asked her to leave me alone. I tried to push her off of me and all of a sudden she started walloping me, punching me, smacking me over my face. I tried to save my face with my hand and she grabbed me by my throat and was choking me. Somehow I got my voice and screamed with all my might. She grabbed me, choking me again.

Mrs. Michalski heard my scream and came running up, hollering, "Victa, down with you, Victa. Leave her alone."

When she came up and got Victa off of me I was gasping for breath. I was sick. I didn't care if my father came right then and made his promise good and shot me. Later when I went downstairs, Victa was out in the yard at the tub washing her pants as usual. Her mother was getting my breakfast, trying to cover up for Victa.

"Victa is a lovable girl, but she gets a fit of some kind once in a while, but she's harmless."

I looked in the mirror and saw Victa's harmless finger prints on my throat.

After breakfast I went to the pump to wash my hands and looked over the fence into Szeleski's yard, in hope that I would see her. She saw me from her kitchen window. She waved to me to wait. I did. My screams must have been pretty loud because as soon as she came out she asked, "What happened there last night? Somebody screamed so frightful!"

I showed her my throat.

"Goodness," she said. "You can't stay in that house any longer with that awful girl. Michalski will be in a good mess some day when that girl murders somebody. She is not right in her head. They never can send her to school because the first time she was brought to school when she was ten years old, she beat up the Sister and wanted to choke her. The school doesn't want her there anymore because she is dangerous to other children. She should be put in a special house," Szeleski told me.

We heard Michalski come from the street, wherever she was. She came to her kitchen, Szeleski went to hers. That evening I saw Szeleski crossing her yard into Winowiecki's yard. Then that evening Geneveve Winowiecki came to Michalski and said, "My mama sent me to bring you over to our house. She has something to tell you."

I followed Geneveve all around the block and into the house. I met the whole family there. Mr., Mrs. Winowiecki, then Marion and the smallest, Anastasia.

Mrs. Szeleski was there with her three children and Mr. Winowiecki said, "Are you still living? We were talking about you two girls as soon as Michalski let out her secret that you were coming. We were thinking if you had a good mother and if you girls were decent anyway, you shouldn't be left in Michalski's hands, but we didn't know how your father was going to take it and act with you."

I told Mr. and Mrs. Winowiecki what had happened from the time we came here of my father's actions.

"In that case, you are staying here," said Mr. Winowiecki.

The next day I removed my belongings from Michalski's house. I told Michalski I was going to stay with Winowiecki's. She got mad and called Winowiecki and Szeleski snoopers, and said they don't mind their own business.

Then she said, "Your father wasn't here for a couple of weeks. If he doesn't come to pay me for your being here you have to pay for it. I see I don't get much thanks for my good work!" She was raving.

I took my things and said goodbye and never did I nor my sister ever want to see Michalski again. I told the Winowieckis and Szeleskis what Michalski had said about me paying her for my staying in her house. Mr. Winowiecki and Mr. Szeleski said,

"Girl, what Michalski got already from your father, what rightly belongs to your mother and you girls, she's been well paid. And she can't sue you for a penny because she would put herself out for her good work that she admitted to both of you girls what she got from your father and how she picked his pockets. If she picked once or twice, then she is sure that she can pick some more. Now your father doesn't come around so often. Her Victa also was told not to molest men on the street, saying 'Come on uncle, mama wants to see you.' Any man that passed her house was Victa's uncle and she dragged him to mama. So Michalski was told by the sheriff that if Victa didn't stop bothering men she would be put away."

On Saturday when Geneveve didn't have school, Mr. Winowiecki told her to take me to where my sister worked and to tell my sister that she didn't ever have to go to Michalski's, and we never did. Thank God for good friends and that God was with us. But it wasn't over yet.

CHAPTER 12

The Wrong Potatoes

Father didn't show up for five months and we didn't care. We had a home to go to, whenever we were off, and any time we were with Mr. and Mrs. Winowiecki we were their daughters and we loved them both and their three little girls.

The Winowieckis and Szeleskis had their own friends. Their company, visiting one another's houses on Saturday or Sunday evenings, having nice parties, music and dances. Charles Winowiecki played a violin and they had entertainment in churches. My sister and I were always invited on our days off. We even for the first time in our lives saw a circus when it came to town in the fall. Mr. Roberts gave us that treat.

We were getting used to people around there and getting along with everyone nicely, even though we had a difficult time with our language. Mrs. Winowiecki got me a job like Victa, with Mr. and Mrs. Greligh. I was so glad. Mr. Greligh owned a big sawmill a little ways across the street from Winowieckis. On one side was Bay Street and Michigan Bay on the other side. A boat was bringing timber right to the mill. They lived a little out of the city and had a baby about a year old. They had a cow, but Mr. Greligh did the milking so I just kept the house clean and did a little ironing, as Mrs. Winowiecki used to do our washings on Fridays.

One day Mrs. Greligh was out of potatoes. She gave me an empty basket and showed me a potato. She spread out her hand and I understood from her what she meant. No potatoes. She took me by the window, pointed her finger to a farm house, then she showed me a telephone, motioning that she was going to telephone someone to expect me and fill the basket with potatoes for me. I understood what she wanted, but when I went on the road I saw a couple of houses and the road twisted. I didn't know Mrs. Greligh was pointing to me, so I went in to the first farm I came to. I knocked on a door and an old lady opened it with an old man following the old lady. They looked at me. I looked at them. They said something to me I didn't understand and I got tongue tied. I forgot to say "potatoes". I said, "kartoffful, Mrs. Greligh," and handed them the basket. The old couple gave me another surprised look, took the basket and went in. I waited for a few minutes. Then they came out with a full basket of potatoes. I knew already how to say thank you, so I said it.

I came home and Mrs. Greligh gave me a surprised look. Well I brought the potatoes, but she said nothing. About an hour later the telephone rang.

I don't know what was said on the other side of the telephone, but Mrs. Greligh said, "She is home already with the potatoes."

Mrs. Greligh probably thought that it was no use asking me for an explanation of how I got the potatoes. She waited until Friday, Mrs. Winowiecki's washing day.

We were sitting at the dinner table, Mrs. Winowiecki, Mrs. Greligh, talking and laughing like anything. Then Mrs. Winowiecki asked me how I got the potatoes that day. I told her and they laughed some more. Mrs. Winowiecki said Mrs. Greligh showed you the farm of Mr. Greligh's parents about a half mile from the first farm house. Mrs. Greligh called there to expect me. When I didn't show up there they called to find out what happened to me. Mrs. Greligh told them that I was back with the potatoes already. They all were surprised where and how I got them. Then Mrs. Greligh called up the first farm to explain to them of the incident.

I was at Mrs. Greligh's a couple of weeks when I was told she couldn't use me. Mrs. Winowiecki said Mrs. Greligh expected another baby soon and needed a girl that would understand her. She said if I wanted to go to her brother's on a farm for a month or so, she would call for me after she gets well. She was satisfied with my work but not with my language. I cried. I said Mrs. Greligh didn't like me and her brother wouldn't like me, so my new mother, Mrs. Winowiecki, took me home.

Mr. Winowiecki had a brother, Paul, who lived the next house from him. Paul had six daughters and two sons. Three of the daughters worked in three different hotels in that city as waitresses. The youngest one, Geneveve worked in Whiting Hotel, and when she heard that I left Grelighs she asked me if I wanted to work in that hotel as a dishwasher for two and a half dollars a week. I took it. Oh my! Two and a half dollars a week! I'm getting rich! I was so happy over it that I started to sing and nobody told me to stop. I kept on singing louder and louder until my voice and my songs came to me and I sang through the mealtime. The echo was ringing through the big dining room. The hotel bartender brought two bottles of beer, handed them to me through the window where I was washing the dishes and asked my name. I told him Antonia.

He said, "That's Nettie for short. Drink it Nettie."

I told him I didn't drink. He didn't believe me. He left the beer and went to his work. The waitresses spied the beer. There were eight of them that shared the beer among them, but two bottles weren't enough for all of them. I told them that I refused the beer but he left it. They said you don't ever refuse anything you get. If I didn't want it they would drink it. So after that, no matter how many bottles he left on my window I put them in the icebox for the girls.

Then one of the cooks (there were two men cooks and a woman baker) who was a boozer himself, asked me for a bottle of beer. I didn't give it to him and he told the barkeeper. The barkeeper came to my window and said, "Nettie, I don't mind giving you all the beer you can drink, but I won't give it to the other girls. They are rich. They can buy their own beer. Some of the customers are paying for your beer. If they find out that you are giving it to the girls they would blame me that I'm treating the wrong people for their money."

I said to him, "I said don't bring me beer, I don't drink. You are buying beer and now you are mad."

He turned to the other dishwasher, a Polish girl who was American born. (Her father was a farmer and her older sister Anna, who worked there before her, went away to become a Nun and Julia took Anna's place.) He said to her, "Nettie is a good girl and has a nice voice. Too bad I don't understand the words she sings."

I worked there two and a half months and got sick. I couldn't get up. Julia went to her boss and said she couldn't do the work herself, the waitresses would have to chip in to help her. They asked about me and Julia told them I was sick. They told the bosses and Mrs. Whiting came up to see it if was true.

There was a doctor living in the hotel and Mrs. Whiting told him to see what was the matter with me. The doctor came up after nine in the evening. Julia was in bed after her work. The doctor took my temperature and said something in a funny way.

Julia said, Give him your shirt to wipe off – he's kidding you."

I looked at him, tears pouring over my face. Then he put his hand on my head and said, "Now, now, you are a good girl." After he left I went to sleep.

I woke up on the fifth day. I didn't know that – Julia told me. All the four days and four nights the eight waitresses, English, Irish, and German girls watched over me. (Geneveve Winowiecki wasn't there anymore. She went to the Colombia Hotel where her sister worked.) These girls didn't know my language and were watching over me two at night and two in the day, changing off. I was crying, raving, getting out of bed, running out of the room, and God bless the girls, all as one, and each and every one that put their effort in to help me. Good deeds are never forgotten in my heart.

The bartender and some of the hotel customers missed my singing. They found out that I was sick and they sent some wine and beer which I never touched. I was glad that the girls enjoyed it because I couldn't pay them any other way.

When I got better they brought my meals to me. Even Mrs. Whiting brought the tray herself a couple of times. In the meantime when I was sick they got another girl who had been working there before, but went home to have a baby. She sent Julia's sister in her place, and she came back. She was probably afraid when I got well they wouldn't keep her. I was talking to Julia and she was worrying how long I would have to work there to pay up for all the doctor bills, as he had visited me several times when I didn't know he was there. I was there two and a half months working and I took out one month's pay. That girl put a scare in me that I would probably have to work a year to pay for everything. She said I had a month and a half pay coming to me, and I should leave it there and get out.

I was still sick. She somehow notified Winowieckis. Little Geneveve went for my sister.

CHAPTER 13

Christmas in America

In Sosnova we had plenty of trees in the big forests, but we never had any Christmas trees decorated in our house. We had nice Christmas time midnight church masses, we sang Christmas carols in every home, but no Christmas trees, and nobody was getting or giving presents. Here, Mom Winowiecki put her girls to bed and I was dressing the Christmas tree. She baked all kinds of cookies and cookie animals. We hung them on the Christmas tree. Packages were under the tree and the beautiful star on the top filled my heart with gladness, just as if showing me the way to a better life (if not for my misery).

On Christmas morning we went to church for the early mass. When mom and I came back, the girls were up. We were opening our packages and there was something for all of us. Even Victa wasn't forgotten. We got fancy aprons to serve on tables at parties. I bought dolls for the girls, but I didn't know that the big people were getting presents. I didn't give anything to mom and dad (they said they didn't expect it). Dad kidded my father that he got his before time. I learned to call them mom and dad, and since I came back from the Whiting Hotel they all called me Nettie.

For the New Year I asked Geneveve if I could buy mom and

dad something. Geneveve said they don't give presents for the New Year, but she said I could make a surprise for them and she said we would have a neighbor's party on New Years. She said they didn't have many glasses, so we went to a store and I picked some fancy glasses and we put the package out late on New Year's Eve under the Christmas tree. On New Year's day I asked dad to open the package from under the Christmas tree. Dad thought we were playing a trick on him and wouldn't open it. Evening came and dad was looking for glasses. He told Geneveve to run to Uncle Paul's to borrow some. Geneveve told him to look under the Christmas tree. Then he looked at me, smiled and opened the package, and after that every time he drank out of those glasses he said the beer tasted better because it was from my glasses.

After New Year's my father and I had another talk. He asked me how much money I had. I told him I had none, I gave all I had to mom and dad Winowiecki. He was mad because I called them mom and dad and told me I must have too much when I could give it away. I told him that they were entitled to all I had. I said, "They took me in the day Victa Michalski almost choked me. They took me when I was through at the Bakers. They took me when Grelighs didn't need me. They took me now when I got sick in the hotel and I am here over two months and have no other home to go to. I told him Victa and I were brought here. We came to our father and thought that after fourteen years he would be able to give us a home to live in. With the money you spend on Michalski and her home and her house furniture you could have made a home for us!"

"Oh," he said. "So you know more than you should."

"Yes," I told him. "Michalski told us and showed us everything she has from you, our father, while mother and we children were working for our own bread, and never having enough for our hard work over in Europe."

"If I make a home for you," he said, "How do I know that you won't kick me out of it? When you grow up you will get married soon. Let him worry about your home."

Then I asked him why he was not wearing his new shoes. He

said they were too big for him so he got his money back for them. I knew he didn't get the money back from the store after wearing the shoes for two weeks on his feet. Dad walked in on the rest of the argument when father said I was too smart for him, but he was my father so he could kill me or do anything he wanted to do.

Dad said, "Mutkoska, as long as the girls are in my house I dare you to lift your hand on anyone."

So father left Traverse City and didn't show up until just before the Fourth of July again.

I told mom I felt strong enough and I wanted to go to work. Mom said she didn't hear of any good place to work yet, but one, and she was a mean one. Girls didn't want to stay in her place. I told her I would try it. I thought she couldn't be any worse than Brzuska, so Mom brought me to Mrs. Sprague.

Mrs. Sprague was a tall, strong woman. Mr. Sprague was a little man. He was a publisher of some paper in that city. Well, if Mrs. Sprague wasn't just like Mrs. Brzuska, she was just as bad. Mr. Sprague was grouchy, but not bad. If I was late with his breakfast, he was the one to come to the kitchen and help me out.

When I was there for a couple of weeks Mrs. Sprague told me to wash windows outside on the second story and I went to do what I was told. There was a little porch just big enough to stand on. I did not have a warm coat on, just my regular clothes. I got out on that porch and she went and shut the window on me. I touched the window with the rag and the rag froze to the window. I could neither turn or bend on that porch to open the window and I got so cold I was afraid I would fall off. I knocked on the window to let me in, and she made believe she didn't hear me. I hollered and cried and she left the room.

Mrs. Sprague had a woman, Mrs. Louis, boarding with her, and Mrs. Louis heard me screaming and came out from her room and let me in. Mrs. Louis saw how cold I was. I couldn't open my fingers to let the rag go out of them.

Mrs. Louis said to Mrs. Sprague, "Look here, Mrs. Sprague, you can't treat that child like that, no matter who she is. If she gets sick you are going to pay her doctor bills. I'll make sure that you will. I saw what you did to her."

Mrs. Sprague wanted to talk herself out of it, but I guess she was afraid of Mrs. Louis, because she came to my room with clean linen and made my bed while Mrs. Louis made me a hot tea and poured some of her whiskey in it and told me to drink it. Then Mrs. Louis got hot irons and they both were ironing the sheets and Mrs. Louis tucked me in bed where I was for the next three days while Mrs. Louis was bringing me meals to my room.

When Mr. Sprague had a big argument with Mrs. Sprague I went to mom and dads or to Victa's where she worked on the same street, half a block away. If I didn't come home at eleven she shut me out and kept me freezing until she felt like opening the door. I didn't complain to anybody because Victa was always worried about me when something happened to me.

Mrs. Sprague didn't have a woman to wash her clothes. I had to do them on Mondays. When I wanted to wash my clothes with hers she came and threw the wash water out and she always found a new job every minute so I didn't have a chance to wash my clothes. I told my sister about it and she told me to bring my wash to her, and then Victa was doing my wash.

One Sunday I was getting ready to go visit mom and dad to see them for a while. I usually was spending my day off with Victa as I did many times on bad days when we stayed in Victa's room. Mrs. Sprague brought out a coat and a pair of shoes, too big for me. She told me to put them on. I did and went to Winowiecki's. Mom asked me where I got that hundred year old style coat. I told her Mrs. Sprague gave it to me to put on when I was coming here. Mom told me to take it right off as soon as I went back and throw it at her. She said Mrs. Sprague was scheming to pay me with old junk instead of money. Then I told mom how Mrs. Sprague treated me. Mom said she would be there tomorrow before she went to see Victa, as it was wash day at Roberts.

Monday mom was there alright and told Mrs. Sprague to have my money ready for me on Saturday and make sure that every penny was there for all the two months or she would talk to Mr. Roberts. Mrs. Sprague said she would, and anyway she said she was getting a new girl, one who could understand her.

So on Saturday I left Sprague's and kept on walking. I came to Winowiecki's and mom asked me if I wanted to go to Mrs. Parks, the ones that lived in the house before you come to Greligh's house. I knew Mrs. Parks. I saw her many times in Greligh's. Mr. and Mrs. Parks, two children and Mrs. Park's parents, Mr. and Mrs. Chase. I went right out with my suitcases that were pretty heavy. Dad had company. An old bachelor, a musician. Dad said to him, "Joe, if you were a gentleman you wouldn't let the girl carry that heavy case so far."

Well, Joe was a gentleman, but I wasn't a lady. I didn't say a word to him and he didn't say anything to me, as I supposed he waited for the lady to speak first. We walked all the way through in silence. When we reached the door I rang and Mrs. Parks opened it. I flew in and left Mrs. Parks out with Joe. Joe was a gentlemen. He didn't tell on me. When I told mom and dad about it they laughed at me. Well, I was so scared of Joe. He was a scrappy, husky fellow, and we were on the dark road. I was afraid to open my mouth.

I was with the Parks a couple of weeks. I liked Mrs. Parks, the children, and especially Mrs. Chase. She was going around showing me things, teaching me and never scolding me if I made a mistake. She was a big woman, but a hunchback, and not feeling well. Mr. Parks worked in Greligh's sawmill. Mr. Chase looked like seventy years old and felt like thirty-five. He always hummed, sang and jigged and always felt happy. Then all of a sudden all went sad. I had picked up a little more English and asked Mrs. Parks what was the matter. She said Mrs. Chase's brother died and Mr. Chase would have to go away and nobody could milk the cow. I told her I could milk the cow. She looked at me and said, "Oh, that's fine."

Before Mr. Chase got up the next morning the cow was milked. He was coming out with the milk pail and I was coming in with an armful of firewood. "The cow is milked already, Mr. Chase," I told him.

He dropped the pail. "Oh, you sweetheart," he yelled out and kissed me on both cheeks. I dropped the armful of wood on both our feet. Mrs. Parks was standing in the door saying "Our Father".

While Mr. Chase was away, dad's niece Geneveve came to visit me and said they needed a dishwasher in the Columbia Hotel. She said I would get fifty cents more a week than I was getting here. I was thinking that dishwashing wasn't as hard as I had it at Parks with seven of us in the house. I had to do the family wash all by myself, take care of a two-story, ten room house, with a cow to milk and fire wood to bring in. Mrs. Parks' work was the hardest I had so far in America. So I told Geneveve I would take the dishwashing, but I had to finish up the week here.

Mr. Chase was away two weeks and the evening he came back was the evening I left Parks' place. Mrs. Parks jumped on her father and blamed him for my leaving her because of his foolish kissing. She came to Winowiecki's and told them so. She said she would have given me fifty cents more a week. She was satisfied with my work, but her father had to get foolish. Mr. Chase said he didn't mean anything by it. He was just glad that Mrs. Chase was saved from the work of milking the cow.

I didn't stay long at the Columbia Hotel. Columbia was more of a working man's hotel – more for men than for women. Brakemen, firemen and engineers from the railroad lived in the hotel. On their hours and days off they were idling around the place chasing girls. They even were nervy enough to come into our rooms when we were in bed. There were four girls in two beds in one room. I slept with Geneveve. Mr. McCormick (or McCarthy), I don't remember - anyway, the hotel owner, his wife's sister, Dilia, who worked there as a waitress, and one dishwasher. Columbia Hotel was smaller than Whiting Hotel, but the work seemed harder. My job was dishwashing and fixing lunch boxes for the railroad men, some on day work, some on night work.

When I started working there I was a new girl and people tried to take advantage of me. The first one who started on me was the boss's wife. I didn't know her until Mr. McCormick himself told me. Every time she laid her eyes on me she handed me a dime and a pail and sent me down for beer. The bartender didn't know me. I knocked on a little side window and he opened the window, filled the can and took the dime until one day he asked the boss who the girl was that drank so much beer.

The boss got suspicious because his wife was drunk every day and he was wondering how she was getting drunk. He told the bartender the next time that can is put in the window to let him know. I put the can in the window as usual, and it took the bartender a little longer to hand it to me. Then I saw my boss by me in the hall. He smiled and asked if I liked beer. I said, "No sir."

"Who are you buying it for? The girls in your room?"

"No sir."

"Who is giving you the money to buy the beer?"

"Sometimes Dilia, sometime another woman."

"Aha!" He said. "Nettie, don't ever buy any more beer for them! The other woman is my wife. When she gets drunk she fights with everyone around. She makes Dilia get the beer for her, and the bartender won't give Dilia beer anymore, so she's taking advantage of you."

I didn't get any more beer for Dilia or her sister.

Then one day I saw a show. Whenever she got her drink the boss's wife was full of it and came to the kitchen and started a fight with one of the cooks. They exchanged some nice words between themselves. Dilia tried to stop her sister but the boss's wife was a boss for a while. Dishes were always piled up in front of the cooks so it was handy just to grab one and fill up the orders and the waitress carried it away. Mrs. McCormick reached for a dish, the cook grabbed a cleaver and said, "You! You throw that dish at me you'll never be able to throw one at anybody else!"

Dilia saw she couldn't do anything there so she got the boss. He came and calmly took his wife gently by the arm, smiling, and said, "Come dear to your room, you need a rest."

The men who were idling again heard of the fight and came up to the girls to find out who won. Then one of the men said, "Say, which one of you girls fixes my lunch box? For the last three weeks the lunches are fixed just like I like them."

Geneveve pointed at me. "It's Nettie."

The other men admitted that they too noticed. "Let me kiss her for that," said one.

Geneveve said, "You'd better not."

"Why not?" he asked. "Does she bite?"

That gave me an idea. He put his hand out to reach for me and I stuck my teeth in his hand. "By jingo, she does!" He said, and pulled his hand back quickly.

The girls laughed at him and the man (one that made me cry) came and said, "Leave the kid alone!"

"Kid?" he said, "She may be a kid, but she's got teeth of a grown pup!" He was mad.

That evening Mom Winowiecki, on her way home from Victa's place, stopped at the hotel to see me and told me the first chance I get to go see Victa, that she has news for me. So I went to see Victa that night after my dishes were done. "What's the news, Victa?" I asked.

She said, "Do you want to come to work for Mrs. Bates?"

I said, "Oh, Victa, does a kitty want milk? "When do I start?"

"Finish your week. Mrs. Bates's girl who worked for her five years is getting married to the farmer they were buying vegetables from. She won't be here next week and you can start on Monday."

Victa told me Mrs. Bates called Mrs. Roberts and they talked long with mom and mom told Victa, and Victa told them that I would take the job.

When I came back to the hotel I told Geneveve that I was leaving them. Geneveve got mad at me because she got me this job and I didn't appreciate it. I told her I did, but I would sooner work for a private home where there were no men around.

The next afternoon I was looking for a broom to sweep the kitchen. Geneveve said she left it in the dining room. I went in for it and Mr. McCormick was sitting by one of the tables in a corner where Geneveve left the broom. I was taking the broom and he reached for my hand and pulled me to him. I thought he was going to tell me something, and he kissed me. I said, "Mr. McCormick, I'm leaving Saturday."

He looked at me and said, "Now look here, child, I didn't kiss you to insult you, I just kissed you like a father."

"My father never kissed me," I told him.

"And why not?" he wanted to know.

I bit my lips first, then I told him, "Because my father is always drunk like Mrs. McCormick, and your mother. My mother got killed at work trying to support us children."

He didn't smile. He put his hand on my head and said, "Good girl, good girl, good girl."

Why is it people tell me I'm a good girl when fate treats me like I was a bad girl?

The end of April I started to work for Mrs. Bates. When I first walked in I fell in love with the place and the people. It was just across the street from the Roberts' place. Mrs. Bates was taller than I and weighed more. She weighed about three hundred and fifty pounds and was not well. She used a cane in one hand while walking, and was bracing herself with the other hand on chairs and walls. Two daughters, the younger, Clara, was always with her mother. She was older than I but not as tall as I. Mabel, the other daughter, was taller and was working with Mr. Bates.

Mr. Bates was a publisher, but was just the opposite from Mr. Sprague. If Mr. Bates said "yea" in his paper, Mr. Sprague would say "nay". If Mr. Bates said "no" in his paper, Mr. Sprague said "yes" in his. I don't think they liked one another, and their houses were just one lot apart. Mr. Bates looked more like an aristocrat. A little slim man. There was a son, but he was married and lived in Chicago. That home was a peaceful home and the family adored each other. If somebody asked me how I liked it there I would have an answer like Pani Graboska when I brought her to Pani Piekaski, "I don't want to go to heaven." (I was in heaven already.)

I was to keep the house clean and help with cooking. Mom Winowiecki did the washing on Tuesday and the rest of the work I was left to do as I liked. I made up my own routine for every day.

On Mondays I didn't have much to do, just the everyday touching up, sweeping and changing bed linens and getting them ready for Tuesday wash. Tuesday I helped mom with the wash. Wednesday I scrubbed my kitchen. We had oil cloths in the kitchen and had carpets in all other rooms. The rest of the day I was ironing. Thursday I cleaned half of the rooms and spent my afternoons with Victa, or sometimes went to mom's as Thursday was her day off as well as some Saturdays. On Friday I finished the rest of my house cleaning and pulled out all silver, big and small, and cleaned it. Saturday I scrubbed my kitchen clean, cleaned my room and prepared things for Sunday. Sunday, while getting breakfast ready I took care of the dinner at the same time so we all could go to church. When I came from church I just fixed the rest of what went with the meat and gravy, got through with dinner and dishes and spent my afternoon and evening with Victa or mom and dad and the girls.

Our meals were very simple. Breakfast everyday was oatmeal or pancakes. Sundays were bacon and eggs. Dinners mixed varieties, suppers were leftovers. Sometimes Clara and Mabel made something different. The girls were honeys. Mrs. Bates was the sweetest woman on earth (next to my mother dear) and Mom Winowiecki. Thursday and Sunday afternoons she was pulling the chair over to her to rest on it every step she took as she was coming to the kitchen. At first I didn't know what she wanted to do. I asked her, "What do you want, Mrs. Bates?"

"Oh, mother is going to help with the dishes so you can have more time with Victa or Mary Winowiecki," she said.

I told her I could do them myself, but she insisted on helping me. I ran to her every time I saw her try to walk. I put her hand around my neck and told her to rest on my shoulder. She didn't believe that I could help her walk that way, but when we made it she found confidence in me. I was helping her to the garden where it was full of flowers like a little park, on two lots between their house and Mrs. White's house. Mr. Bates used to come often to see how his wife was. He came one day and saw me helping Mrs. Bates off the steps into the garden to her chair. He smiled at me and gave me fifty cents. After that he often gave me quarters or fifty cents. I never was tipped before in my life no matter what kind of work I did, nor given many presents either.

When I came to work there, Mrs. Bates asked me how old I was. I told her I would be sixteen on May 8th, and I forgot about it. Nobody thought of birthdays in Europe. Some of the older people didn't remember their age, and didn't know how old they were. But Mrs. Bates and the girls didn't forget mine on May 8th. When I went in to my room to change for dinner, I put a clean dress on to wait on the table. I found on my dresser a big basket of fruits of all kind and boxes of goose berries and currants. I don't know where they got them so early. In Europe those berries were ripe in June. That was a surprise for me! And there was also a fancy apron and a velvet flower to wear in my hair. I thought that fruit was for the table and wondered what should it be doing in my room. I asked Clara if I should put the fruit on the table. She said, "Why, Nettie, happy birthday to you! Mrs. Bates says this is all for you, Nettie! You and Victa can enjoy it!"

I thanked them with tears in my eyes and I kissed Mrs. Bates' hand. She said, "God bless you my child!"

I thanked God that I found a home that I could be happy in, but I didn't know for how long. I tried to do everything to please them. I tried to do more cooking so Mrs. Bates didn't have to come and show me how to do it. When Clara wasn't around I felt bad because I couldn't make bread. I was taught to do hard work every place I've ever been - and in a short time – two or three weeks here, two or three months there, but no one gave me a chance to learn any good or easier work. Victa already baked bread in Europe, and now she could bake tasty pies and cakes. Mrs. Roberts taught her. Mrs. Bates was encouraging me in everything I made, saying, "Nettie made this! It's good!" I didn't know if they really liked it or were making fun of me. When I made a chocolate layer cake it laid flat like two pancakes together, but they said it was good and I had a good cry for myself in my room.

I had a lot of time in the evenings and I went to help Victa with her dishes. One day I just got an idea and made a proposition to Victa. I said, "Victa, we know how to read in Polish, why not teach ourselves to write?" She didn't believe it could be done. I told her, "Listen, we learned our reading without school. Aunt Mary taught you and I swallowed Jozef Kowaleski's education. We can help one another! Let's try it, Victa, please!" She wanted to know how we were going to do it and when we could do it. I said, "Listen, I am coming here every evening to help you with the dishes, so we both have a little more time to talk. Why can't we use the idle time for something that will be much valued to us. Now we have to bother dad to write our letters and we don't write often because we don't want to bother dad. How nice it will be when we can write to Aunt Mary and to Maryanna!" Victa doubted it could be done, but I talked and pleaded until she said she would try.

The next day I bought boxes of paper, two dozen pencils, pens and ink. Aunt Mary and Maryanna were in Brooklyn then, Wladka, who became our cousin by marriage, was in Pennsylvania. We sneaked into Victa's room and shoved the things under her bed. When we got our work done that night we planned to take an hour or two every night for the writing, but we were forgetting the hours and it lasted to two, three, four and five in the morning.

How we started the headlines on Aunt Mary's letter were the same words on every letter that we knew by heart, "Niech Bedzie pochwalony Jezus Christus mamy nadzieje ze list was dojdzie wdobrym zdrowia I od powiecie nam na wiekow Amen." In English it sounds like this, "Praise be Jesus Christ. May this letter reach you and find you in good health, so we hope you will answer us, for ever and ever, amen." We took the letters apart, n i e c h b e e d z i e p e h w a l o n y j e z u s c h r t u s – and so on and on, and we got ourselves so mixed up we didn't know which letter belonged to which word. We tried to work them out, figure them out, to three o'clock in the morning, but couldn't figure them out.

Victa overslept that morning and got mad at me. She didn't want to do the writing that night. I pleaded, I begged, "Victa, please, we got the letters separated, we've got to figure out how to put them together!" We stayed up late another night. The next night I gave Victa off so she could have a good night's sleep. Then we got at it again. We wrote some more letters. We kept at it off and on for a month, writing and re-writing and couldn't make out what we wrote. Some nights I slept with Victa just to wake her up in the morning on time so she wouldn't oversleep. Mrs. Bates saw me one morning coming home at five. I didn't know she had seen me, but she didn't say anything to me. The next night I went out and she watched me to see what time I came home. I came in at three, then later again. Then she thought something wrong was going on. She called Mrs. Roberts to see if Victa was home nights. Mrs. Roberts told Mrs. Bates that when we went to sleep as late as midnight Victa was still in her room and we were doing something. Mrs. Bates told Mrs. Roberts that I came home sometimes just on time to cook breakfast. Victa and I didn't know that our mistresses were worrying over us as nobody said anything to us.

We kept at our writing for another month. We wrote a letter to Maryanna and the answer came back, "Get someone else to write your letter. Whoever wrote this one for you didn't pass the first grade." She was right! Now Victa wouldn't write anymore.

"Look, Victa," I said. "This is the first letter! The next one will be better!"

We wrote the next one to Wladka. She wrote back, "No one can read it. Who is doing the writing?" Wladka said she believed if we wrote the letter we could do just as good!

Victa and I got thinner and felt lazy. Mrs. Bates and Mrs. Roberts got worried over us. One night we were so busy we didn't hear Mrs. Roberts walking in on us quietly. She stood for a while watching us and found out our secret – how we were spending our nights. She saw Victa get mad at me and I was pleading with her, "Please, Victa, please."

The next day Mrs. Roberts brought us a couple of books that William, Alicia and Marian, her children used when they were going to school years before. Mrs. Roberts said to Victa, "Nettie speaks English better than you and you have been with me so many months and can't speak. Here are some books. See if you can learn something." Victa got more ambition and we went on.

Mrs. Bates found out why I was spending the late nights and didn't mind it at all. My work was always done right.

Then our writing improved. Maryanna said so. It was getting better. We passed our first grade! We would probably have done nicely in English, but trouble began. My misery came back.

CHAPTER 14

The House in the Woods

As last year, everybody was coming to the city to enjoy themselves on the Fourth of July. One day Victa was running across the street to Mrs. Bates' house. Mrs. Roberts saw Victa running from her window in her room upstairs and was wondering what happed to Victa. Don, their big dog was barking downstairs, so Mrs. Roberts came down to see who Don was barking at. She found two drunken men in her kitchen and asked them what they wanted. One of them said, "I am Victa's father. I want to see her. And this man (he pointed to the other man who looked older and much drunker than father) is going to marry Victa."

Mrs. Roberts thought quickly and said to father, "You can't see Victa for a couple of days. I sent her with my daughter to visit an aunt." Victa and I were in Mrs. Bates' room, scared like rabbits. We saw them come out from the Roberts' house and go away. Victa went home. She saw the two men coming through the house from the kitchen window, recognized father and guessed who the other man was, and shot out through the dining room and ran to me. Father didn't know that I was working right across from Victa. He couldn't keep track of me as I had so many places that I worked, while Victa was always in one spot, and mom and dad wouldn't tell him of my whereabouts.

Victa and I stopped our writing at night. We had suspicions that Roberts' house was being watched. We kept quiet at our homes nights and worried about one another. Mrs. Roberts saw how we were scared and all nerves and called Mom Winowiecki to find out what's the matter. Mom told Mrs. Roberts that our father wanted Victa to marry the old man for the money father owed the man. "He can't do that!" Mrs. Roberts said. "I'll talk to Mr. Roberts!"

When Mr. Roberts heard the story he said to Victa, "What does your father want to do, sell you to someone you don't want, for the money he owes him? Doesn't he know that he would go to jail? Don't you worry about that, Victa, you don't have to marry a man if you don't want him."

Father came back again after the Fourth, but Victa ran when she saw them coming in to Mrs. Roberts' room. Mrs. Roberts told father again he couldn't see Victa. Father got nasty, told Mrs. Roberts she was lying and said he knew Victa was in the house. He said she was his daughter and had to do what he wanted her to do. Mrs. Roberts told him, "My husband is a lawyer, and he said if you are coming and bothering people, he will have you put in jail."

The other man was arguing with father on their way out. "It's money or the girl, Frank!" And they left.

We didn't hear of father until after the 15th of August. I was shopping downtown. I thought lightning struck me. A woman stood before me and grabbed me by my sleeve and hollered with excitement, "You are Flinta's girl, aren't you?" I looked at the woman. I didn't know her – never saw her before in my life. How did she know me?

I said, "Yes, I am Mutkowski's daughter, if that is what you mean."

"Yes," she said. "I went to see your father – your father and another two men are building a home in the woods where he is working. The house will be ready about November. Then your father will come to take you girls there to live in the new house. Just imagine what a good time you girls are going to have with all those men there. There are about fifty in one gang and about seventy in another gang. They all want to come board with you. There are no other houses for four or five miles around. What a good time! I will come to visit you sometime."

She slapped me on my back and disappeared as she came. I stood on that sidewalk for a long while, her words ringing in my ears, "fifty, seventy, fifty, seventy men – father coming to get - fifty, seventy men, fifty, seventy men – father coming after you to get you." Instead of going home to Mrs. Bates, I turned and ran to mom and dad crying.

Mom saw me running and seeing me crying got scared and said, "What happened?"

I said, "My father!"

"Where?" she wanted to know.

"He is coming here to get me."

Mom ran to the door and locked it. "He's not coming in here until Charles comes home!"

Poor mom! She thought that father was right behind me. She remembered when my father was threatening to shoot me.

Dad came from work, I had my good cry and calmed down. I told him and mom of the woman and what she told me. Dad said to me, "Don't worry. November is far away yet and by that time we might think of something. Go home or Mrs. Bates will be wondering what became of you."

I went home. I was too late to fix the supper, so Clara and Mabel had done it. Mrs. Bates and the girls noticed that I was sad and upset and asked me what had happened, and was I hurt. I told them about the strange woman and that I was scared and ran to Mom and Dad Winowiecki. Mrs. Bates said all we had to do is ask Mr. Roberts' advice, and told me not to worry now.

Sunday I called for Victa and we went to Winowiecki's. I told Victa about the bad news. Victa was mad. She said he couldn't be our father or he wouldn't be so mean to us. Mom and dad were thinking things over before we got to their house. Dad said to us, "Victa and Nettie, I don't want to put you girls on the wrong side of your father. We all found you two decent and respectable girls. Your mother must be a decent woman and brought you up in the right and respectable way. We all know your father, and he wasn't so bad when he first came to this town. The place he is in now amongst the lumberjacks – not all could be bad, but the gang he's in I wouldn't trust. The only thing for you girls to do is if you have relatives somewhere in another city, go there, or to your sister, if he doesn't know where she is." brotherbro said I told father that Maryanna was in New York, but he doesn't know the address, because Maryanna is in Greenpoint, Brooklyn, New York, and she is working in a carpet factory and boarding with a private family. Dad sat down and wrote a letter himself to Maryanna so she would understand it well. He didn't write anything about father, just that we are lonesome for her. He wrote to Pennsylvania for us too so if we didn't get an answer from one place soon we might get it from the other.

But we got our answer from both at the same time, so we picked Maryanna. She wrote that she is lonesome too, and if we come there we can be either together or at least near one another, not so far away.

Well, we had a place to go, so we started to plan our trip – what we needed, what to buy. We needed trunks. A little over a year ago when we came from Europe we both brought our clothes in one small basket, now we needed trunks. Well we need new shoes and new hats, skirts and blouses for each one. But how far is Brooklyn? How much money will it be for the tickets and how much do we have?

Victa was with Mr. and Mrs. Roberts all the months since we came here, and that's close to fifteen months. She started with a dollar a week, then a dollar fifty, then two, then it was as high as two and a half dollars a week. She wasn't taking her pay every week. She thought the money was safe with Mrs. Roberts. She took a few dollars now and then so she figured out she must have sixty five dollars cash. And I? What did I have with all the places I had, even though I was getting more money in some places than Victa? I spent it more than Victa. Every once in a while when I bought myself a skirt or a blouse I bought Victa the same thing. I didn't want to be more dressy than Victa. And then the debts to mom and dad? I had been with them for two months when I was sick, and a week now and then when I was out of a job. My bigger money I owe to them because I didn't want them to feed me for nothing. If the tickets cost a lot, then we have to stay another month or more till we have enough.

Again we went to dad for advice for our troubles and he didn't say a word until we were finished. Then he told us he already found out how much the tickets cost and he went on figuring for us. The tickets were nineteen dollars each to New York. Let's keep the change and say twenty. That's forty dollars for two. I don't know how far New York is to Greenpoint, Brooklyn. Let's make it five dollars each – that's fifty dollars. Then he was joking, "You have to act like ladies and tip the porters or somebody. And I was told it's going to be two day's ride. You will need something to eat. Then we'll add another five dollars for each. That will make sixty dollars. Trunks will be five dollars each, that makes seventy dollars."

We sat listening to the adding with our hearts going down in us. Then Victa said, "Yes, and all I have is only sixty five dollars."

Dad was always slow moving, never in a hurry in talking or walking. He looked at Victa, looked at me, then looked at Mom, smiled at us, got up off his chair and went to the closet and pulled out something and came back and laid it in my lap. I saw a little book and I opened it, looked it over and saw the numbers $68.00. I looked again. A bank book with only my name on it. I cried. I said, "Dad, mom, and my debt to you for the time you took care of me and my staying with you for weeks at a time!"

Dad said, "Nettie, in your life you may come to find somebody that will be needing help. Don't forget him. Even with what little you think you owe us, to us you owe nothing now. God bless you both and good luck to you. Get somebody to go with you to the bank as a witness tomorrow morning and get your money."

I said, "Come with me then, dad."

Dad said, "Oh, no! I put it there for you, but I don't want to be seen taking it out for you."

What did I do? I kissed their hand, both of them, mom's and dad's.

The next day I asked a check girl to go with me to the bank. I had become friends with her when she worked for Mrs. White, next door to Mrs. Bates' house, just past the two flowery lots. She worked for Mrs. White while I had worked for Mrs. Bates for five months. I think the name of the bank was HANNAH & HANNAH. I got my money.

Then Victa and I went out, bought our trunks, our shoes and the hats and skirts and blouses and put our trip money aside. We didn't have much left, but we thought it would bring us to our sister in Brooklyn.

Then the day came when we had to leave our beloved friends. We had to get the seven o'clock train in the morning. I said goodbye to dear Mother Bates and her family the night before. I got handkerchiefs and an apron from the girls and a brand new cook book from Mother Bates. God bless their souls, each and every one. I wished I could stay with them forever. Then I asked them for their photos. They gave them to me too. I said goodbye to the gardener, Mr. Ross, who was taking care of the lawn and the flowers and kept enough firewood on hand for me. Mr. Ross said, "Nettie as soon as you hit New York you will get married."

I said, "Are you going to follow me?"

He said, "No kidding. Any girl that works for Mrs. Bates, as soon as she leaves Mrs. Bates, she gets married."

I took his words lightly and went to stay with Victa over-night so she wouldn't oversleep.

The next morning at five we were ready to go. We had to walk about forty minutes to the station. Victa had the breakfast ready for the family for the last time. The Roberts got up early - before dawn. Mr. Roberts looked out the window on the porch and said, "What are you going to do with your trunks?" Victa had helped me to bring my trunk to her porch the night before and forgot to call the express man. Good thing Mr. Roberts got up early. He called the express man to take our trunks to the station. The express man said the trunks have to be strapped or tied with a rope. We did not know that. We didn't buy any straps or rope - now what? The express man said he had a piece of rope on his wagon that may be enough to tie one trunk. Mr. Roberts grabbed Mrs. Roberts wash line and tied Victa's trunk. The trunks were ready, and the express man took them away.

Mrs. Roberts handed us our basket. It felt kind of heavy, but we carried it with us to the train. We didn't expect anybody to be by the train as we said goodbye to Mr. and Mrs. Winowiecki and Szeleski's families Sunday. Tuesday morning, we were leaving, and when we got to the train, Dad Winowiecki was there with his bicycle waiting for us to see us off. We just had time to kiss him and left Traverse City behind us. God bless our dear good and bad friends, but misery followed us and arrived ahead of us to greet us at our new life.

Riding on the train from Traverse City to Grand Rapids we had to change trains. One train we were on stopped and a black man in a white coat with red cap was calling, "Anyone going to New York to change trains? Anybody to New York follow me." Several people got up ready to follow him.

I got up and pushed Victa out of our seat and a woman grabbed me by the sleeve and said, "You going to New York? Don't go on the train. I'm going to New York too. I'm going on a boat. You come with me. It's much better to travel on a boat than on a train."

We blocked the alley arguing and I said, "I'm going on the train, and so is my sister." But the woman held me.

The man with the red cap came to us and said to me, "Are you going to New York on a train? You'd better hurry. We have no time to wait for anybody. The train leaves in half an hour."

I said, "We are going on the train. We have tickets."

The red cap turned to the woman, "Hey, lady, will you mind your own business! These girls are big enough to know where they want to go!" and he took my and Victa's suitcases and people behind me pushed me out from the woman hurrying out.

We followed the red cap to a car like the buses nowadays. I think they took us from one end of town to the other end of the town, because we rode quite a while. Then they stopped before a big station and put us on a train. The man in the red cap put our suitcases up above our heads and left.

We were making ourselves comfortable when Victa looked around. I said, "Aha, hungry, aren't you!"

She looked at me and said, "Yes, how did you guess?"

"Because I'm hungry too, and you're looking, wishing for somebody to come around with a basket." I wanted to put our basket somewhere because it was in our way. It felt kind of heavy as she was taking care of it. I didn't know what was in it. I asked her, "What have you got in that basket?"

She said, "I don't know what's in it. I would have left it there if not for Mrs. Roberts handing it to me when we were leaving."

"Let's investigate what's in it," I said. And we stuck our noses in the basket.

Victa opened the basket and I whistled and said, "God bless them! They even thought of that!" There it was – a loaf of bread, box of cookies, bottle of milk, two pounds of frankfurters and oranges.

"Oh, look!" Victa said. Then we both burst out in a giggle. A bunch of bananas – seven in a bunch. "And we don't have to eat them with the skin!" We learned how to eat bananas in Traverse City. "This is going to last us till we get to New York," Victa said.

We had our lunch. Victa spread herself out and made herself comfortable to get her beauty sleep. I was sitting, thinking how just over a year ago coming to America, uncertainty, half hungry, but glad in our hearts we were coming to father. We found father and we found disappointment and heartache. And we found dearest friends, the dear people we have to leave, and we have to run away, run away in fear from our father. Now what disappointment, what heartache will come to us in the future?

I rested my head on my beloved sister Victa, who always worried over me and promised never to let me out of her sight, always willing to help me. Yet when something came suddenly, she was more scared than I. We were near in age and nearer than our oldest sister Maryanna. Maryanna was always somehow jealous of us, especially Victa. I don't know why. Maybe because Victa is the pretty, round-cheeked, apple-like face. My face was long, always pale. Maryanna was nice looking but smallpox left marks on her face and darkened her skin a little. Maryanna liked me somehow – a little. When she was a younger girl, when Uncle Julian bought her material for a dress and she knew she had plenty of dresses, she made a smaller size so it fit me. Then she told Uncle Julian she made a mistake. She knew that uncle would say, "Give it to your sisters." Maryanna gave it to me.

How is she now? She asked us to come. She wrote to us that she is lonesome. I got drowsy and closed my eyes.

All of a sudden, the train stopped. Conductors called something like "Detroit". I woke up. Then the cars started to push at one another, hammering, bucking. Then another train stood by our side. Trains generally passed one another quickly. This one was standing right even with our car. I saw the same faces on that car through our windows when it was light, yet, now it's dark out. Cars lighted with lights, then the lights are out and the both trains seemed to stand in one spot. Every once in a while a sound like somebody splashed a pail of water on something. I thought it probably rained outside, and as I couldn't see anything anymore, I went back to sleep.

I don't know how long I had been asleep when I heard some one's voice, "Are we out of the water yet?" Our train was standing still, but we were going. The boat was pulling it. That's why I heard the water splashing. Then we came to Buffalo. When the train started to move again a conductor came to us and said, if we wanted to see a waterfall, to sit in the other seat across from us. We did and we saw the big falls, but we didn't understand what it was. Later we found out that it was Niagara Falls. I asked the conductor how soon we would be in New York. He said around one o'clock.

When we arrived in New York the train stopped, the conductor came, took our suitcases down, helped us to the ground and we were left on our own. Before I had a chance to pick up my suitcase from the ground, Victa was running somewhere. I went after her. "Hey, where do you think you are going?" I said to her.

Victa said, "Come on, follow the people."

I said, "Victa, we are in New York now. Do you remember what Mrs. Roberts told us? New York is a very big city. We can get lost easily! And don't ask anyone for anything – only the men in blue coats who are cops, with an eagle on their caps. We can follow the people, but we don't know where they are going. People are going in different directions. Where would it get you?" I then looked around and saw lots of blue coats with eagles on their caps. We went to the nearest one. I showed him my address. Victa had one paper with the address and I had one, in case one would lose it. The man took his cap off his head, scratched his head, put the cap on again, turned around and waived to another blue coat. The other took a slow walk to us. The first said something to the second, the second nodded his head. The first one put his hands on my and Victa's shoulders, pushing us across the street.

Cars, wagons, bells ringing, he was pushing us through. He got us across safely to the corner, stopped a car, spoke to the conductor, gave the conductor our address and went back. The car was an open car with benches across the car and the conductor was walking on a board outside the car, holding onto the posts collecting money. I sat on the farthest end, Victa next to me and two more girls got on and sat near the conductor. I told Victa to watch what they were paying for that ride. Victa watched. She saw one of the girls give the conductor a dollar bill. We were smart now. We knew the American money already, so Victa watched the girl give the dollar to the conductor, but she didn't watch what the conductor did with the dollar. Did he give any change to the girl, because she was facing me, demanding two dollars! "Give me two dollars!" I took out two dollars and gave them to her. She handed them to the conductor. The conductor looked at us and yelled, "Hey! Where do you think you are going?" and kept on collecting from the next customer.

One of the girls (God bless her) came out and said, "Listen, maybe the girls never rode on a trolley car before!"

Victa turned pale. I was looking for more money and thought we didn't give him enough. He was taking money from other customers. Then he counted out $1.90 and handed it to us and went on. "Phewww!" the girl said. "If we weren't sitting here the poor girls would have been minus two dollars."

One of them asked us if we spoke German. I told her that we couldn't. She said it was too bad, but she asked us in English where we were coming from. We told her from Traverse City. We had never been on a car like this, we told her. Coming to America we saw cars like this in Bremen, Germany, but never rode on one.

Later on the girls got off and the car came around some building where other cars were coming from one side and turned around and went back in the same direction, only on the other side. All the people got off the car we were on. As the conductor hollered, "Last stop!" Victa and I were getting off too, but he stopped us. I was already looking for a man in a blue coat with an eagle on his cap, when a car came in and turned around and the conductor came to us and this one pointed to us and said to the other conductor, "Hey, will you keep your eyes on these two dummies. They're going to Greenpoint," and handed our address to the conductor.

People getting off and getting on cars looked at us and laughed aloud. I don't know what the second conductor thought of us or of the other conductor, but he was very nice to us. He helped us with our suitcase onto his car. It was an open car too. He told us to sit. When his car was full he collected his money. He told us, "Two nickels." We gave them to him. When we were going over a bridge he asked us if we were coming from afar. We told him from Traverse City. "Got somebody in Greenpoint?" he asked.

"Sister," we said.

"Married?"

"No, widow."

"Ohhh!"

The car got off the bridge, people started to get off and get on again, but he told us not to get off until he told us.

We were riding quite a while. Then we were out from one city. Then we rode over dumps and then came into another city. The conductor looked at our address again and said, "You will see your sister pretty soon, it's almost five o'clock. We'll be there soon."

Then he said, "Listen to me good. When you get off the car, walk two blocks straight, turn to your left and look for this number that's on this address, on your right. You got it? Now repeat it after me." We did.

About fifteen minutes later we were knocking on the door where Maryanna was boarding. A tall woman came out and said, "Come in, your sister will be home in a few minutes for supper."

So we were in Greenpoint. Victa and I, while walking the three blocks of that city found that we didn't like it a bit.

In the house, before Maryanna came in, we had a chance to look the place over and we decided we didn't like it. Victa said to me, "How could Maryanna live in a place like this! If Aunt Mary ever saw it she would have heart failure! A filthy city and a filthy house. A man, woman, three children. The city and the house need a lot of cleaning," Victa said.

Maryanna came in. We greeted each other with tears in our eyes and asked of one another's health. We all knew that we missed one another.

After supper when we were alone in Maryanna's room we told her we didn't like neither the town nor her boarding house. "Dirty houses, dirty streets, no flower gardens around. How can you bear it?" Maryanna looked sad. She looked older than she was. She was twenty four years old and looked like she was ten years older.

She said, "I am getting sick of it myself. I just waited until you came and we will go somewhere to find work here in the carpet factory. I make from three to five dollars a week on piece work. I spend it on my board."

I told her it was better to work in homes. You get your pay and your food and board. She said she would try it as she never worked for anybody yet. She said she already told her boss she wasn't coming to work anymore. Maryanna told us that she expected some visitors, as she had told them of our coming.

The company came. A few girls from her workplace and a fellow who had come together with Maryanna to America. He said he saw us walking on the street but was ashamed to meet us because he was coming from work in dirty clothes. So he went home, ate his supper, cleaned up then came to greet us. One sneaky one was there amongst the company. He asked me to show him my rings. I never thought anything was going to happen. I had them off my finger many a time when people wanted to see them. I took them off and gave them to him to look at. He put them in his pocket without taking a look. I thought it was a joke, but when he was going I told him I wanted my rings and that skunk slammed the door behind him and ran off with my rings. I didn't care for the one that Baker gave me, but the other one I got at the shrine. I thought the fellow was known by the company, but it happened that nobody knew him and everybody thought that he was with somebody else. The fellow that we knew promised me that he will watch out for the crook, but he never saw him.

Then another young man was there that Maryanna introduced to us as her boyfriend, and said they would marry soon. His name was Frank Gawronski. Maryanna asked Frank to take a day off work and help us to go on a ferry boat from Greenpoint to Jersey City, as Frank knew the way better than she did. One of the girls' uncles that Maryanna came with lived in Jersey City. Maryanna got acquainted with the uncle and his wife through the girls. Maryanna didn't know them well, but she had made occasional visits as she didn't know anybody else. So she thought she would take us to the people named Motileski and look for an agency there so we could get a job quickly. (If I and Victa knew that Motileski's place was something like Michalski's place we never would have gone there.) Frank told Maryanna that he would be there bright and early the next day to help us and he was.

Frank came all dressed up and we started for Jersey City. We were on the ferry for a while. Frank asked us if we wanted to see the Statue of Liberty and Victa said we had seen it when we were standing all day that Sunday before we got to Baltimore, coming to America. So Victa sat on a bench. Frank, Maryanna and I crossed to the other side of the boat and I sat on a bench there. Frank and Maryanna were standing near me. Frank looked at Maryanna and said to her, "Maryanna, I'm not going to marry you. I'm going to marry your sister."

Maryanna jumped at him with her hands, fingers curled, and said to Frank, "I'll scratch your eyes out for you!"

Frank backed off a little from her. Then she said, "Which sister?" Frank said, "Antonia."

"Oh," Maryanna said. "If it's Antonia, it's alright – Victa, no!"

I thought, those two are just joking. I laughed and got up off the bench to see if Victa was all right, but I thought, my poor sister, Maryanna. Victa never had harmed her. Why was she so hard on Victa! I was glad Victa didn't hear those words.

We were in New Jersey now. We got to Motileski's. There was Mr. and Mrs. Motileski, four girls, two boys, ages from two to seventeen years old. They lived on Steuben Street in a three room house. The living room was used as a kitchen too. There was one small, light bedroom and one small, all dark bedroom. Three girls, fourteen, twelve, and nine, and the boy, six, slept in the dark room in one bed. The mother and father with the two-year old one slept in the light room, and the boy, seventeen, slept in the living room.

That evening when we came there the house was full of girls and young men. Motileski's two nieces were there and other girls on their day off, because it was Thursday, and men came to meet them there. One of the girls was a nice girl we knew from Europe, but they were like us – without another place to go. They came to Motileski's because they knew the two nieces.

When the house was thinned out we went to sleep with the four Motileski children. Three of us squeezed in that dark room. We slept across the width of the bed instead of lengthwise. I couldn't sleep, neither could Maryanna. The place was too crowded, the bed had too many heads and too many feet. Frank Gawronski slept on the floor in the living room-kitchen.

Friday morning when we got up I was worrying how we would get our trunks. We forgot what station we came into. We were advised to get a private person who had a horse and wagon to pick them up. We found a Jewish man who kept a little express wagon and he took the job to look for our trunks. Maryanna told him she wanted him to go and pick up her things too. Victa and I went through our purses. How much money do we have left? Victa noticed she was missing twelve dollars. She couldn't figure out how and where she could have lost it, but it was gone. So we had to depend on the rest of the money I had left. The express man took eight dollars for his job.

We needed to find work in a hurry – we were out of cash! Maryanna was going back to Greenpoint to pack her things so the express man could pick them up. She asked Motileski to go with Victa to the agency to find three places for the three of us to work for Monday, if possible. Maryanna took me with her to help her with the packing. Frank brought us to Greenpoint, back to Jersey City. We came alone. Maryanna had an argument with Frank. Frank told her that he was leaving for Pittsburgh. I overheard him say, "I will make more money in Pittsburgh inside of three months, and I will send for her." Maryanna cried, but didn't tell me anything, and I felt I was in the way.

We packed her trunk and she asked the woman to give it to the express man when he called for it, and Saturday morning we returned back to Jersey City.

I found Victa all excited. The agency promised to call for us Monday morning to bring us to the places to work, but she said to me, "Do you know who lives in Jersey City?"

"A lot of people," I told her.

"No," she said. "Do you remember the woman who lived next door to us for one year? People used to call her the lame Wasielewski."

I didn't think I remembered it, so Victa tried to bring it to my memory. She said, "The one that had Jozef, Jan, and Mary with a hunch back, Anthony, Wladek and Aniela. A young man was here last night and said he is a cousin to the Wasielewski cousins, and he says they live on the other street on Railroad Avenue. She said she would like to see Mary some time."

If my poor sister could know then what hunchback Mary would do to us she wouldn't want to see Mary. All that evening Victa was watching for the man who told her about the lame Mrs. Wasielewski, but the man wasn't in the crowd that evening. We, seven of us, murdered the one bed in the dark room again.

Sunday a crowd started to come early in the afternoon. Girls and a man. The nieces were there again. Then the man came in and brought another man with him. The other man had never been in Motileski's place, but everybody knew him and he knew all the boys there. The man was introduced to us as John Wasielewski, and his cousin was Adam Stawski. Adam excused himself for not being there last night because he was searching for John and couldn't find him. He finally found him at his brother Joe's house. Adam and John joined the crowd.

Mrs. Motileski, Maryanna, Victa and I and the two nieces were sitting in the little light bedroom and two fellows came in also. One was talking to Motileski and Victa, and seemed like a nice fellow. His name was Nawrocki. The other's name was Bogusz. Bogusz was talking to me, telling me that his mother was in Austria and was a very rich woman. He showed me a silk handkerchief that his mother sent him. I got tired listening to Bogusz's silly bragging and told him he should have stayed in Austria and not taken a job from another man who was poor and needed it. I wanted to get away from him, from that room, and I don't know if he tripped me or I tripped over his feet, but I flopped right in John Wasielewski's lap.

John held me so I wouldn't fall and looked at Bogusz and said to him, "That will do you!" Bogusz excused himself and went to the other girls. I jumped out of John's lap and sat by another window. Then they started to play and sing. John played a little harmonica and the girls sang some song with some naughty words in it. John came to me and said, "Now you sing something."

I sang a holy church song and the nieces didn't like it, and passed a remark around that I was "holy".

Chapter 15

No Job for Antonia

Seven o'clock Monday morning before Mr. Motileski went to work the agent was there already. We three sisters were getting ready and glad it came so quickly. Mr. Motileski said to me, "You're not going to work, you are going to get married!"

"What?"

"Sure," he said. "The fellow who was here last night told me not to let you go to work – he is going to marry you."

I said to him, "Mr. Motileski, if anybody asked you to marry him, you go and marry him. No one has asked me and I don't want anybody to ask me. I came here to make my living, not to get married."

They all looked at me. "I'm sorry," the agent said, "But I was going to tell you that I have only two places today, and you look kind of weak for that kind of job, so I'll take your sisters and look for easier work for you."

I started to cry and begged the agent to hurry up so I would get work too. My dear sister Maryanna said to me, "Well, if you are going to get married, get married, or go to work, nobody is going to feed you for nothing!"

I almost fainted. I felt sick around my heart and cried all the more. "My God," I said, my father's first words – "Go to work, nobody is going to feed you for nothing.'" Why the hard words from Maryanna? She knew very well that I always did work for myself.

At that time not all people had toilets in their houses. Motileskis didn't have a toilet in theirs. We had to go to the first floor, then to the cellar and through the cellar far back in the yard, so some nights weren't so pleasant to smell the odor in Motileski's. I was a light sleeper and had a better chance to think at night than in the day and the dark room was right off the kitchen and it had to be open because there was no other ventilation.

One night I heard somebody walking in the kitchen in the dark. Then I heard a faucet open and water pouring somewhere, and then a voice. Motileski's son who slept in the kitchen hollered, "Pop, that's a pot with sauerkraut! You are going all over the stove!"

The next night I didn't eat any supper – sauerkraut. Frank ate sandwiches, the younger children finished the sauerkraut. They didn't know what was in it. Motileski couldn't afford to throw it out.

I didn't ask Victa for any help yet, and Victa pulled me to the dark bedroom, stuck two dollars in my hand quickly and said, "Don't cry, sister, this is the two you gave me Friday for the carfare when you went to Greenpoint. As soon as I get my pay, I'll pay Motileski for board. Maryanna is jealous of you. Don't mind her!" and she went with the agent and I was left to wait.

I guess everybody was tired after Sunday because we had a quiet night Monday and I was glad to put my head in the bed among the Motileski's four heads and after the past few disturbing nights I slept soundly. The bed bugs were crawling all over me, biting me so that I had bumps and lumps all over. The other night I couldn't sleep I had been chasing them away from me. Monday night I just slept. There was another night when I could not sleep and I saw things and heard things in Motileski's house that had no toilet.

Wednesday, Mrs. Motileski packed a couple of washtubs of dirty, and I mean dirty, clothes from her six children and hers and her husband's. We were also taking the wash of three men who kept rooms for themselves in the next apartment. Mrs. Motileski left me by the tub and went outside to sit on the steps gossiping with the other women until the children came from school. She didn't have to fix dinner because the children, Mr. Motileski and the boy that worked were taking sandwiches with them. She bought something from the near store for the little girl and was sitting out there chewing on something while I was sweating inside. For supper she bought some baloney. She, her husband and the boys had some sandwiches. I had one. The other children – whichever one grabbed the skins first, ate them. The rest filled themselves on bread and coffee or beer (which they had plenty of when the guests were around).

On Thursday when Victa came in the afternoon I still had the full basket. She took the iron from me and told me to sit down and she kept ironing until ten o'clock when she went home. She asked me if I was sick. I said, "No." I didn't tell her what I was doing in Motileski's house and that I was starving. Victa asked if the man called again and did I know who he was. I told her Monday and Tuesday nobody was there, and Wednesday just Bogusz and one of Mrs. Motileski's cousins, and those you see who are here – just the nieces and their boy.

I told Victa that I was asking Mrs. Motileski where the agent was and I would go to him and ask him to find me work. Mrs. Motileski just smiled and said he would come when he had a job, and so for the rest of the week no extra man came in, not even Adam Stawski showed up, neither that Sunday nor Monday.

Mr. Motileski was sizing me up from the corner of his eye as if to ask himself what is she waiting for? Maybe the man was drunk and didn't know what he was saying, or maybe he himself was too drunk to hear what the man was saying.

Then on Tuesday night, October 9th, the man came. The man was John Wasielewski. John brought with him a bottle of whiskey and sent Frank Motileski for a can of beer, and while the family was enjoying themselves John took a glass of beer and came and sat by me and asked, "Get a job yet?"

I said, "No, but I wish I had."

He said, "Don't look for one, I want to marry you."

I said, "I don't want to get married."

"Why not?" he asked. "Every girl wants to marry."

"I'm one that doesn't," I told him.

He said, "Two years ago a gypsy read my hand and told me that I will marry a girl that just came from over the ocean and she will be a good wife."

"Then I'm not the one," I said. "I'm here in this country over a year and I'm not good for anyone."

"Maybe you price yourself below your value," he said.

"One should know his own value," I told him.

He said, "I want to marry you just the same. Tell me your reason why don't want to marry?"

"I have many reasons," I told him, looking him straight in his eyes. "I am too young. I'm only sixteen years old and I never had a chance to learn to cook a decent meal. All I know is to wash the dishes and scrub the floors."

John said, "In this country you don't worry about cooking. You go to the butcher, get a pound of steak, fry it, open a can of tomatoes and a loaf of bread and the meal is ready."

I said to him, "I am an orphan. I have no mother to make my trousseau and I have no father to help me with money."

John said, "Money? I have two hands and ten fingers. Today I have money, tomorrow I haven't – today I haven't, tomorrow I have."

I said again, "Every girl getting married wants a least a nice dress to marry in. All mine are black skirts and blouses."

John had an answer for that one too. He said, "I think I have a few dollars saved. It will be enough for a suit for me and a dress for you."

"Listen," I said. "You see my sisters. They are both older and smarter and both prettier than I. Why don't you marry one of them? Victa is the prettiest one, and a good girl, and Maryanna is a widow."

John looked at me and laughed. "You are a funny girl," he said. "If I wanted your sister I wouldn't ask you. I want you."

I got out of the argument. I didn't know what to say anymore. "But," I said. "I'll ask my sister about that and see what she will say."

"All right," John said. "I want the answer by Sunday." Then he went to Motileski's table, sent for a couple more cans of beer for them and when John was leaving, Motileski said to him, "How is it? Everything all right?"

John told him everything would be all right.

When John didn't show up for the rest of the week, Mr. Motileski changed his mind about me. Wednesday I did Mrs. Motileski's laundry. Thursday Victa didn't come, so I did the ironing myself. I didn't know why she didn't come, and thought that Sunday she wouldn't come either because it was her day off. I might have had to wait for Victa until next Thursday if Mr. Motileski didn't change his mind about me.

On Saturday he told me, "What are you waiting for? Do you think that fellow is going to marry you? He has better girls here than you. You had better get yourself a job before he makes a fool of you."

Get myself a job? After I had been begging Mrs. Motileski every day to take me or show me where the agent lived? And that Monday if Motileski didn't open his mouth the agent probably would have had work for me. So I decided to go to see Victa. Maryanna didn't come to see how I was. She didn't even let me know of her new address, like Victa. Sunday I asked Mary Motileski, the fourteen year old girl, to take me to the street where Victa worked, but Mary was just as bright as I was, so we both got lost.

We took the Courthouse Street car from Newark Avenue and First Street. The conductor let us off at the junction and told us to go straight up. We did. We went straight up, but we didn't follow that street, we crossed the street and went straight up. We walked as far as the street was going, then the street disappeared and only a small path was there. Next the path disappeared, and we came to a river. It was getting dark. I said to Mary, "Well, I'm sure Victa doesn't live here."

Mary said, "No, I don't think so."

She didn't think so? I said, "Mary, were you around here before?"

"No," she said.

"Well, all we have to do is go back the same way that we came from, and hurry before it gets too dark."

We came back to the place where we got off the car and an old man stood on the corner. I showed him the address and he said, "See the big house straight up? This is Summit Avenue. You will see the number on that big house."

We were right there, walking miles looking for it. I saw Victa and cried my story to her. I told her the man who asked Motileski about me is John Wasielewski, and the talk we had Tuesday evening, and what Motileski said about me last night.

Victa thought about it for a while and then said to me the nice name she called me when I was a baby. "Toshulma, if that fellow wants to marry you, don't send him away."

"But Victa, I don't want to get married. I always had in my mind that when you get married I will come to stay with you and never get married. Won't you marry him?"

Victa said, "He didn't ask me. If he wanted me he would have asked me. He wants you. That's what he said."

I said, "Maryanna is mad at me. She won't even come to see me. Maryanna was supposed to marry Frank Gawronski. She told me."

I told Victa that Gawronski went to Pittsburgh the Friday when we went to Greenpoint.

Victa said that was what she was probably mad about and wants to take it out on you. How right Victa was! I didn't tell Victa about the accident on the Ferry the day we were coming to Jersey City.

So Victa said, "Don't mind Maryanna, you marry John."

I told her I was afraid, and then she started from another point. She said, "Listen, sister, we are two orphans and no matter where we go we are just orphans. We have no home to go to. I don't like you staying in Motileski's house. He already told you that you are not good enough, because we are not like his nieces, Valera and Stefa, because they have five acres of land in Europe. And if Motileskis will keep on drinking like they do their children will be worse than we are. You know that I can take hardship better than you can. If you get married, I won't have to worry about the two of us. You will have your home and I will always come to you like to my own."

"You know," I told her, "That I haven't a cent left."

"I will help you always," She said. "You marry John if he wants you."

I left Victa and it was nearly ten o'clock when Mary and I got to Mary's house. John was there waiting for his answer. He asked me why I was so late and I told him how we got lost and got to Victa's about eight-thirty. Mary told her mother the same thing, so we weren't questioned any more.

John said, "What did your sister say?"

I said, "She told me to marry you."

John said, "That's fine."

John went home early and forgot to throw a quarter on the table and say, "Here Motileski, get yourself another can of beer." Motileski got mad and took it out on me. He called me a bad word in Polish and said, "You think that fellow is going to marry you? He will stick his rear end at you. You'd better get out quick and get to work."

I looked at Mrs. Motileski and said, "I've been begging you to please show me the agent's place for the whole two weeks, why do you keep me here? With all the work you lay out for me in your house I have no chance to go out to find somebody else to help me. I'm not staying here because I want to, you're trying to keep me here to take insults from your husband."

She said, "Well if you want to go to work, go tomorrow to the cigar factory. You may get a job there."

I didn't know if she wished me good or bad then, but I jumped to that. I thought now maybe it's a good idea. I might get to know some good girls there that would help me to get out of Motileski's.

Monday morning, I got dressed and went out without breakfast to the cigar factory, which was near Steuben Street and I got a job. I came home for dinner, but there was no dinner. No Motileskis in the house. I had my two dollars that Victa gave me and went to the nearest store and asked the store lady to make me a sandwich and I went back to work.

Throughout the evening the boss was going around looking at how the work was done. He came to me and said, "Good work, new-comer! Where did you learn it?"

I told him I never worked in a factory.

He said, surprised, "No! We have some of them two and three weeks before they do as good as you on your first day!"

I went home for supper and saw the children fight over the baloney skins. I went to the store, bought bread and cheese and milk and shared with the children. Tuesday Motileski gave me coffee for breakfast and a roll. I went to the store and got me a sandwich for dinner and worked all day. My work must have been good, I got another praise. I tried to get a word with some of the girls in there but they were all so busy working piece work that none cared to talk.

In the evening John came again, putting a bottle before Motileski and a quarter for beer. He came and sat by me and said, "I told you not to go to work and you did. Why didn't you listen to me?"

I said to John, "I don't know who to listen to. Motileski told me Sunday night to get out and look for work and not to wait for you because you will stick your rear end at me and marry the rich girl. On Saturday I owe Motileski board for three weeks. I have to work to pay her."

John looked at Motileski and asked, "How much are you charging her for board?"

She said bashfully, "Well, she was helping me around a little so I think six dollars will be enough for three weeks."

John took out six dollars and gave it to Mrs. Motileski and said to me, "Don't go to work anymore. Pack your things and have them ready for Thursday. My mother will come for you in the afternoon, and come for your trunk in the evening."

But I went to work Wednesday as I had two day's pay coming to me. I thought I would put in another day and finish. While I was working the floor lady came to me and said, "Your work is pretty good. The boss said to put you on piece work next week."

She was a Polish girl by the name of Jankoski. I told her that I was not coming next week, I was leaving tonight. She wanted to know why. I told her I was going to get married and I told her she will be one of my bridesmaids. She said she would be glad to and gave me her address and where to find her when I needed her. I received my pay of three dollars. Three dollars to start married life with.

When I got home that night I started to gather my loose things to put in the trunk. I asked John now that I got a good job and they said my work was good, couldn't he give me at least six months or so, so I could make a little money for my own dress and get to know the people around here. John said, "I'm sure if I let you have six months then somebody else will have you, and if I don't get married this month I will catch the first freight to Buffalo and become a first class bum."

I didn't know what to answer or what to think. He was headstrong, aggressive. Just likes to tell you something and expects you to do as he said. But I went to work.

I know I had them clean on top of my trunk, some were hanging on a nail. They were not there now. I asked Motileski what she did with my clothes. She said she thought they were dirty and put them in the wash. She never touched my wash before. What's the idea? Oh, that was Wednesday, her wash day. I thought she did the wash, but when she lit the lamp I saw that if I wanted to get my clean clothes I would have to wash all her dirty ones. So I stayed up half the night to wash her "little work" as she told John, and pay her two dollars a week to stay there. I did much less in dear Mrs. Bates and got two dollars fifty a week. Well, it's the last week in Motileski's.

Thursday John's mother came in. Mrs. Motileski said, "This is Mrs. Wasielewski." I went to greet her. They both talked for a while, then John's mother said, "John sent me here to bring you to my house. I might as well. People are already talking that if John doesn't marry you, you will take him to court so he will have to marry you."

I stepped away from her. I said, "No! He doesn't have to marry me. I don't want him, he wants me!" Then I stood there speechless, thinking what to do, what to say. If I had a better place than Motileski's I would have told her to go home and keep her John.

If I didn't tell the floor lady in the cigar factory that I was going to get married I would go back there. Now I was ashamed. I wished I wasn't so green, but I was a silly, young girl. I wished I had dear Mom and Dad Winowiecki here to advise me what to do. And then I went like a lamb on a string to the slaughter house.

John didn't tell me that the Sunday I was at Victa's, Motileski tried to discourage him. Motileski told John not to marry me because I was only a girl who worked for rich landowners - that people didn't have a good opinion of girls who worked in big places. Motileski told John he should marry one of his nieces whose father had several acres of land in Europe and the girls worked for a saloon keeper's wife in New York and made good money. They were good girls from a good family, Motileski said. John didn't tell me that he, John, smelled Motileski right then and there, that Motileski was trying to hold John not so much for his nieces as for himself. John noticed that the other men didn't throw so many quarters for Motileski's beer and John caught on to Motileski's schemes. John remembered the first Sunday when he asked Motileski not to let me go to work because he wanted to marry me – how Motileski had praised us three sisters up to the sky, and John didn't tell me then what was going on in his house. John didn't tell me that the evenings he didn't come to visit me as Motileskis expected him to, to throw his quarters for their beer, that he was working overtime. He was having a war with his mother and his sister Mary. John didn't tell me that Mrs. Motileski, while I was washing her dirty clothes, found time to meet Mrs. Wasielewski on the street corners coming from the grocery and butcher stores. And Mrs. Motileski was smearing me from my nose to my toes with mud that there was not a white spot left. And that John's mother liked it because she had picked him a girl whose father promised to give the fellow who married his daughter five hundred dollars cash and new furniture.

The girl was Tilly Lada, a good friend of Mary's, and that Sunday John asked Motileski for me he was supposed to have an engagement party with Tilly. When John told his family that he was going to marry another girl he set them all on fire – John's mother and Mary got mad at John and Adam Stawski for bringing John to Motileski's. Tongues went to work all around. John's mother and sister went for information and advice and Motileskis caught a foolish one and tried to hold onto him as long as they could, and get him to marry one of their nieces first. John's mother forbid John to bring me to their house. If he didn't want Tilly, she didn't want a girl with bare ends.

John packed his grip and went to his brother Joe, who lived with his wife and two children on Canal Street in Jersey City. John told Joe and his sister-in-law Stella, his troubles. Joe and Stella told John he could bring me to their home and have a quiet wedding. John asked his mother for his money. John was the only one who was earning good money at that time – eighteen dollars a week steady, and with overtime he got from twenty to twenty-five dollars a week. His father had started with nine and got as far as fourteen dollars a week in Forbes Foundry on Communipaw Avenue, or somewhere near the city hospital.

When John's father went for the job as a cupola tender, Forbes asked his name. He said, "Stanislaus Wasielewski."

"John Smidt from now on," Forbes told him, and gave him the job. And from then on the young children called themselves "Smith".

Mary was working in a tobacco factory for three dollars a week. Wladek (Willy) worked for a half dollar a week and Antony didn't want to work at all – anywhere. He got a woman to sign for him and his mother and got himself in the Navy. Then there was Leon, Ben and Frank who were too young to work. John's father knew that John was giving his mother money to save for him, but mother had one daughter left who was a hunchback. They were taking advantage of John to save for Mary. She wanted to marry Mary away too, so when John asked for the money his mother refused to give all of it to him. John's father told him to come home and have the wedding in their house. Then they decided to make a big wedding.

Years ago people invited to a wedding collected money among themselves at the table. They took a platter and passed it around from one to another buying a bride to see who gives more, buying one another out. The bigger the wedding the more they collected. The bride gets all the money to start her home. If girls had homes their parents or relatives made the weddings. I had nobody, so after the three weeks' war, while I was in Motileski's and didn't even know what was going on around me, John's mother and Mary decided on a big wedding for themselves to have one on me.

The one who greeted me nicely in John's home was John's father and John's grandmother. At least John's father acted like a human being to me. Mary ignored me and carried her head high, over her hunchback as if to try to show me that she is something and I'm nothing. Both Mary and her mother were passing signs and signals with their eyes between them which the little grandma was catching. Grandma was John's mother's mother. She didn't measure five feet and she was a little deaf, but when she pinched her nose tight and held her breath she could hear good. First her action seemed funny to me, but I got used to her and we understood each other well, and grandma was there all the time. She saw and heard and knew what was going on in the house, but I had a feeling that grandma was afraid of her daughter and granddaughter, because she only talked to me when the other two were out of the room. Many times she shook her fist in their direction.

John's family lived in a six-room apartment. Three bedrooms, a living room they called a front room, and a kitchen. On the second floor they had plenty room to turn around. John's parents with the youngest boy Frankie, slept in a light room off the kitchen. Grandma and Mary had their room between the kitchen and the front room. Willy, Leon and Ben had a bedroom off the front room where there was no window. John had his light room off the front room, so I had the pleasure of sleeping in the front room on a couch.

John came from work that night and took me to his brother Joe. I met Joe's wife and fell in love with her. Stella was about twenty-seven years old and she was a grand person. I felt that I was going to have a friend to the end.

The next day John asked his mother to take me to the store and get me a dress. Mother thought it would be cheaper to buy material, so she bought silk good enough so Mary could have a dress too. The material for my dress was four dollars, the dressmaker took eight dollars for making it, and the veil and trimmings came out to a total of fifteen dollars. John got his suit made to order. It cost him eighteen dollars.

Saturday evening John and his father went to Priest Kwiatkowski in Saint Anthony's church on Monmouth Street to notify him to prepare for our marriage ceremony. John forgot to tell the Priest my age. We came back from the Priest and went to get the rings. Father picked out our rings, heavy plain fourteen karat gold bands. Mine turned my finger green in six months' time, but it was gold at that time. John paid nine dollars for both of them and the lady there gave me six silver teaspoons for good luck. The teaspoons got rusty on me in a few weeks, but anyway I got something for my own.

Then Sunday we had the engagement party and the next week everybody was busy preparing for the next Sunday wedding. Everybody did something without asking me if I liked that way or this way. So, mother and Mary were running around, then sent me and Mary. I didn't know anybody, so they were inviting people. They asked thirty families to that wedding. All I had invited was Victa and Maryanna and Stella Jankoski, the floor lady from the cigar factory. Maryanna didn't come.

I wanted Victa as my first bridesmaid, but mother said, "No, Mary is going to be the first."

I had to be satisfied and have Victa second, and Stella third. The brides walk the aisle differently today than they did in my time. John picked his best man.

Then Sunday came – the wedding day. Guests were pouring in from early morning and the musicians came at noon. The ceremony in church was to be at four in the afternoon. I don't know why. I didn't see anybody and I didn't care what was going on. I cried all day. The first bridesmaid was supposed to assist the bride with her veil. She was busy curling her hair, so Victa helped me with it. Victa didn't need curly hair. She was pretty without it.

CHAPTER 16

Three-Day Wedding

When I had my veil on, Victa said, "Oh sister, you have your old shoes on!" They had to wait for me until I changed shoes. Then we were ready to go.

John said the Priest would be mad if we didn't get there on time. We couldn't find the second best man and we went without him. The Priest called us first to the office to get our right names, right ages and the witnesses. The Priest asked me my age. I said, "Sixteen."

John's mother said, "Seventeen."

Victa said, "Sixteen."

Mother said, "Seventeen."

The Priest turned on us mad and said, "Make up your mind, which one of you is getting married, sixteen or seventeen?"

I knew mother would have her way anyway, so I kept my mouth shut. Priest Kwiatkowski knew the Wasielewski gang and he took her word for it and we went before the altar. Since I was minus the second best man to help the first best man bring me before the altar, one had to do it, so the first one brought me there. John had his two, Mary and Victa, to bring him there, coming from the altar to go in pairs. Well, I had John. Mary got her best man and Victa was left alone. Stella Janicki was a lady, her best man was a gentleman. Stella left with John's mother and pushed him to Victa to save Victa the embarrassment of walking alone in the aisle.

We came back home. Our second best man was crying that we didn't wait for him. He was in Motileski's the night before and overslept and forgot to shave himself. It took him so long. The wedding was going full speed all day. At midnight they set me on the table, took my veil from my head, spread it on a big platter and the people had their fun throwing their money on the platter with words like, "For the bride, for her pots, for her dishes, for the baby diapers," and so on. There were ones, twos, fives and tens. "Let's buy the bride from the bridegroom!" And more money came in. "Who gives more?" When the money stopped coming John threw ten dollars on top and bought me out.

I never saw a wedding as successful since Tyburski in Zamosc was marrying off one of his daughters. The bride was supposed to take the money herself and count it and thank the people for it. I thanked the people for it, but I didn't get the money. Victa took the platter off the table, carrying it to me. John's mother took it off her and went to another room to count it. Victa went with her. Mother didn't like Victa following her but she couldn't say, "Get out," so Victa helped to count it without any suspicion of what was going to happen to the money.

Victa came to me and said, "Oh, sister, one hundred sixty nine dollars in bills and some change too!"

People were going home shaking hands with me and leaving ones, two, and fives in my hand. I was thinking they are safer with mother than with me and didn't count them, just handed them to her.

The party went on for two days and two nights and then came the third day to finish the food and the beer. They ate, drank and only two men got drunk. They were then brought back to their homes.

Tuesday morning brewery trucks came to pick up the empty kegs. They got eight and were looking for the ninth one. I told them one on the first floor. A man kicked if off last night. The man said that one was full yet and the brewery man went out. I went down to see the keg, and yes, it was full. I brought the keg up. I had two steps to climb when John's father opened the door wanting to go down and saw me. He almost fell when he felt that the keg was full. He didn't believe that I just picked the keg up and carried it – Nooooooo! I tilted one end, rested on the a step, pushed it, tilted it on my knee, caught it on another step, pushed it and so on to the top, always resting it on my hips again. I braced myself on the banister and if the keg made up its mind to go down I would have gone down with it too. Father said if he didn't see me come up the two steps he wouldn't have believed I did it. Well, I was a hero for that day!

Mr. Ross predicted that any girl who leaves Bates gets married! I left Traverse City September 23rd, arrived in New York September 24th and October 28th was married!

Well, the wedding was over. If that's what people called married life, then I didn't care for it. Why didn't somebody tell me the truth about it. Maryanna could but she didn't. Maybe she was glad that I took John. Maybe Frank Gawronski came back to her. Well, I'm married now, and in Europe people said once you get married it is yours for keeps – good or bad. I knew I wasn't as good a wife as John expected of me. Maybe John didn't love me either, just got his satisfaction running away from Tilly and from his mother, just to have his way. Tilly, we heard, afterwards took her father's five hundred dollars and ran away with another man. The man took her five hundred dollars and she came back to her father. Then we didn't hear of her any more.

John and I were looking ourselves over, what's for us in the future. John asked his mother for his account. They were counting and recounting and the more they counted the more John owed his mother. I told John that we collected over two hundred dollars with the money I added to the platter that people gave me. Mother couldn't deny it because Victa counted it too. John claimed he gave his mother two hundred dollars to save for him. They counted our wedding cost as one hundred fifty dollars. Food, beer and whiskey, our clothes, the Priest, the organist, the three coaches, flowers, and small things were one hundred, so if two hundred fifty dollars was taken from the four hundred we still should have had one hundred fifty dollars coming to us. Mother insisted John owed her board. John wanted to know who had been helping to support the family for the last five years?

John was twenty-two years old and went to learn his trade at fourteen. From then to eighteen years old he was steadily helping to buy things for the house – furniture, a sewing machine and a lot of other things, but mother said that didn't count.

His mother told John she would take me to New York and buy some feathers to make me a feather cover and some pillows. Well, she did that. The next day she took Mary and me and we went to New York somewhere on Broom Street where she bought nice goose feathers – forty-five pounds – for me for a cover, and two bigger pillows and one little pillow and the same amount for Mary. We dragged the bags of feathers home, and we each, Mary and I had made a feather cover, two big pillows each and one little pillow for each of us. Mother paid thirty-five cents a pound for the feathers, which John and I didn't think that it took the whole hundred fifty dollars for ninety pounds of feathers, but she insisted that she paid seventy dollars for each. I didn't argue for the money, knowing that she would get back at me and ask me what I brought here. So, I said nothing.

Whenever John was out she was telling me that he owes her for board. I didn't know who to believe. John came home with his first pay after our wedding and divided it between us. He gave his mother ten and me ten and left five for himself for his car fare and beer. Mother said to John, "Is that all you are giving me?"

John said, "Yes, that's for her and me for a week."

She didn't say anything anymore.

When John was home the next day she told me to give her the other ten before I lose it. I was afraid not to give it to her so I did. That evening a peddler came with a bundle on his back and spread the bundle out. He had curtains, tablecloths, and different linen. I said to John, "I wish I could buy some of this."

He said, "Buy what you want."

Before I had a chance to tell him that his mother got the ten he gave me, mother said, "What do you want to buy things right now to lay in your trunk and rot? You've got plenty of time for that." I didn't know what she meant by that, and she had the ten, so I didn't buy anything.

Then John wanted some money. He had to go to a meeting. I told him mother had it. He didn't say anything. Mother wanted me to go to work, to the tobacco factory with Mary. I told her that I could go back to the cigar factory. Mary made three dollars in a week, while I made a dollar a day. She didn't want me to go to the cigar factory. I don't know why. Maybe she was afraid that I would get richer than Mary. Grandma told John that mother was chasing me to work. John asked me if it was true, and I said yes.

John said, "That's enough mother – you've gone too far with me! When I was a young boy I did everything to help you when all the others didn't want to work. I went to learn my trade so I could make more money so you wouldn't have to keep five to six boarders in the house with all of us and to wash and cook for all of them. Every boarder paid you five dollars a month board. For that five dollars you washed for them, you cooked for them, you served them. Each one of them had his own account book with the grocer and butcher and paid for their food themselves there. You were lucky, your boarders trusted you. You kept their books and they gave you their money to pay for their accounts. You bought their goods, you paid with their money, but you made sure that out of every pound of meat you bought for them was a bit of it left for our gravy. They had the bigger pieces while we had the chips of every one of their bigger pieces for soup. Otherwise, no matter how hard you worked we would be starving with pop's weekly pay. I started to work in the tobacco factory when I was eleven for a dollar and a half a week and got as far as three dollars a week when I was fourteen. From fourteen years I went to learn my trade and brought home from nine to eighteen dollars a week steady. Willy is sixteen years old and still getting a dollar and a half a week. Mary is nineteen and still gets three dollars a week. Pop started at seven dollars a week and got as high as fourteen a week. Isn't it about time I get a chance to live for myself, or do you want me and my wife to stay here and work for you and the ones here that should start thinking and working for themselves? Leon is thirteen years old and all you have left is seven year-old Ben and two-year old Frank. Pop can take care of them. I want to pay you ten dollars a week food and board which gives you more than forty dollars a month until we save a little to go on our own."

John's father, who was sitting, listening without a word until then said, "John is right, and you have no right to take advantage of the girl, so let them alone," he told mother.

But did she? When John was working, I was afraid to come to the kitchen when his mother was in unless it was to help her with washing, ironing or scrubbing the floors. Then I got my meals. Other days, no work, no eat. In the morning when she went to church, she was a very religious woman. Almost every day to church, once a month to receive communion. When she was in church, Grandma and I had our breakfast. When John was working overtime and was late for supper I had to get bread and ham and with his beer, he had supper. Then John's father again stepped in. Father didn't see me at the table. He called me to come and eat with him. He got a plate, a spoon and said, "Come and eat with me, I didn't see you eat." Then you could see the fire in mother's and Mary's eyes.

"Why don't you take a teaspoon and feed her!" they were saying. "Nobody is stopping her from eating, and nobody is going to feed her if she sits in her room and doesn't come out to eat."

John and I went to Joe's again as dear Stella had said, "Come again soon!"

I told Stella what was going on. Stella said, "Didn't she shake your bed yet? When we got married, we lived with her three weeks. Every Sunday she came to our room where you are now, at seven in the morning, shaking our bed and calling us bums and all kinds of names and chasing us to church." Stella said, "I wonder why she's going to church when she can't get that devil out of herself. We didn't have much money, but my friend helped me out. My friend was married a little sooner than I. She had nobody, he had nobody. They took four rooms, had their wedding there and lived in the rooms afterward. Four rooms was too much for them and they didn't have enough furniture to fill them, so they let us have two of the rooms and we lived there for three years together until my Aniela came. They had a baby too, so we separated. You two get your own place and wait until Mary gets married, then they will have new meat to bite and will leave you alone. I had my share of them too. I know what they are."

I told Stella that we would get out but have to save a little because mother took all the money. Stella said, "I knew she would, too bad I didn't warn you about it. She did that to us too."

Sunday Victa came and I told Victa about the start of my married life. No money. Victa wanted to know about the wedding money. I told her what had happened. Victa felt kind of guilty and took out twenty dollars and said, "That's my month's pay. Next month I will bring you more."

Then Maryanna came. She was sorry she didn't come to the wedding. She worked for people who owned a big grocery store with three children and she couldn't get a day off. Victa walked out of the room to the kitchen to talk to John's father. He kind of liked Victa. I told Maryanna that I'm moving out and am just waiting to get a little money. Maryanna pulled out twenty dollars and said, "Here, sister, if it was for Victa I wouldn't give.

My God, if I wasn't in such dire need of the few dollars to get away from John's mother I wouldn't have accepted it from her. I felt like throwing it back at her but I took it and promised her as soon as I was able I would pay her back.

John got his next pay and we sat to count what we could buy for our money. John paid his mother hers and we had fifty dollars cash left. There was a little furniture store three houses away from where we lived. We went and priced the things we needed the most. We picked a bed spring and mattress, paid for them and told the storekeeper to hold them for us until we called for them. The man said he would even move them for us when we got the rooms ready.

I got two letters from Pittsburgh in one week. They came in my name, at Motileski's address. I sent them back unopened. John's mother and Motileski got mad because I didn't open them and let them read what was in there, so they made their own story up about it. "She says she came from Michigan. She was in more towns than one. This one fellow is from Pittsburgh. How does the fellow from Pittsburgh know her? And if she came to her father why did she leave the poor old father and come here? No, those girls are bad girls," the two decided.

Then the third letter came, registered in Maryanna's name with a note to the postmaster to find that person. It was to Motileski's address from Pittsburgh. Motileski told the mailman to ask the agency that gave Maryanna the job. They found her. Maryanna went to the post office but she couldn't speak enough for herself. They told her to bring a witness and she came to me. John was home and she was going to Brooklyn to look for a new job and rooms. John went with Maryanna and got the letter. Maryanna opened it and found that the letter that cost her so much trouble to get was meant for me. Frank demanded my address of Maryanna. John didn't know anything of Frank Gawronski but wanted an explanation. I told John of the accident on the ferry and told him, "If you don't believe me ask Maryanna. I thought they were kidding that time."

Maryanna shamefully admitted it, but John's mother and Motileski didn't believe it.

CHAPTER 17

The Move to 115 Barry Street

John's new boss lived in Greenpoint. The mister lived the next house to John's parents. John went to the man to help find a job and rooms. I told John I didn't like Greenpoint. He found rooms in Williamsburg. 115 Barry Street was our first address. The rent would be seven dollars a month for three rooms. Not bad, I thought. John got the rest of his pay from his work, told the furniture man to get our furniture ready for the next day to move and picked up my and Victa's trunks too (I had Victa's trunk, she told me to take it wherever I went).

The next day I was all ready to go. The man came to take the trunks and John went down to the back yard. As the man was taking the trunks mother ran out from her room and sat on one trunk and held the other by the handle. "You're not taking these trunks out until John pays me eighty-six dollars board he owes me!" The man looked at me, looked at her, and didn't know what to do.

Then I got mad. I said, "If John owes you eighty-six dollars, let him pay you. This, what I have in this trunk was bought by my own money from my hard work. Victa and I owe you nothing, you made money on me since I was in your house. You can keep his pants, you can take the wedding dress that didn't bring me any luck and you can keep your John. I'm taking what belongs to me and getting out of here!"

John was coming up the stairs and heard my words. He came in and saw his mother sitting on one trunk and holding the other. He took mother lightly off the trunk and set her on a chair and held her there. He told the man to carry the trunks out. I kissed grandma goodbye as she shook her fist in mother's direction. The man took the other trunk out and I went out. John's mother was kicking John, biting him and threatening to call a cop. She was going to arrest the man for carrying the trunks out, but John held her until we were out. The man was fixing the trunks on his wagon when John came down. We were going to take the car and ferry to go to our new home, and the man said, "Why pay for car fare? It is good and wide – sit here! I can take you with the furniture for the eight dollars you pay for the ferry." So we did. We went on the wagon in addition to the furniture, for the same price.

Well, we got our own three nice rooms. A kitchen, living room and a dark bedroom. I put my bed in the bedroom, the stove in the kitchen and the six chairs – two in the kitchen, one in the bedroom and three in the living room, and used my trunk as a table. There was a big pantry for dishes. I had none. I put my six silver teaspoons on the shelf. There I found a pitcher with a broken-off handle. I said, that will do to boil water for tea or coffee. I was looking around the rooms, getting rich in my mind – what to buy – how to dress up the rooms. But when I paid the rent, I knew I was poor.

John was out every day looking for work, but no man was needed. We were on our last money and I went to the grocery and got some bread, a can of salmon, a pound of coffee, a can of star milk, a bag of hard coal, a bag of charcoal, and I came home without money.

John came home. He said he was doing the traveling on foot to save on car fare and all he had was a quarter. Now what? John took the quarter and went to the man in Greenpoint, borrowed one dollar, went to Jersey City to his brother Joe. Joe lent John twenty dollars and warned John to pay it back as soon as he could. Then Victa sent me her November pay. We were safe for at least two months on the forty dollars if we were careful. I bought two knives, two forks, two spoons, two plates, two cups and saucers and two pots for cooking.

We spent our Christmas and New Year as every other day – in our home. Right after New Year we were invited to Mary's wedding. So of course, being John's only sister, he wanted to go. We went. John promised to come back the same night, as he was offered a job for the next day.

Mary's wedding wasn't as successful as ours. They got a fellow working in the Standard Oil Company making nine dollars a week, who just came from Europe a few weeks ago. His name was Mick Burczynski, and they called him Buszki. Mick's drunken uncle knew the Wasielewskis and heard what a big wedding the Wasielewskis made for a strange girl and thought they must be rich, so he got Mick and Mary to get to know one another and the wedding was on.

Mary invited mostly young boys and girls she knew from the factory – very few older people, just from Mick's side. After the ceremony things started to get noisy. Somebody mentioned a girl's name who just came from Europe and she was visiting Motileskis. That girl was a friend of mine. She had her three brothers in Jersey City who had already been living there for some years. Everyone was single and boarding out. The girl also knew Motileski's nieces from her home town, so she was making her visits to Motileski's. When I heard the name I went to Motileski in hope to meet the girl, but she wasn't there. Then the house was full. The two nieces were there. I asked Motileski if Yuzia Agurzynski was coming that day, and she said no, so I didn't want to stay long.

I was going out when I was caught with a sudden cramp in my stomach. I said to Motileski, "Please come with me to the back yard."

She said, "You know where it is, go ahead."

I figured she wouldn't go, and I just had to, so I went down through that dark cellar to the back yard. Coming back to the first floor there was Adam Stawski sitting on something under the hall window without a coat or hat. I said hello to him and asked why he wasn't at the wedding. He said he wasn't invited, they were mad at him because he brought John to me. I didn't stop by him. I was talking to him while I was walking the long hallway. I said, "Better put your coat on."

He said, "I'll be all right, just cooling off from too much to drink."

As I came to the front door to go out, I heard giggles on top of the stairs. I looked up and saw Motileski and the two nieces sitting there. When they saw me, they jumped up and ran in to the rooms. I felt a funny lump around my heart and went back to the wedding, wondering what made Motileski act so strange. Then I forgot all about it.

My sisters weren't invited to the wedding, so I didn't enjoy it. I saw in John's face that he was not enjoying himself either. John told his father he was going home early because of his first job offer the next day. His father didn't like it and his mother put the blame on me that I wouldn't let John stay. We stayed until after one o'clock – after the collection, and John saw the disappointed, greedy look on his mother's and sister's faces. There weren't tens on the platter, few fives and mostly ones and twos and quarters and fifty cent pieces. The younger people weren't as generous as Mary thought they would be.

Then all of a sudden noise, screaming! What's happened? One of Mary's friends cornered Mary and was kissing her. Mary's new husband didn't like it and punched the fresh guy in the eye and others jumped at Mick and there went a free-for-all – bottles, glasses flying high. I thought John was going to help one side or the other, but John saw his sister's action, got disgusted, handed me my coat and said, "Come on!" Nobody noticed us with all the screaming. We got home after three o'clock. John sat down for a while, thinking, then cried and said, "My sister! If I didn't see it with my own eyes!"

I didn't ask him what he saw.

We went to bed and Mary and Mick stayed in John's room for a couple of months and Mary never went to work anymore. If Stella and I thought that we would have one more on our side, we were mistaken. We gained another for scheming, for Mick was as greedy and scheming as Mary and her mother. They would go over a dead body to get where they wanted to go.

John got his promised job. It was not much of a job. Anybody could do that piece work for ten, twelve dollars a week. John was a molder and wanted his trade, but he had to stick it out for a while till he got acquainted with the town and the people. He was working there a week and a half, pouring the hot iron in the ingots, when he poured some in his shoe. Before he took his shoe off the hot iron burned the flesh almost to the bone, right on the instep. John was a union man, but he never reported it for anything coming or going, just sent his dues and never got any benefits. A man brought him home from the foundry and for what I had left of Victa's money still yet, our landlady sent us a doctor.

The doctor looked the foot over and said it was bad. He gave his prescription and went out. I got the medicine from the drugstore right across the street. I did what I was told to do but the foot got worse. John's foot swelled up to his knee. The doctor came again and looked over the foot and said the foot had to be amputated, maybe to the ankle, maybe to the knee. He left the prescription, and going out said to call him tomorrow and he would see.

I took the prescription and went to the drugstore crying. The druggist man spoke to me in Polish and asked me what the matter was. I told him what had happened and what the doctor said. He looked at the prescription and said, "Then this prescription is not for that kind of burn. I was a doctor in the Russian army before I came to America. I'm only a druggist and I'm not allowed to go visiting. My son is a doctor, but doctors cost money and you said you haven't the money. But if you can somehow bring your husband here I would see what I could do for you youngsters."

I was thinking how could I get John down here? I went to the grocery store. They were Polish people. They said no, the druggist wasn't Polish, the druggist was Jewish. The grocery man came up with me when I asked him for his help. We put our shoulders under John's shoulders and carried him across the street to the drug store. The druggist took us into his side room, looked at John's foot, got some luke warm water and poured some kind of liquid from a big bottle. He got some wads of cotton, bandages and some salve. While he was fixing John's foot he told me to watch him to see how he was doing it so I could do it every day until the foot got better. Then he gave me enough of the liquid, salve, cotton and bandages for two weeks, and all of it for one dollar. He told me to keep him informed and keep our mouths shut to anybody else.

It took John over eight weeks, but it saved his foot. Thank God and the Jewish druggist! In the meantime, while John's foot was healing, I told John I was going to Jersey City to see his parents and tell them about his burned foot. I fixed everything for John and put it near him so he wouldn't have to walk far to get it and went.

I came to the old folk's home and knocked on the door. John's mother opened it and left the door open and kul-tit, kul-tit on her lame foot, ran to behind the stove and grabbed a broom and kul-tit, kul-tit back to me, lifted the broom over my head and then the words started to flow from her mouth. "How dare you come to my house! Don't you dare come through that door, you disgraceful thing! You disgraced my house," she screamed, shaking and swinging that broom over my head.

I was dumfounded and didn't know to run out or dare to come in, but I shut the door behind me and stood inside and demanded she tell me what this was all about. Grandma was standing with her nose pinched, holding her breath in the doorway to her room. Mary stood by the stove laughing. John's father was sitting by the table. John's father said to the old woman, "Wait a moment, now. She is here, let her explain herself."

"But to explain what?" I asked.

The old woman hollered to John's father, "Oh, you! You are always taking her part! You know she won't tell you the truth! Motileski told you that she was in the cellar with Adam! Motileski and the two nieces were watching them!"

Something hit my thought. That's why the three women were sitting on the top of the stairs giggling the night of Mary's wedding when I went to ask for my friend Yuzia! I wasn't in the house, just standing in the hall when I came up from the back yard and we both were surprised to meet there and I didn't stop to talk to Adam, just talked to him as I was walking. Motileski, knowing where I went, must have followed Adam when she saw him going into the hall so she could watch me. And when I came up she could have something to say about me that would be fresh news to Mrs. Wasielewski so Mrs. Wasielewski forgot her own daughter's disgrace at her own wedding! Better people to remember something of John's wife from that wedding than Mary!

I turned to John's father and tears came to my eyes. I said, "May my tears bring hard luck to the ones that are telling untruth about me. I am innocent."

Father said, "I thought that Motileski was making out something! It isn't necessary to explain anymore to them."

I told father I came here to tell you that John has burned his foot so bad that the doctor wanted to amputate. Father wanted to say something, but a wild, "Ha, ha, ha, ha," came out from mother. "I'm glad, I'm glad," she was saying. "I was praying to the Virgin Mother to punish him for not listening to me when I told him not to marry you!"

I said goodbye to father, waved to poor grandma and went out the door. I was upset. I didn't go to see Stella, I went to see Victa. I told of John's foot and Victa gave me her December pay and promised me that if she could talk to Maryanna to show her the way they would come to see me at Easter.

Maryanna somehow learned the way to come visit. Victa once in a while spent a few hours with Maryanna on her day off. Hearing that made me feel better and I was happy going home.

Coming home I found John all right. I told him what a reception I got in his parent's home and what it was all about. I told him Victa gave me her month's pay again. John didn't open his mouth. Not a word came out of him if he believed what Motileski said about me or not.

The day before Easter, early in the morning, both my sisters came. They asked for the holy day because they didn't take a couple of Sundays before. John's foot was healed and he was walking. Maryanna took us for a walk on Grand Street to show me where the bigger stores were, and then in the stores both of them gave me a surprise. They bought for me a nice big mirror that I could see myself in from nose to toes, one second-hand rocking chair that I liked, enough dishes to go around and some pots and pans. Victa got me a set of knives and forks, not like you get them now that the handles stay on them only while they are in the store – handles on those knives broke only when you put them in the fire and burned them! Oh, my trunk was used for clothes only! My sisters called it my wedding present, which I accepted happily because I didn't have to owe them for that. I was glad that we were together at Easter.

John went to his trade again. He was working in New York for a couple months and Victa asked me if she could stay with us for a while and maybe she could find work in Brooklyn. I asked John if it would be alright to have Victa with us, and John said yes, she could come. She came and it wasn't a week later she got a job in a rope factory through customers of the Polish grocery store. As we got more friendly with them – their name was Smolinski, they tried to help us through other people.

Victa didn't care for a job in a factory, but she wanted to stay with me for a while. She got introduced to a man at Smolinski's baby's Christmas party when she was with us for about two months. The man asked Victa to go with him to visit his sister in New Jersey one Saturday when they both didn't have to work. Victa asked me if she could trust the man and I told her that he seemed to be a nice man. Victa went with him early so they were to be back early, but ten o'clock she wasn't in. John and I went to sleep and didn't hear her come home at eleven. The landlady let her in. We were sound asleep.

Sunday, I woke up, and before I got out of bed I said to John, "I wonder what's keeping Victa in Jersey City?" What I heard from John I never forgave him for all the years we lived. No matter how mean and bad he was to me through our life I had forgiven him, but what he said about Victa left a scar in my heart against him forever in his life. My dear sister who was a mother to me even when my mother had to go to work and locked us two inside for all day to take care of me. Victa, a baby herself, two years and five months older than I. Victa who sacrificed so much for me since our dear mother was killed. Victa who kept us living and our rent paid for all the months we were married. For the weeks John was suffering with his foot, and paying his doctor bills and for his medicine, when his mother was praying to the Holy Virgin to punish him. And when his mother was glad when she heard of John's suffering, John showed he had his mother's tricks in him.

"Where do you think Victa went? She went whoring! She is doing a dirty business somewhere right now!" he said. "And you worry where she is?" And he kept on laughing and saying filthy words.

I jumped out of the bed, "John, how could you say such things about my sister? Is that your thanks to her for what she has done for us? For all the months you have not been working now, I paid your brother his twenty dollars that he wanted back in a hurry and Stella said they didn't need it. And I paid half of your eighty-six dollars to your mother for your board as she claimed you owed her, while Victa is still helping us by living here paying her board and food!" I cried, I dressed myself in a hurry, came out from our dark room to the living room, and there, my dearest sister was sitting in her bed crying. She heard every word that we were saying. I came to her bed and fell on my knees and put my head on her hand and cried more with her. I had no words to say to her. For some reason I couldn't say to her the way she always said to me when I cried, "Don't cry sister." We just cuddled each other and cried.

We were still holding each other when John came out of the room. He stood in the door a while, puzzled, and said, "Oh, you're here! How did you get in? We didn't hear you come in."

We spent most of the day in silence. Later on Victa said to me, "I'm going back to Jersey City to the agent to get me a job, sister, but don't you worry, I won't forget you. I'll come to see you every once in a while." She was packing her suitcase.

We had our water sink in the hall and I went out to get the water and met my landlady who was coming to fix her son's room in the front. I asked her if she knew any agency in Brooklyn and she said she did, but she said, "If your sister wants, I would give her work. I would bring her there tomorrow." Mrs. Nathy said, "I went to visit a friend of mine last night, Mrs. Hughes, on Keip Street in Brooklyn. She just lost a girl. There are three growing daughters and a son who is a lawyer. With Mr. and Mrs. Hughes that's six adults, but they only pay thirteen dollars a month."

Victa said, "I'll take it if you bring me there."

So my dear sister Victa went to work for Mr. and Mrs. Hughes on Keip Street, as patient as ever, and worked herself up to twenty dollars a month and worked there for three years.

One of John's cousins sent her husband and another man to us to see if maybe they could get jobs in Brooklyn. John sent them to a paint factory where they got jobs, but they didn't last long. I didn't like putting them in the bedroom because they were getting up at night passing our living room where we slept. I was leaving them in the living room and then I was embarrassed when I had to get up at night. They were with us just two nights.

John got restless and wanted more rooms, so we found four rooms, but the tenants were bad. We lasted a month and a half. The janitor's sister kept a house like Motileski's all around. People lying in the hallway, having to walk over them, going to the toilet in the yard. I never went there myself, John had to bring me to the toilet. Then the filthy woman told Mrs. Smolinski's brother who also had a store on another street, that she saw me going to the toilet with a man. The woman didn't know John was working in New York and left early and came home late.

Sundays we were going to find rooms and stopped to visit some friends. I asked John to take rooms out of town somewhere. John had an Aunt living in Maspeth, Long Island. He took me there to meet his aunt, and we found five nice rooms for the same rent we paid to watch the drunken men and women fight every day. Ten dollars a month.

Then John found a job in Brooklyn at his old pay of eighteen dollars a week. I paid his mother, squared with Maryanna – everybody except Victa.

Maryanna went to Pine Island, New York, with some people who were buying some land there and I didn't know her address and she didn't know where Victa and I were scattered to. I thought I would have some peace in this third place. I thought? At least I saw Victa on Mondays. I went to see her and helped with her washing. Hughes had nothing against it. Thursday afternoons Victa was at my house.

Victa sent for our cousin Aniela. We knew how hard she worked to keep herself and her mother. Aniela was my father's sister's daughter, the one who was supposed to play a piano. Aniela was a good girl. Victa and I liked her. Aniela did appreciate what Victa did for her and we three were getting along nicely. She was about ten years older than Victa.

I visited Stella often. Joe and Stella bought a grocery and butcher store. I used to help them a lot. If Stella was sick I worked in the store or helped her with the children. I had Stella's daughter Nellie stay for a few weeks at a time with me in Maspeth, which John's mother didn't like, and she tried her best to keep us apart. I from my part tried to be friends even with her. I couldn't believe that she would be so mean all the time. I tried to please her. I took John's brothers for weeks at a time for vacations. She sent the boys with one pair of pants and a pair of shorts, whatever was on them without extra to change. I had to wash every night to have them clean the next day. When the children went home they went home with brand new suits and extra clothes to wear to school.

CHAPTER 18

Grandma Thrown Out

One day I went to see Stella. Grandma was there. When she saw me she started to cry. Grandma said to me, "Tonia, I wanted to ask you for a long time if you would take me with you, but I thought you might not want me, but I see you are taking the children and they are praising you. Would you take me away from that awful woman?"

I didn't know who grandma meant. Stella said, "What she means is take her away from our mother-in-law!"

I asked grandma what happened. Grandma repeated a bad name for her daughter and said, "She put me out! She and Mary are always fighting with the old man. No matter how much good you are doing for her she always finds something to say about you. I took your part and Mary caught me taking a cup of coffee from her coffee pot, because Mary's coffee is stronger. Mary grabbed the cup and poured it back in the pot and accused me that I was eating everything of hers. The old man just came from work and they both jumped to him with lies, telling him that I'm a trouble-maker in the house and taking and stealing things – Mary's food."

The old man grabbed grandma's belongings, opened the window and threw them out two stories down. A man from the top floor was down in the back yard and it happened that he saw the bundles coming down and heard grandma screaming. The man thought that they were going to throw grandma out of the window too. He went up to find out what was going on, and he was told to mind his own business, but he saw grandma crying. The man told grandma if they had no place for her to come to his house. Grandma was with the people upstairs and every time the people were passing the second floor someone was always standing by with a bad remark, insulting them. Grandma asked them to bring her to Joe and Stella.

Stella took grandma, but she had only three rooms behind their store, and with three children and three of Stella's cousins boarding with her, by luck working nights. So, grandma was waiting for us to ask me to take her.

Grandma was seventy-two years old when she came to live with us. Grandma told me when she was living with me that her mother died giving birth to her. Her father married again and got sick shortly after and died too. So, she was left an orphan. When she grew up she knew nothing but hard work. A mean creature attacked her when she was alone at night and she couldn't even see his face to know who he was. Out of that attack came John's mother. Later the ugly creature came to her and admitted that he was the father of the baby and wanted to marry grandma. She refused to look at him and refused to tell anybody of the baby's father. Then she met a widower with three children and married him. The husband and his children were very good to her, but John's mother was the troublemaker between them right from small as she was growing.

Grandma said when Jadwiga (John's mother) was working in the field with her stepsisters and grandma brought their meal to them, Jadwiga ran first to the package, grabbed the slices of bread and weighed them on the palm of her hand, and the heaviest slice was hers. Grandma called her a greedy hog. The husband's daughters told her, "Let her have it, mother."

Jadwiga got married to John's father who worked in Germany as many Polish people from Russia did. Bismark, or whichever one was the ruler then, wanted them to become German citizens. Many did, many didn't. Jadwiga's husband didn't, so they were put out of

Germany. Jadwiga and her children who were born in Germany could stay, but Jadwiga didn't want her husband to go without her. That's how they got to be our neighbors in Zamosc. Joe, John and Mary came from Germany. One girl died in Germany. Antony, Willy and Aniela were born to them on the Russian side, then they went to America and had more children. Grandma said they had Felix, Leon, Benny and Frank in America.

Grandma said she didn't have to come to America because she had it good with her stepchildren even after her husband died. But here when Jadwiga didn't want Mary to go to school, people were talking against Mary that "that big girl stays home". Jadwiga was taking Mary's side, putting the blame on little Felix that Mary had to stay home to take care of him, as her mother kept nine boarders and could not care for Felix. Then Jadwiga was sending promises and promises how good grandma would have it if she would only come here.

Grandma was fifty back then, and she took a chance and came to Jadwiga just to take the blame for Mary. Mary still didn't want to go to school so they blamed it on grandma, saying that she didn't want to take care of Felix, so Felix died. Mary grew up and still didn't know her A-B-Cs and grandma told me that John's aunt at Maspeth was not John's rightful aunt. She is about three years older than John. When grandma got married to the widower she had another girl with him at the same time another woman had a baby girl. Grandma's baby girl died at birth and the other baby's mother died. Grandma and her husband adopted the girl and raised her and all the other children alike, and named her Julia.

When Julia was fifteen years old Jadwiga got her. But Julia was an educated girl. She spoke, read and wrote in Polish and German and caught on to English quickly too. Julia didn't want to listen to Jadwiga's way, so Jadwiga forced Julia to marry one of Jadwiga's boarders named Stanley Zegler, and was making trouble between them afterwards. Jadwiga was talking against Julia to Zegler, and putting in bad words to Julia against Zegler. Julia told her husband to get away from Jadwiga and they moved to Maspeth.

Julia liked John, and so we called Julia Aunt Zegler. And Aunt Zegler liked me too. When we got to know each other Aunt Zegler told me that John's mother was treating her as bad as she treated Stella and me. Aunt Zegler said she would keep Grandma, but Zegler was mean too, and wouldn't let her. He was always saying that grandma was not Julia's mother as Jadwiga told him, and he didn't have to keep her. But Zegler took a liking to John when John saved him from two bums that would have beat him up when Zegler was drunk.

As I was gaining friends my misery stood fast with my enemies. Aunt Julia had such a good head for business that even her husband couldn't think as fast. They already had three houses with two stores and a saloon in one. They bought six more lots when we moved to Maspeth and Aunt Julia was advising us to buy property there as at that time you could buy a lot cheap and people were buying them fast. John couldn't make up his mind if we should or should not. In the meantime, John scattered word in Jersey City that we were buying a house in Maspeth.

Mary and Mick were living in Bayonne, New Jersey for some time near his work. They found two houses on Twenty-Fourth Street and Avenue E. They liked one nine-room house but the agency wouldn't sell one separately. Both houses had to be sold together. The other house wasn't as nice looking, but had thirteen rooms. Mary and Mick heard that John was buying a house on Maspeth and set a trap for John. All of a sudden everybody was good to us, visiting us, inviting us to parties every week, and Mary and Mick spent their Saturday nights trying to find out how strong John was.

They wrestled and fought just for fun. Mick was saying that John was fighting in some club as a lightweight. Once he fell and broke his right arm below his elbow and gave up the business. Mick must have found out that John would be harmless and then they started to work on John. "The houses are nice. The thirteen-room house is the same price as the nine-room. You can pick either one after we buy it, but we have to put our money together now to buy them both."

I didn't like their talk and that kind of deal, but they got to John

Antonia Wasielewski

and John wouldn't listen to me, nor to Joe and Stella. I had been trying to delay the deal. I told John to count how much he would gain by living in Bayonne. I said it would cost ten cents car fare a day from Maspeth to his work; from Bayonne it would cost him fifty cents a day, twenty cents to the ferry and thirty cents through the ferry from Jersey City to Brooklyn. I told him he would have to get up two hours earlier in the morning and he would be coming home two hours later in the evening. I told him if there was any work to be done around the house he wouldn't be able to do anything, but Mick promised to help John. I told John I didn't have enough money as I had been paying his debts. All I had bought for myself in two years was an icebox for seven dollars and a dress for ten dollars.

Mary then said, "Mick, I'm a _real_ housewife. I put one hundred dollars away each year."

But I knew Mary didn't save that one hundred dollars a year on Mick's nine dollar a week paycheck. It was a little of my wedding money and John's board money. Mary moved away from her mother and took all the furniture that John bought for his mother when he was home, and left mother with only beds and chairs and a table. When mother went to visit Mary she brought bags of food to last for a week, Stella told me. Anytime they came to visit John, like on holy days, the whole gang came. John had to have enough for them to eat and drink or I got the blame that I was starving John and he was getting thinner.

So, Mick was coming more often to feed John on beer. John had stopped spending his evenings in pool halls and playing pinochle in saloons since we moved out of Jersey City, and we found new friends who didn't care to throw their money away foolishly. Mick wasn't used to spending his own money when he went out, but just when he came to coax John to move to Bayonne. He got John acquainted with saloons in Maspeth. John began to like it, and I didn't because from there I found John to be a liar, deceiver and a braggart besides. When I gave him five dollars to go to church on Sundays, he spent it in a saloon - and right three doors from where we lived! He told me he met a friend at the church!

From Maspeth John had to take the Flushing Avenue car to Brooklyn, change to the Graham Avenue car and go to Greenpoint to church. That's the only church we knew at that time. Our friends, Molinskis, moved from Barry Street, Williamsburg, with their grocery store near the Polish church. When we went to church there, we went to visit friends after church. Then we got home ten or eleven o'clock. A couple Sundays it happened that I didn't feel well. John wanted to go to church himself. I said all right and gave him five dollars. We had to start at ten o'clock in the morning to be in church at twelve, so John started at ten from the house and was back home at five o'clock in the evening. I was too sick to ask questions and forgot the next day. John took an interest in church and went out the next Sunday, but the next Sunday when he came home at seven I asked him for change from the five he took in the morning. He said he met a friend. I know when a man meets a man – I didn't say anything.

Come the third Sunday I was feeling better and wanted to go to church, but before I had a chance to dress myself after I got the breakfast dishes done, John was gone. Well, I said to myself, I'm not going out by myself. I stayed home and my cousin Aniela came in that afternoon. Victa had gone with the Hughes to their farm in Smithtown, Long Island for four months. She got a two dollar a month raise. It was too far for her to take Sundays off. Aniela worked in Brooklyn.

Aniela and I were sitting peacefully when my landlady's daughter came up. Mrs. Szymanski asked, "Where is your husband?"

I said, "He got religious and went to church without me."

She started to laugh and said, "I'm sure he wouldn't want you to go the church he is going to. Do you know what church he goes to when you're not going? Do you want to know where your husband has been going for the last several Sundays and some evenings? Your husband, my husband and my brother John, the three Johnnys go to entertain the redheaded woman in Hoffman's Saloon. I can't get mine out, maybe you can get yours. I'm tired of waiting for him with dinner every Sunday.

I got mad. That man was lying to me a long time and I didn't know it. And I didn't know that he was teaching me to lie for him. He told me something and I took it for truth. Then he told someone else who doubted him, and John said, "Well, if you don't believe me, ask her!"

Of course, when I was asked I said yes, until a good friend told me once, "It's either that you are as big a liar as John, or you are so green that John is making one out of you!" So afterwards, so as not to get myself in trouble and be embarrassed, and to keep peace at home, if John sent somebody to "yes" to his lie, I would say, "I don't remember", or "I'm not sure".

John wanted to make of himself a big man. He was spreading word around in Hoffman's Saloon that he worked in the Navy yard. Of course, I was proud to know my husband worked for the government until a squealer came and said it wasn't true. The man was Hoffman's good friend who really worked in the Navy yard as a molder. Hoffman told the man that John was working in the Navy yard and the man said, "Well, he might be a new man just coming there a day or two, because all the old molders are known to me."

My landlady said to me, "I thought you said your husband worked in the Navy yard?"

"Well," I said, "That's what he told me."

"He is a lot of wind," she said. "A man who works there for years said he never saw your husband there."

I told John what people were thinking of his working in the Navy yard, and making a liar out of me too. John said he would prove it to me. He told me to go and stand by the Navy yard gate at five o'clock when all the men were coming out of work. I picked one day and told John I would meet him at the Navy yard gate – to watch out for me if I should miss him. "All right," he promised, and went to work at 4:30.

I was at the gate until five-thirty, until all the men went out and the gate closed behind them. No John. He promised to watch for me if I missed him. I was looking around thinking maybe he was standing somewhere waiting for me when a car from Flushing stopped by me. People were getting off and there was my John on the car. A man got off, the seat was empty and I jumped on and sat by him. I didn't say anything as he was looking the other way. When he turned his head and saw me his face got red and then pale. I said to him, "That's all right, John. I don't care if you are working for the Navy yard or for Mr. Micik's foundry. All that matters is that you are working." John had to work overtime that day and forgot that he told me to meet him at the Navy yard gate.

When John found out that I caught on to his lies and wouldn't tell him "yes" any more and he couldn't be a big shot in my eyes, he turned around and started to belittle me. When our friends asked us to parties and weddings and asked me to sing or recite or do something, and praised me when I did, John was telling them, "Why, she is getting a little smarter now. When I married her she was so green like tobacco in a horn," or "She was so blind she couldn't tell number two on the clock."

People who knew me long enough were giving me credit, because if I was as green as John said, then I was doing fine with everything now.

We hadn't been to visit Joe and Stella for some time and so we decided to go visit them. John didn't work Saturday so we went Friday night. Stella was always glad to see me. When we went there for one or two days I took care of her children and she was taking care of the business. We got to Joe's old place, the grocery store. We were told that Joe sold the grocery store and bought a saloon now. We got to their new address and I helped Stella with the house and the children all day Saturday. At night, as Stella was tired, she slept solid through the night. She was a good sleeper like my sister Victa. I got up at night to change the baby and give him a bottle, or when one wanted to go to the potty, or one wanted a drink. I did this without awaking Stella. And John? He was in the saloon all the time helping Joe.

Sunday John's father and mother came to Joe's with another woman that Stella knew. When it was time to go home, I said to Stella, "Will you get that bum of mine – it's time we went home." I wasn't mad, and I didn't say it to insult anybody, just jokingly. I never thought I was pulling a fire alarm, but I did.

Stella whispered in my ear, "Oh, oh, you stepped on her corn!"

John's mother got up out of her chair steaming. "How dare you call him a bum! I didn't raise no bum!" she hollered.

I said, "I didn't mean to hurt anybody." But, I said, "Maybe I did mean it! Yes, I do!" And I told them all that was going on for the past few Sundays when I was sick. When John was supposed to be praying in church how he was entertaining a red headed woman in Hoffman's Saloon. How I gave John five dollars every Sunday so if he met somebody they wouldn't call him a tight wad or that his wife had him under her foot, but I expected a little change out of that five spot for his car fare. And how was he supposed to buy a house if he spent five dollars in one day?

John's father got up and said, "John can spend three dollars a day. He has no children."

Stella answered for me, "How about Mary? Mary is married just as long as John and they have no children, and you are helping her with all you can give."

"Mary has to save for her old age," said the old man.

"Oh, oh, oh," Stella said. "Mary has to save for her old age, and John can starve when he gets older?"

Mother started to argue with Stella. Mother said, "Mary could have children, only Mick is no good."

Stella said, "Tonia is much younger than Mary, and it is not three years yet since they have been married. Tonia still could have a baby."

The old woman said, "I don't know where Tonia comes from and how she lived. Mary is good because her father examined her, and he said she is all right."

Father walked out of the house. The strange woman opened her eyes wide and her mouth still wider. "Her father had examined his own daughter?" she said.

Stella said, "Don't be surprised, they had eleven children and never had a doctor or midwife for any of them except the last one."

"No wonder that she is limping," said the woman. "He must have pulled a ligament from somewhere."

"And that's not all," said Stella. "When Joe and I got married they wanted us to have a baby in a hurry and blamed me. The old man said a tree that doesn't grow fruit should be cut down and burned, and in the third year when I was having my Aniela, Joe went to get his parents for me instead of a doctor. I was in pain. They were walking me up and down the kitchen floor. My friend heard me screaming and she wanted to come in through the hall door. The door was locked with a key from the inside so nobody could come in. She opened her bedroom door next to my bedroom and came to see what they were doing to me. She saw father and mother with both their sleeves rolled up above their elbows, full of blood. They both had their hands in me trying to tear Aniela out of me."

My friend grabbed Joe by the collar and told Joe, "If you don't go to get the doctor in a hurry, I'll get the cops after all of you. Do you want to have your wife murdered by these butchers?"

Joe then ran out for a doctor and the old man said, "In Europe they tie a woman to a door and she has to bear it."

"That's why every eight women out of ten die there giving birth to children. Not because every man is mean, but because the women die in childbirth and the men wear out three or four wives before they die," my friend was saying.

Stella said, "The old folks didn't wait until the doctor came. They went home mad. The doctor came, put me to bed and gave me something to calm me down so I rested from the traveling all around the kitchen and my Aniela was born."

When John's mother was gone Stella told me that she and Joe were buying a house on 1008 Newark Avenue in the last block of houses near the Hackensack River, and that they would open a grocery store and a butcher shop. They would have to build an extension in the front of the house. Stella asked, "Why don't you and John get a house there? A saloon man there has a lot of houses and he wants to sell some of them, and I think it's a good buy for the future. I have a feeling that someday that place will be good for business."

While Stella was telling me of her hunches, in which she was right, Joe was trying to get John not to buy a house together with Mick, as the ones on Newark Avenue were much cheaper even if they were only six and seven room houses.

But the devil stuck to John and on our third wedding anniversary we were in Bayonne. Mother and father were so nice around John that they even lent John the shortage of one hundred fifty dollars. John had told me to go ask Victa for it. I told John to first pay her the three hundred dollars he owed her before I ask her for any more. "I paid everyone we owed but her, and you have the nerve to ask her for more! Some thanks you give her!"

John then told his father we were short one hundred fifty dollars. Father gave John the money and John bought a house without me. John went with Mary and Mick to the real estate because it was supposed to be only John and Mick's name on the deed for the two houses, but by a mistake (on purpose) Mary's name got on the deed. Of course, I didn't know their scheme then.

We were living in another house and paying rent until the people that lived in our new house moved out and they were taking their sweet time moving too. I gave my address to my cousin Aniela and to Victa, as that's the only relatives I had. I wanted them near me as badly as they wanted to be near me themselves.

Aniela came to visit first. Victa was going to stay until New Year's and then take a vacation after putting in three years with the Hughes.

CHAPTER 19

Abandoned Baby

One day a woman walked into our house with a little boy a year old. The woman was about forty-five years old. She asked me if I would take care of her boy. She said she was going from house to house to either find work for herself with the child, or a home for the child. Nobody wanted the child and nobody wanted to give her work with the child. She was desperate. The woman had come from Austria some years ago. Who the child's father was I don't know. She claimed she was a widow. My cousin Aniela and I both had the same thought, but she said it first, "Tonia," she said, "Your in-laws want you to have a baby. Here is one ready-made for you!"

I told the woman to come back that night when my husband would be home. If he said it was all right, then she could leave her boy with us. She did. She came when John came home from work at eight o'clock. I asked John and he said, "If you want to, go ahead, but you will have to wash his diapers." I found out later that as far as John was concerned babies didn't have to exist on earth. John told the woman to stay with us for a week or so until little Joe got used to us, but the woman slept over-night and disappeared.

I kept Joe and I fell in love with him, but I wanted to find out more about him. I asked people in stores if they knew of a woman with a little boy. I finally found her sister-in-law and the sister-in-law said she wouldn't have the woman in her house. The woman's husband was working in the Standard Oil Company and fell in some hot oil and was burned to death three years ago. The boy's father was a New York Jew. I wanted to know if the boy was christened and she told me to go and find out from the Polish Priest, Reverend Swider on Twenty-Second Street in Bayonne. I found out that he was christened there.

As Mary lived next door in the same hall, she knew of our baby. The next day John's mother knew of it and she took a ride to Bayonne right from church where she was praying curses to the Mother Virgin on me and John. As soon as she walked into my kitchen she dropped on her knees in the middle of the floor and she prayed and she prayed, "Oh, Holy Mother Virgin, punish her for taking that brat in until John comes home! Punish John for not listening to me and marrying the world runner."

She demanded we give the boy back to the woman or she would report us to the police. We had no right to take it without notifying the police. "When that boy grows up," she said, "He will put a noose on John's neck like one boy did in Germany to his foster father!"

Aniela was sitting there listening to her raving. Aniela picked up little Joe and said, "Joe, take a good look at your new grandma. When you grow up, don't forget to put the first noose on her for the curses she is spreading on your new mama and papa."

John's mother got up off her knees and ran to the open door, slammed it behind her and went to Mary's.

When John came home Aniela told him the story. John had it in for Aniela, but I knew John was going to keep the boy to spite his mother.

After New Year's we moved into our thirteen-room house while Mary and Mick took the one that they were after. Victa came to take her vacation. She was with us two weeks, then we got visitors from Greenpoint – Mr. and Mrs. Smolinski. They brought with them Mrs. Smolinski's brother, John Blazeski. John Blazeski was a widower about thirty-seven years old and had a son nine and a daughter seven years old. John Blazeski first saw Victa when Victa and John stood up as Godparents to Smolinski's son, and was after his sister to come with him to visit us. So they brought him with them, and when they did, John Blazeski asked Victa to marry him. Victa didn't love him, but she fell in love with his children, as my Victa always was ready to help somebody. The children, William and Agnes were three years without a mother. Mrs. Smolinski was praying to God to make Victa accept her brother John for the sake of his children, and Mrs. Smolinski won.

Victa was good to the children even when their father was bad to them, and the children loved Victa better than their own father. Once when William came back from the army and World War One he pulled his father out of a saloon by the collar and said he would always appreciate the mother that raised him and took care of him and his sister, but he wouldn't give his father five dollars if he saw him starving in a gutter. Mrs. Smolinski and Victa were good sisters-in-law like Stella and I. One of Mrs. Smolinski's sons was a policeman in Greenpoint. I never asked about him, but he was Victa's Godson.

Our thirteen-room house had no cellar, no fence around it like Mary and Mick's. John couldn't do anything to improve it because he was out of the house before six o'clock in the morning and came home after seven in the evening.

When our friends in Greenpoint found out that we were living in Bayonne they told other people who came to visit with Maryanna and a man who came to America with us. He came to visit and brought another man as a surprise. He didn't tell the other man who he was going to meet, and it was a surprise to both of us. When they walked in the other man stopped and stood still and said, "Oh, my God! May I come in, or should I run out?"

I said, "Hello, Tony, what are you afraid of?"

He said, "You! The time you wanted to strangle me when I wanted to smoke me, you weighed about ninety pounds! Look at you now!"

"I'm only a hundred forty pounds now," I told Tony.

Tony said to John, "Aren't you afraid of her? She was a wild tigress in Europe. She wouldn't let any man come near her or she was ready to wring his neck!"

Tony asked John if he could stay with us for a while as he wanted to get into work in Bayonne. John told him he could stay.

Aniela found herself work in Bayonne and just came home on Sunday. Mary had a boarder, a young man who took a liking to Aniela. Aniela told him that she was ten years older than he was and it wouldn't be fair to him, but Mary didn't know that Aniela told the boy herself. Mary criticized Anilea as an old maid and told the boy that he was too young for her. The boy got angry at Mary and wanted to come live with us because he said Mary was making passes at him. I told the boy that if I took him on to board then all John's family would be on my neck. He understood and moved somewhere else.

Mick had a younger brother in the Russian Army who was sent out to war with Japan. The soldiers didn't want to fight for Russia and were escaping to Japan themselves wholesale. Mick's brother escaped also with seven other men. The Japs helped them to come to missionaries and the missionaries helped them to come to Canada. From Canada the men wrote to their relatives in America for help. Mick's brother wrote to Mick for help and Mick was mad at his brother for running away like that. Now his brother would never be able to return to his homeland any more or he would be sent out to Siberia, and he had left his mother, wife and baby behind. It was hard to tell what the Russians would do to them there when they found out about his escape. John told Mick that it was just as much a duty of Mick's to help his mother by helping his brother and then the two of them could do something for the mother and the brother's wife and baby.

So John and Mick got Mick's brother Teofil to America from Canada in a few weeks. Teofil came, Mary took one look at him and liked him better than Mick. He was younger and nicer looking than Mick, but another look made her scream. Everything on him was full of lice. She refused to let him come near her door. Mick didn't know what to do, so John told Teofil to come to our house. I got scared too when I saw things crawling, but I told John to get his underwear and shorts and pants and I told Teofil to go to the back yard house and take his things off him carefully and put John's on. When he was ready I washed his hair in kerosene and boiled his clothes real good. John told Mick to take his brother out and buy him top clothes and get his hair cut. He slept overnight in our house and the next day Mary accepted him to her house.

Teofil was with Mick about three months when Mick came to us asking John if he could stay with us. I told him no. I said Mary was mad at me enough as it was and I didn't want any more trouble. John asked him what the problem was and Teofil said, "John, it's your sister and my brother. Your sister would be all right to me if I would keep my pants loose in my hand all the time for her, and I won't do that to my brother."

So Teofil went to live with his other relatives in Jersey City. In later years Teofil came to visit us with his grown son and two daughters and introduced me to his children this way, "Children, this is the woman I was telling you about who washed the lice off me when I first came to America." Well, Mary did get madder at me. She went to Jersey City and heard a bad story about herself and blamed me for it. She told me that I was not a decent woman because I knew what Teofil was saying about her and I didn't tell her. I told her that Teofil was telling John about her, I wasn't. I told John he had better get our house separated from Mick before they put us out.

I didn't know how near the truth I was. John had a hard time to get them to sign off. Mick wanted the nicer house for himself and three hundred dollars cash from John for the bigger house. John said, "No, give me the smaller house and I don't want a penny from you."

Mick said no. Mary got her father and mother to come to her house and told her father that John wanted to rob them and cheat them and to take everything from them. John's father came to argue it out with John. John said, "Listen, pop, if the big house was worth more we would have paid more for it, but the real estate man told us that the small house is the better house. It has nine rooms but it is newer than the big house and has a good cellar. The big one is much older, has no cellar, no fence and it stands right next to Brady's ice house. That's why they didn't want to sell the small one unless they sold both of them together, or the big one first, so why should I give Mick three hundred dollars? Let Mick take this one and I won't ask for a penny from him."

The old man said, "Mick, John is right. You picked your choice, don't ask for everything."

Mick and Mary were mad but they gave John the big house without the three hundred dollars, but they were looking for something to put us in trouble to revenge on us.

Mary asked me a couple times to help her to bring some packages to Jersey City. I did until I found out that if I got caught with them I would be put in jail. I didn't know what it was or where Mary was getting it from. It was black like iron and almost as heavy. Small pieces like stove covers, smaller and bigger ones. Mary used to bring them to a junk man who had his junk shop on the same street where her mother lived and Mary used to collect from three to seven dollars apiece for them. Stella warned me not to carry that stuff for Mary.

I wanted to improve my house since I knew it was ours and John couldn't work around it because of his late working hours. We bought a carload of wood for the fire from the railroad company and we had the tracks coming right to our back yard. The railroad man dumped it right into the yard. I found some wood not only for a fire but good strips and posts for our fence. So I took an ax, saw and planer and went to shape up the strips and posts. People were watching me, wondering how I was going to come out with them. Tony was coming home at five o'clock and I gave him his supper and after supper Tony and I were working until John came home. We fixed the porch and we put the fence up. Mary didn't like it.

We had a passageway between Mick's and our house all the way from the street to the yard so we could walk that way to the kitchen and save our front hall. The walk was made of boards. One day Mick started to rip the boards out of the passage way and I asked him what he was doing. Mick said the passage way belonged to him and he didn't want anybody to walk through that way and he blocked the passage. John saw that but said nothing, but Mick and Mary wanted trouble. Mary started on me again. Mary was telling the neighbors things about me and the neighbors started to watch me and watch Mary at the same time. Mary went on picking on me when I was on the front porch with little Joe. Mary came to sit on her porch and talk to herself quietly, but to make sure the neighbors were listening. "Look at her, come out to sit on the porch to show herself!" Mary said. "What is it that she is so proud of that she is showing off because Tony is more boss in the house than John!" Mary kept saying this and laughing to herself.

When I took Joe in the yard Mary was sure to be in the yard to point her accusing finger at me. "Oh look where she hides herself, she doesn't sit in front, she's ashamed to show her face to people!" Mary was talking to herself and the neighbors were listening.

One day coming from the grocery store I heard somebody calling my name. I looked around and a young woman who lived three doors away from Mary caught up to me and said, "But you must be a very patient woman to put up with that one, or are you afraid of her? Why don't you get a pot of boiling water and pour it on her head!" The woman then said, "Mary is just like the thief that robbed a man and as the man was running after him, the thief hollered, 'stop thief!' and it was the thief who was running and pointing his finger. The thief got people confused and the thief got away. That's what your sister-in-law is doing with you. Does she think she is fooling the neighbors? Sue her and the neighbors will be your witnesses. Even Mick himself said once at his uncle's house when his uncle warned Mick not to bother girls, 'If my wife can, so can I!'"

I said to the woman, "Thank you, lady, I'm glad to know that my neighbors are thinking decent of me. As for suing Mary, God will judge us some day and I'm sure that God is fair."

Mary was quiet for a few days and I thought she had settled down, but that was only quietness before the storm. On Saturday evening, John, Tony and I were sitting on our porch. Tony was playing with little Joe. Suddenly Mick and Mary came out and sat on their porch. They had company too. Some young man and Mick took a can and were going for beer. They passed us and said aloud, "Look at that woman!" I thought he meant me, but I didn't say anything and John didn't say anything. But something was brewing in John's head that Mick was looking for trouble and didn't know how to start. He was picking on someone to start first, so John ignored Mick. Mick got mad. Standing on his porch he pointed his finger in our direction and was talking louder and louder, "See that old woman!" And he was sure that we all were afraid of him so he was being braver and braver. Mick had been trying John on Maspeth to see how strong John was, but now Mick wanted somebody else to start the fight. As no one wanted to grant Mick's wish, Mick went for another pint and passed us again. I knew Mick meant business. He pointed straight at Tony. "You, old woman!"

Tony never had any trouble with Mick, and thought Mick meant John, but when Mick pointed at him, he wanted to make sure, and said, "Who, me?"

Mick said, "Why sure, you fool! Who do you think I mean?"

Tony said, "What's got into you Mick, picking trouble with me? I've done no harm to you." And Tony sat where he was.

Then close to eleven o'clock Mick's company got up, said good night to Mary and went to the street. Mick was right behind him so the man stood at our gate and said to Tony, "So you are the old woman?"

Tony tried to talk the man out of the fight. He said, "Listen, fellow, I don't know you, you don't know me. I'm sure I've done nothing to you and you didn't do anything to me, so why not be on your way in peace?"

Then John went out and said, "Why explain things to him? Don't you know he has been looking for trouble all evening? Go out there and give it to him, Tony!"

That made Mick happy, so he said, "If he gives it to him, then I'll give it to you!"

"Oh, you will?" John said, starting for the street.

Mick didn't wait for John to get out of the gate. Mick made an aim with his foot under John's stomach. John knew Mick would go for that, so John tripped Mick's foot. Down on the street John went on top of Mick. They were pounding one another but Mick couldn't get up from the ground. Mary was watching her brother getting the best of her husband. She ran out to help him – Mary on top of John on top on Mick, showing their brotherly love to each other. Mary tore John's shirt to strips, but that didn't help, so she bit him on his arm and shoulder and Mick was still on his bottom.

Then Mary started to holler, "Police, police! Help, police!" When she saw the police coming she ran home as quick as she could, calling, "Mick, the cops! Mick, the cops!"

John got off Mick and came home. Mick got up slowly bracing himself on the fence and went into his house. I looked off the porch, how far Tony was. The two men were beating themselves all the way to the corner of the next street where there were few houses. Cops were gathering around them. I didn't want to be seen by anybody. I picked Joe off the rocker and went in. When I was by my door I saw Mick coming out of his house again with a big knife in his hand. I stepped in quickly and locked the door. John was in his bedroom. I put Joe in his bed and blew out the lamp and went from window to window to see where Mick was, but I could not see him and didn't see him for two days after.

I didn't tell John that Mick came out on his porch with a knife, but I was wondering, would Mick throw that knife at John if John was still on his porch? Sunday morning a man came from the court and asked if we wanted to bail Tony out. John told me to go. The man told me where to find the judge. The judge asked me if I owned a house. I told him yes. I told the judge a lie and didn't know it. I brought Tony home. Tony said it felt funny to hit a man and not to be mad at him. Tony said he wasn't mad at the fellow. When the two of them were in jail Tony said to him, "Now that we are both in jail, tell me what was your reason to start this monkey business with me when you don't know me? I don't know you. We both did no harm to each other. The other fellow was mad now; not at Tony, but at Mick, and promised himself if he caught Mick up around his way again he'd break Mick's head off. The man was in jail until Monday as nobody came to bail him out Sunday.

Monday before the judge, the fellow told that Mick promised him ten dollars to start the fight with Tony, so Mick could finish the fight with John, and although both men were telling the court the truth no one believed them.

CHAPTER 20

Death Comes

A letter came to us from John's family. I handed the news from Jersey City to John. "Look at Joe's letter here. Joe is demanding to know if it's true, because somebody told him that I fell in love, so I want children. Stella is mad at me. When we were in Jersey City, one of your relatives, a woman, told me that I should do as one of her sisters did to her in-laws. When she didn't have children for three years after her marriage, she went to the forest and got herself a gypsy and a baby came as black as that gypsy was. When her in-laws were mad at her for doing that she told them, "But now I'm sure that I am all right."

Then I told John what had happened to me. I went to the priest and I told the priest I wanted to have children. He told me he could help me, and his eyes went almost red. He told me that in such a voice and manner that I got scared of him and I jumped up. His eyes weren't shiny when I went in there first. I told him I do want children, but with my husband, not with anybody else. I didn't know what to do or say anymore. I just stood there and his eyes turned mad, and he hollered almost loud, "What do you eat? tar? that you can't have any children?"

I went out. I kept walking all the way from Newtown to Maspeth, crying, and I finished crying on my knees in my room, "Merciful God, why are you punishing me this way? I'm trying to live the way my mother taught me. If that is wrong, teach me the right way, but what right does the priest have to send temptation? And when I told him what I thought, that he should turn and condemn me because I have no children?" I promised myself it would be a very long time before I went to another confession.

I don't know how you feel," I told John, "But your family - they won't leave me alone."

John said, "Who asked you to have children? I don't care if you have children or not. If they come, they come, if they don't, they don't. I'm not asking you to have children for me."

We lived with Mudrzicki three months. John got a notion to open up another business. A junk shop. John went to Zegler and rented a cellar for that. Zegler had empty rooms, so we moved into Zegler's. Zegler took me to Long Island somewhere and I got a license for the junk shop. John was working with Mick again. I was in the junk shop. When John had a day off he went all over Maspeth to all the hardware stores, plumbing shops and saloons and he bought all the scrap they had – old and new. I kept a book of what I bought and from who. One day three fellows came with heavy bags of iron in them. We were paying ten cents a hundred pounds. I bought it off them and they went and brought some more, and some more yet. In one day they filled the cellar full. I gave them the book, they signed their names and addresses. I thought I was safe. The next day the three men were back again with the goods. I was weighing the bags and Mr. Zegler ran in and said, "Oh, no, don't you buy that!" The fellow left the bags and ran out without his pay.

Zegler said, "You know what you have been buying? Long Island Railroad! These iron plates the railroad company is putting on the ties and laying rails on them, and the fellows took enough of the pile for the detectives to notice and search for it!"

"My God!" I said. "Please help me to get rid of it!"

Zegler and I worked hard to carry the iron to an empty lot. I don't know where it went from there. I lost a few dollars, but when the cops came to search for it, my place was clean. I told John, "That business is too dangerous for me! If not for Zegler, I would be in jail!"

We sold the business. A big junky from Grand Street came with his big truck, took the whole business on it for forty dollars.

We hadn't been to Jersey City for some time. Then on August 15th Mick came in and right from the door shouted, "John, your mother is burned to death!" John, who never got excited, quickly said, "Oh, yes." But it struck him funny. Mick wouldn't have come here unless something did happen, so we got ready and went with Mick.

"Oh, please, God, don't let anyone suffer like that!" I forgot the suffering for all the years she cursed me. I cried over her suffering.

That day, the fifteenth of August is a Polish holy day. People offer their prayers to the Virgin Mother. John's mother had gone to church that morning and come back from church and was getting dinner ready. She was frying fat in a frying pan over the hot stove. Some sparks flew on her thin, starched dress and it caught on fire. Mother didn't notice that until it started to burn on her back. She panicked. Instead of throwing something heavy over her and rolling on the ground, she ran out the door and across an empty lot to Joe's store. That time when we moved to Maspeth, John's parents had bought a house by Joe's and didn't live there long. Mother lay suffering in pain for three days. John and Joe sent mother to St. Christ Hospital.

Mary was hollering, "Don't send her there, they will give her a black bottle!" The ambulance men looked angrily at Mary but didn't say anything. They had mother in the hospital two days and didn't give her any black bottle. They brought her back and told the family that nothing more could be done for her, she was burned too much. The fourth day she died. God have mercy on her soul.

After mother's funeral the family held a conference – what to do with father and Ben, eleven, and Frank, seven years old. Somebody had to take care of the three of them now. Mary and Joe wanted father to sell the house and board with them. Mary wanted him, Joe wanted him, John wanted him. Stella said, "The old man needs that home for himself and the boys and they would be better off to have their own roof over their heads."

"Then who is going to do their cooking, washing and house cleaning?" Stella said she couldn't do it, she had a business to take care of and her own children. Mary said she won't do it, she has her own house to care for and she is not going to come from Bayonne to care for the old man. Stella said, "Johnny has no house now, they can move to father's house. Father can give them rent free and Tonia will do the work for them."

I said, "No, I don't want any more trouble, I'm peaceful where I am."

The old man looked at me bashfully. Others said nothing to that.

Benny had spent his vacation with me many times, for months at a time. Mary had him for one week, and he bit his fingernails so that they were bleeding. Mary had to bring him back home at night because he wouldn't stay there any longer. I knew I would be in trouble again, but I felt sorry for them. I said all right, and back to Jersey City we moved.

I worked. I tried to satisfy the old man. It was dandy for a couple of months, then Mary started visiting him. She pointed out my faults to the old man. I didn't do this thing right - I didn't do that thing right. That's not like mother would have wanted it to be done! Stella dropped in daily, helping me to find what would be the best to suit father, but Mary openly criticized me to people and wanted father to sell the house. She said John was taking advantage of father. The work is not work enough for rent. John paid his father his rent and said to let Mary take care of him. John said, "We'll leave grandma to do pop's cooking for him."

Poor grandma grabbed me by the neck crying, "Please. Tosia, don't leave me here. Please take me with you."

I said to John, "Grandma is staying with us John, if you like it or not." I didn't let grandma do his work. I sneaked down every once in a while to show Benny how to do the cooking and cleaning. Benny got used to it and then I left them alone.

I had more time to spend with Stella again and I found out who made the story up about me and Joe. Stella told me it was her own sister Kaminski. Mrs. Kaminski was about fifteen years older than her husband and she was jealous of me. Her husband was praising me for my singing at a Christening party in Joe and Stella's and her sister didn't like it.

One day Stella was in her sister's house and her sister had a couple women in her house telling their fortune. Stella was a lovely woman, but she had one fault, that was believing in fortune tellers. Her sister knew that and she knew how Stella and I liked each other. She wanted to hurt us all, so Kaminski told Stella a fortune that I fell in love with Joe. Stella didn't want to believe it, but the way she was told it convinced her. Kaminski took a prayer book, found the psalms of David, put the end of a door key in the spot where the psalms were and tied the book so the key wouldn't slip out. The top handle was hanging on one of Kaminski's fingers from one side, and on one of Stella's finger from the other side, and every time Kaminski or Stella asked, "Psalm of David, does Antonia love Joe?" the book moved around. So poor, dear Stella didn't know her sister's scheme and came to believe it.

Joe bought a live pig at the market and kept it for a pet for the children. The pig was running loose all around. One day the pig disappeared and was gone for two days. It happened when Kaminski came to visit Joe. I was there too and they all were talking of the pig's disappearance. I said to Mrs. Kaminski, "How about if you look to your fortune gazer?" I don't know if Kaminski remembered the nasty fortune she told Stella about me or not, but she said, "Yes, give me the book!" Stella gave Kaminski her book. I stood close to Kaminski and watched her closely how she was going to operate it. Every time Kaminski and Stella asked where the pig was, and did the bums eat the pig, will the pig every return, the book said, "No". When the book turned around, Kaminski said, "You will never see the pig any more, the bums ate the pig." Then Kaminski went home.

I said to Stella, "Come Stella, and we will try that fortune again." Stella sat down watching me. I fixed the book just like Kaminski did. Every time I asked, "Psalm, will the pig return back home?" the book turned, meaning "Yes". Stella got pale in her face, then she got red. "What is this?" she asked.

I said, "Dear Stella, don't believe everything you see in a book, sometimes the book is wrong." Then I showed Stella how her sister operated it. Stella tried it herself. It worked for any way she wanted it to. Stella said a curse and turned to me shaking her head, not believing what she just saw. Two days later, boys playing ball near the gas house found the pig sleeping with pleasure in a swamp and brought the pig back. Joe killed the pig and made good kielbasa of him, and Stella told her sister not to use a holy book for her filthy fortune telling. After that we two were as ever before, loving together.

Mary must have been after her father's money very bad, because she took time to come from Bayonne much more often and stepped on the old man's toes to kick us out.

Dear grandma, if it was her time to go, or from a fear that John would leave her with the old man, got sick on me and told me something I wish she forever took with her to the grave, but she thought she had to tell me. Grandma said, "They are all throwing mud at you, and some day they all will be punished for their sins. When John got married he came to me and said, 'Grandma, forget that incident that you knew about me.'" Grandma said, "Sure, no one else knows, only I, because I caught what he was doing. Of course John was only sixteen years old at that time. He told his father and mother. They did destroy the dog. They had been threatening me and promising me things. They were afraid that I would tell somebody. I didn't tell anyone, but now that I see how they are treating you, I have to tell you."

Grandma wasn't sick long. She was eighty years old when she died, eight months after her daughter. When grandma's funeral came I had no money. I had lent Joe our money as Joe had bought another house and a lot on the next street, VanWinkle Avenue. Father and Zeglers were both paying insurance on grandma. Father said he was not giving a penny out of his insurance. He told us, "She is not my mother, she is your mother's mother, go to her and let her bury your grandma."

Zegler said, "It's silly talk. I'm willing to pay half of the funeral, but I won't pay all. She wasn't even my wife's mother." He turned to the undertaker and gave his half for the expenses.

Stella said, "John's not paying any! They kept grandma several years and took care of her when she was sick. It wouldn't be fair to them to pay when you got the insurance!" Joe already had their grave as they had three children, and they let grandma be put into it. Then father gave in and paid his half.

We wasted another year in Jersey City. We moved to High Street in Brooklyn, where we lived for a year. A new owner bought the house and wanted the whole house for himself. We then moved to Two-Thirty-Nine Front Street. I was looking for rooms and saw the rooms on the top floor of the building. I went in on the first floor to ask for it and was sent to the next house. The bosses were out but their oldest daughter took a deposit and we moved in. I was all settled down, all my things were in the right corners. I brought the rest of my rent down to the bosses who were now home from their vacation. The daughter introduced me to her mother and I put the money on the table. Mrs. Flynn said, "I'm very sorry, but I can't accept your rent. We won't have Polish people in our house."

Well, for that kind of slap in the face I didn't know what to say for a moment. Then I said to Mrs. Flynn, "Well, nobody told me that when I deposited the money for the rooms. Now I am here and I will stay here for a long time until I get the next place!" I took my money and went to my rooms.

John came from work and I told him that we had to look for another place because we were not wanted here. John said, "At least I want to know the reason why!" John took the rent and went down to find out. John found Mr. Flynn in. Mr. Flynn asked John to sit down and went on asking questions. Where was John working? What was he doing? John told him.

Mr. Flynn was a superintendent for W. Bliss Foundry and

Machine Company. He knew Mr. Micek, John's boss, and took the rent from John. He told Mrs. Flynn, "These people are all right."

I didn't go down to pay my rent for two months after that. Little Joe was bringing the rent down. The third rent I brought down myself and asked Mrs. Flynn how she liked the Polish people. She was ashamed and apologized that she didn't know all of them, but she said the ones they knew around here were giving them a lot of trouble. She said the Polish people had church services held underneath their church. The priests let them pray there and when they prayed they were all right, but when they got loose they were drinking, fighting and breaking windows and throwing bottles out the windows.

I said, "My dear Mrs. Flynn, I don't know everybody, but those people who have church service in your church are not Polish."

She said, "Why, they pray the same as you do!"

I said, "Yes, to the same God. So do the Jewish people. They say, *Our Father Who art in heaven,* but in their own language, and these people in our church pray in theirs. They are Lithuanians. Polish people have their own church on Green Avenue. And as to who the worst drunkards are, I can't pick a nation that is worst, but didn't you have your own people before us? They were Irish and they were doing the same thing that you said these people are doing, and it took you five months to put them out of the rooms I'm in now. Mrs. Flynn, we should not judge one person or one nation for the other, because there is good and bad in every nation, race and even in every home amongst one's family."

Mrs. Flynn gave me credit for my saying. She said I was right in that.

We lived in Mr. and Mrs. Flynn's place three years and five months. Not even one bottle went out of our window, and the Flynn's and the Wasielewskis had parties and lived as friends.

That was on Front Street, and there I had someone who lived a half block away from me. It was Victa and her John and his children, and now three of hers. Victa's John, who sold his grocery store, now spent more time looking for a job than working one. He was working here and there, but none of the jobs suited him. He got himself in with the longshoremen. He liked that job. Longshoremen were getting forty cents an hour – good pay at that time, when you worked. But there weren't many ships coming and there were too many men lying on the docks when any ship did come in to the docks. All the men went in on a few hours off and then for a few hours on and then rest for a couple of days. Victa's John was getting lazier and lazier and poor Victa was getting poorer and the children hungrier and Victa's John was going visiting his relatives in Greenpoint telling them of his forty cents an hour job, and in the meantime borrowing money wherever he could get it.

John's relatives were puzzled. What's the matter with Victa? John makes forty cents an hour and is borrowing money. Victa is not a good housewife! So the whole crowd came to visit Victa at once. What they found was that Victa and John lived in three rooms (a kitchen and two bedrooms) with their five children. No furniture, no covers on the beds, the children sleeping under blankets and coats. John's brother-in-law passed a remark to me that he is lucky because his house has plenty of blankets and all are covered. Mrs. Smolinski looked around and said, "I'm sorry. It's my fault. I prayed hard so she would marry John. Even I knew he wasn't any good. I thought he would change if he got a girl like Victa."

William told his Aunt Smolinski that now his mother is making trips four times a day on foot through the Brooklyn Bridge to the Singer Building in New York to scrub floors and clean the offices from four to twelve midnight and from three to eight in the morning. She comes home just on time for him to go to school. William watched his younger sisters and brothers the times mother was at work. The sisters in school knew William had a hard life so they let William come to school at nine o'clock, one hour later than his sister Agnes.

Stanley Blazeski, one of the younger brothers felt sorry for Victa. He came and asked Victa if he could board with them. Victa told him that there was no room, but he said he would sleep with William. Stanley asked his brother John to take him to work with him. John told Stanley the work is not for him. Stanley insisted to get the forty cents an hour. John could not get himself out of it. Stanley went with his brother and hung around like John for his forty cents an hour. After hanging around like that Stanley went back to Greenpoint and told all his family if anyone opens his mouth about Victa he would blacken their eyes. Maybe now they would see their brother in his true color.

Then one winter an epidemic of scarlet fever broke out. Almost every home was attacked. Victa had four of her children in bed with it. God saved William to help Victa.

It came my time to repay my sister, heart for heart. I had paid her the money I owed her after she got married when she complained that their grocery business was going bad, but now, to show her that I didn't forget her help when I needed it. I couldn't give her cash. We had, like Joe, bought four big houses with a store and a saloon on the next street, VanWinkle Avenue and James Avenue from Mr. Dill (who later was a governor of New Jersey, I think). So I didn't have any cash, but I tried to help out on my weekly pay with the food and medicine. The doctor was kind. He told Victa not to worry about his bills. "You'll pay me when you have it," he told her. "But for the medicine you have to have money."

But poor Victa lost her two little sons; Stanley, four, and John, two years old. Both died in one week, and William blamed his father for their neglect. William was fourteen years old then. A very good boy, and smart. He sympathized with Victa. William remembered all the years since his father's marriage to Victa, when he was nine years old and Agnes seven. William came one day for me to give him money for medicine. I gave him a dollar. Victa was at work yet. William went home and put the dollar on the table to have it ready to run to the store as soon as Victa came home, but someone else came home first and took the dollar.

It's a custom, or a habit of the Polish priests, that right after Christmas they go from home to home of the Polish people to bless their homes and mark on the doors the letters of the three wise men, "K", "M", "B". For that job, people are paying them whatever they can, or feel they should. Victa didn't know what day the priest would come to her street. She wasn't prepared for him, and of course William didn't know what to do.

When the priest from Greenpoint came in, the priest looked around and said, "Is your mother home?"

William said no.

"And who is sick?"

"My sisters," William told the priest.

"Hmmm," the priest said. "Children are sick from dirt, from filth, the house is dirty, the mother is out."

The priest marked the door "K", "M", "B", took the dollar from the table and went out.

Victa came home. William told her what had happened. Victa cried. "Dirty house? Did the priest ever try to walk the Brooklyn Bridge four times a night to make five dollars a week to buy bread for children and pay doctor bills and funerals?" William was ashamed to come and ask me for more money, but Victa told him Aunty will understand.

Thank God, Agnes and Jennie came out if it. Then my Joe and I got it. The doctor told John to send us to the hospital and keep away from us so he won't get sick. As John was working, he didn't want to stay home and didn't want to send us to the hospital and we couldn't get anybody to do anything for us as everybody had the same trouble in their own houses.

William and Agnes were our help, and they were glad to do it because the three children were warm and fed in my house and were all dressed up in new clothes and shoes for Easter. Victa was doing my wash and her John still was sticking to his forty cents an hour until William and I went after him.

My Joe and I got over the sickness. I was to see the children going home. I left them a quarter and told William to buy some cakes for themselves. William laid the quarter on the mantel piece. His father spied the quarter, took it and went out. William was telling me that one day in front of his father and William told his father if he was old enough to work he would throw his father out. His father wanted to beat William up, saying "I raised you up until now!"

William called his father a liar. William said, "Agnes and I were full of lice and bed bugs when my mother's sister was taking care of us until you married this woman. She did the raising us, not you, taking the last penny from our mouth so you can have your beer!"

I saved William from his father's fist. I told Victa's John, "Why don't you grow up and go to work for your own meals, not take it out of your children's mouth!"

He told me to get out and keep out of his house. I turned to Victa and said, "Victa, if you think that you and John will be better off if I don't come to see you, I will stay out."

Poor Victa thought maybe to give him a chance.

William asked me to come. I told William if he needed anything to come to me, but he was ashamed to come to ask for anything.

Then my John started an argument with me because I helped my sister. John blamed me that if I wasn't helping Victa, her John would have to work to feed his family. "Tell Victa to pay back what you gave her," John insisted. I reminded John how much Victa helped him when we got married, but John had no sympathy for anybody, so I stayed away from Victa almost a year.

One nice early spring day I took a walk to the Fulton Street shopping district, walking back by a little park on the bridge near Sands Street. I saw Victa sitting on a bench with little Jennie. I went to them and said hello, and nearly dropped to the ground with a pain around my heart. My poor sister was so pale and sick. Little Jennie was skin and bones. I got mad. "Well, sister," I said to her, "Is it better without me visiting you?"

Victa started to cry and said, "Yes, sister, much better. I and the children didn't eat for three days. I can't work anymore as I am sick. John even stays out nights now. William and Agnes at least get milk in school. Jennie and I didn't have anything."

I took my sister and her Jennie to my home. I saw that Victa was going to have another baby any day and she couldn't work in that condition. I fed both of them and gave Victa some money to buy the children supper, but I said, "If you give that dog of yours as much as a crumb, then you're not any better than him! Look at Jennie! The poor child doesn't deserve to be treated like that, and you with another on the way! I'll be there tonight at your house, and if I have to, I'll split his head open!"

I was there when Victa's John came home and asked Victa for something to eat. I got up to him and said, "Listen, you, you told me to stay out of your house, but I won't until I split your head open! Yes, they are eating after three days of fasting, but they are eating my food! You go and get your own if you don't want to work!"

He said, "You go and get me work and then I'll work!"

I said, "Brother, I'll get you work, but if you don't work I will buy a gun and shoot you like a dog!" I wasn't sure if I could get a job for him, but I went to try. I went to Mr. Flynn and I said to him, "Mr. Flynn, will you give my brother-in-law a job? I don't ask for him or as a favor for myself, but for my sister's sake. She is expecting a baby any day now and that skunk hasn't had a job for years."

Mr. Flynn laughed and said, "We don't need anybody just now, but you tell your brother-in-law to go to the machine shop and ask for my son. He is a boss there. Maybe he will put him somewhere."

I thanked Mr. Flynn and ran to my sister, and I said to John, "Here! Go tomorrow morning to the machine shop on Water Street and ask for Mr. William Flynn. He will put you to work!"

The next day I went to Victa and there my brother-in-law was, sitting on a chair. I looked at him, but before I said something, he said, "I was there this morning. I couldn't find Mr. Flynn. Nobody knew where he was."

I didn't believe him. I waited for Mr. Flynn, Sr. to come for his lunch. I went in after him and I told him what John had told me. "Oh," Mr. Flynn said, "I forgot to tell my son about your brother-in-law this morning and as they don't need anybody they told him William was not there. William told me your brother-in-law was there. Let him go there tomorrow morning and William will be watching out for him."

I thanked Mr. Flynn and I thanked God, and I went to Victa's again. I said, "Well, you didn't lie that time. You were there and you talked to Mr. William Flynn himself, but as they didn't need anybody, Mr. Flynn told you he was not there, because the Senior Mr. Flynn forgot to tell him this morning. But make sure that you are there tomorrow morning. They will take you."

The next day Mr. Flynn took John Blazeski. Mr. Flynn asked John if he could write. No. Did he know numbers? Yes. All right. They gave John a pencil and pad to take the numbers of the castings. The first job and first pay John received on the day when little Stella was born. John Blazeski worked in W. Bliss Machine Shop over nine years, until the Depression came. He worked under Mr. Flynn, who made a man out of him over those nine years. John learned not only machinery, he learned to write – to write his own name. His son William taught him.

We heard from Maryanna. She lived in Pine Island, New York and was married. Her husband died and left her with three little girls; one, three and five years old. John and I went there to visit her. It was twelve miles away from her house from the station, Maryanna sent a farmer to the train for us but the farmer had only one seat. I sat with the farmer holding Joe on my lap. John had no seat. The farmer had a box of beer on his wagon so I told John to turn the box upside down and sit on it. The farmer wouldn't let him. He was afraid the bottles would break, so John sat on the bottles and before we got to Maryanna's, John was ruptured. John was in bed at Maryanna's for three days, and two months more when he got home, but there I found out the secret of Maryanna's jealousy.

I said to her, "You are left with three little girls like our mother with the three of us."

Maryanna put her hand on my shoulder and said, "Yes, sister, just like our mother. The three girls put me in mind of that many times. For these years I have been living with hate and jealousy against you two, against mother and against Aunt Mary, because I thought that my mother loved only you two. I thought that she didn't love me because she gave me away to Aunt Mary. I craved for the plain salt potatoes you ate and the wild peppermint you drank as tea, the dough mother kneaded and baked in the hot ashes, the zacierki with vinegar. I wanted to share that with you two and play and cry and laugh and fight with you, but I wanted to be with you and mother. I didn't think then how much mother must have sacrificed, sending me to Aunt Mary, to have you two live and work the way you were, while I had everything. I was sorry for you two eating and working the way you did, while I had all the milk I could drink, all the meat, bread and all other things, but I was glad that you had to suffer because you were together. I was separated from you because I thought you didn't like me. Now my three little girls have made me understand our mother's point, how hard it was for her to bring us up, and how hard it must have been to part with me. She thought at least one of us would have the better life. Now I understand, and no matter how hard it will be for me to bring my girls up, I will never separate them. Let them eat one thing, let them play together. Let them beat each other's heads, but they will love one another like you and Victa!"

"My dear sister!" I said. "You didn't believe us that we always loved you as much! We always have been wondering what made you act like that towards us! You acted that way because you were suffering! But remember, you are, thank God, strong and healthy, while our mother was living with a broken spine, besides other hardships!"

Maryanna said, "Forgive me, sisters!"

We did gladly.

CHAPTER 21

1913 - The Trouble with Family

When I returned to Brooklyn I told Victa. Victa, the always forgiving Victa said, "Poor Maryanna, God bless her!"

Then I came to think of my father. He was fifty-nine and would be sixty soon. Maybe he was sick somewhere. Maybe he needed me. Maybe he was settled down and would stay with us. But who knew where he was now? I thought of Mom and Dad Winowiecki. Dad always said that good things are easily forgotten. I didn't write to them for ten years, but I didn't forget them; I didn't have anything good to write, and I was ashamed to write them my troubles. Now I would write and ask them about my father.

I wrote to Mom and Dad. They were very glad to hear from me, but as to my father, they didn't know, and didn't want to know. Dad said, "He doesn't want to see my face anymore!" Father had made enough trouble for Dad after we left Traverse City. Father had come in November to take Victa and me to his new home in the forest among the lumber jacks and didn't find us in Traverse City. Father blamed Dad Winowiecki for our disappearance and father threatened to burn Dad's house to the ground. He then sued Dad Winowiecki and told Mr. Roberts, Victa's former boss. Mr. Roberts knew from the time Victa had worked there how father was acting with us and how we were afraid of him. Father lost that case and left their city and they never heard of him since.

My little friend Geneveve, who was a grown up lady, wrote me of her hard luck. She wrote that her dad was in the fish business. He had men catching fish for him, he packed them and sent them to the Fulton Street Market in New York and he proved it. Dad Winowiecki sent me one hundred pounds of fresh fish to Front Street. I didn't know what to do with all that fish. The whole block had a party. Poor Geneveve. Three months after Victa and I left Traverse City, Geneveve, who was twelve years old then, got sick with scarlet fever. From that sickness something set in her head and she had five operations on her head and bones taken out from behind both her ears. She said those doctors would have killed her, but her parents found a doctor who came from Johns Hopkins Hospital in Baltimore who cured her and called the other doctors butchers. They ruined her ears and she was deaf now and had to wear a kerchief on her head all the time.

Geneveve tried to locate people who knew my father but nobody knew his address, so I put an ad in the Polish newspaper and somebody saw the ad who knew where my father lived and sent the address to me. Then I wrote to father and asked him if he wanted to come to live with John and me. Father wrote asking me to send him the train fare. I remembered what he had done with the shoes and shorts Victa and I bought him when we first met him. I wouldn't trust him with money. I told father to go to Dad Winowiecki and I would send money to Dad. Dad would get his ticket for him. Father got mad and found money somewhere. He said he borrowed it. But my father didn't come as a father, he came as an enemy to revenge on us. He didn't even let us know what day he was coming.

When he came to Brooklyn looking for our address he had a crowd of children following him like a parade. It was in the middle of July. Father had a sheepskin winter coat on him, cowboy boots, cowboy hat, cowboy pants, red bandana on his neck, and in every pocket of his clothes a pint bottle of whiskey. He was carrying on his back a canvas bag that looked more like a seaman's bag, but I remembered the bag. Father used to have it when he came from Battle Creek to Traverse City for his monthly supply of food. He was hot and sweaty, and the children from Sand Street, Bridge Street, Front Street and Gold Street were puzzled. They didn't know whether to holler *'grease ball'* after him or not. They didn't know if he was Spanish, Mexican, Italian or Indian, but he was very white skinned with blonde hair. He was coming from Montana. So the children were anxious to see where that creature was going. Then father asked them if they knew where 239 Front Street was. The whole parade brought him right in front of Mr. Flynn's property. The children from all the streets knew all the numbers on Front Street as they were attending St. Ann's School on Gold and Water Streets.

My father was walking proudly with all the children around him. He said the children here were very polite and obliging. And so this was also my father. As many people told me that my father is not worthy to be called a father, and my sisters hated him, I somehow loved him. Maybe just because my sister was a little older than I and remembered him from home when we were little girls and I didn't. John took father to the store and bought new clothes for him so he wouldn't be seen in his cowboy outfit any more. Father was with me two weeks, leaving bottles of whiskey all over the house; in the hall, in the toilet and on the first floor where three families were living. I was ashamed to look people in their faces. I asked father, "Please don't do that! If you must drink, bring it into the house and drink, don't disgrace us!"

John didn't drink whiskey since he was living in Brooklyn. The last time John drank whiskey was at Joe's baby's Christening when John was the Godfather. The first glass he drank he almost died from. He was throwing up for two days straight. He gave up whiskey and he didn't like my father drinking, but there was nothing I could do to stop him. I promised father that he didn't have to do a stock of work (although he was only fifty-nine) and good looking yet if he only stopped drinking whiskey.

Father said to me, "So, you wanted me to come here to be under your foot! When a man is born with a habit he'll die with it. I'll put my head under one of the trolley cars and die with whiskey in my hand!"

One Sunday morning father went to the toilet on the first floor. I went to fix his bed and I saw a big book, twice the size of the biggest Bible, lying on his bed. I was curious to see what kind of book that was. When I opened it I got scared. I couldn't believe my father read that and believed in it! The pages were full of pictures of devils with horns and tails on them with all kinds of names, Satan, Beelzebub, and all other different names, and under each of the devils was a prayer, and it told you how to pray to them. I saw it was printed in Chicago. I'm sorry I didn't get the printer's or the publisher's name. I am never afraid of a devil. I don't care what his name is, but that time I wouldn't keep a book like that in my home. I took that book to the kitchen where John was making a fire to make coffee. I showed John the book. John didn't know what was in it and didn't wait for me to explain. He took the book, tore it in half and put it in the fire. I never heard of the F.B.I. at that time, but that book may have brought them on some devil's work as it said in that book how to work out different things to bring you luck, money or love – when you have to kill little and young innocent girls and what to use their blood for. It told when to use a white chicken or a black cat for the dirty tricks.

Father came up and saw his book was missing. John said, "I burned it."

Father turned on John and said, "You are going to burn like that for it! That book cost me twenty five dollars, and if it takes me the rest of my life to get another one I will get you for it! I will be far away from here, but you have to die!"

Father took his bag and went to Victa, and thought he found just the right place. Father and John Blazeski became good friends. They both liked to see the bottle dance from one hand to another. Father encouraged his son-in-law to beat his own daughter and his children. Victa was afraid that if father stayed in her house her John would go "on the bum" again and would lose his job in the W. Bliss Machine Shop.

Then one night everybody was asleep in the house but her. She was just lying there thinking, when she saw father get up and come out from his room and go into the kitchen. Victa thought he wanted a drink of water. He was in the kitchen for a moment and then was going back to bed. He gave a funny laugh. Victa was wondering what the laugh was about. What was so funny? A few minutes later she smelled gas in the house. Victa jumped up from her bed and ran into the kitchen. Ya! The kitchen light gas jet was wide open and gas was filling the house full speed. Victa thought, that's the devil's laugh! She shut the gas jet, opened the door and windows and waked John and William up. They wanted to know what the gas smell was. Victa told them that God saved them this time because she couldn't fall asleep. Victa didn't sleep for the rest of the night. She was afraid to go to sleep.

The next day Agnes came after me. I went there to see what Victa wanted and Victa was telling me what had happened in front of father and father laughed, "So you are afraid to die! He, he, he, he!"

Victa said, "Sister, you are the one who wanted that old devil here, you keep him! I won't chance my and my children's lives with him here!"

I told father to come with me, but he refused. He said, "Give me Maryanna's address. I will go to Maryanna."

I told him he did enough wrong to us, why should she put up with him! Let him go where he came from.

He said, "Give me the money!"

My John said, "Come on, Pa, I'll buy you your ticket, put you on the train and off you go!"

He refused. He wanted Maryanna's address. I wouldn't give it to him. Victa wouldn't give it to him. John Blazeski gave father Maryanna's address and he went to Maryanna's.

Maryanna was married to her third husband, John Kwiatkowski. John Kwiatkowski was a quiet, peaceful man and an old bachelor who lived by himself, working in the field growing onions on shares. He saw Maryanna struggling with her three little girls and he married Maryanna and was as good a husband as a father to them all.

When father came to Maryanna he was hanging around Pine Island for a year, but not in the house, because John and father didn't care for each other. So father made himself a camp in the woods until he got lonesome for his friends in the West somewhere and went back, and I never heard of father since that time.

Then it came the year 1913 and it turned John's and my world upside down. John began with coming home from work, sitting on his rocking chair, closing his eyes and rocking and rocking, or just sitting still for hours. First I thought nothing of it. I thought he was just tired, relaxing, but when it went on for days I was worried. "What's the matter, John?" I asked him. "Sick? Why don't you go and see a doctor?"

"Leave me alone," he told me.

I left him alone, but that didn't help any and didn't stop me from worrying. I wanted to know what was eating him. Sometimes I felt like going to him like to a father and putting my head on his lap. Then I wanted to take him in my arms and rock him to sleep like a baby, but the nearer I went to be by him, the farther he threw me away from him with his words, like, "Leave me alone!" or "Get out of here!" If he got mad he would say, "What are you looking for, a lollypop?"

Then I was thinking the other way. Maybe John got tired of me and maybe he's got some other woman on his mind. I told him, "John, if you are tired of me, why don't you tell me? Come out in the open if you think you would have a better life with someone else. I'm willing to give you a divorce."

John said, "Stop talking, woman!"

I didn't look for an argument. I sat down to do my work. I had plenty of work to occupy my mind. I sewed and crocheted for people. Then something happened to me.

Four weeks before Christmas, all during the four weeks, our people used to do a lot of fasting. In Europe they didn't eat any meat at all. Here they just fasted Wednesday, Friday and Saturday. Women from Brooklyn were looking for some substitute to meat. They went in groups and went from Broome Street to Delancy Street in the Jewish section of New York where they could get things they wanted and much cheaper than up around their way. They bought all kinds of dry food like rice, barley, beans and peas by pounds and sturgeon fish and herring. They bought salted herring, pickled them and they were good with a glass of beer any time.

When the women were going around from store to store, Victa was going around too. She asked me to go along and I did. I bought some herring and when I came home I just had an appetite for herring. I fixed it for supper and John ate one. He said it was good. I ate it and got sick from it. It stuck in my throat and stayed there for nine months. I felt like a hair was traveling from my throat to the pit of my stomach and back to my throat. I had headaches, dizziness, fainting spells and I had to spit and spit and spit. I couldn't bring it up. Seeing John moping around in his far moods I was disgusted with him and myself. I took to crying spells. I felt sorry for myself. I'd like to have cuddled up to someone for sympathy and I was ashamed for my own actions, but I couldn't help it. John saw me change like that, but never said a word. Of course I didn't expect any sympathy from him. He had no sympathy for anybody, not even for himself.

One Sunday morning he got up and said, "Everybody is getting rich on my money. All I do is work and lend it to others. They all go in business and I'm helping them. I am going to open a business for myself too!"

I didn't ask him what kind of business he had on his mind again, and I didn't dare to either persuade or dissuade him because he wouldn't listen to me anyway and did as he pleased always. He always told me, "Who would listen to someone like you?" or told me I was not smart or not right in my head. I told him once, "Do as you please. If you live, I live, if you starve, I'll starve with you."

John went to Jersey City as I was sick and couldn't go. John came home with his mind made up for business. John's head was always full of business. The only trouble with him was he didn't know how to run it by himself and always depended on someone else to help him. So John said, "Joe's making out pretty good in their new place they bought from Dill and has the whole house empty on Newark Avenue. I will pay Joe twenty-five dollars a month and open up a junk shop there. We will move right after New Year to Jersey City."

I thought, "My nice peaceful four years, five month's life in Brooklyn, back to Jersey City".

John said, "Only, I can't get a license on my name. I have to have a least six month's residential rights."

"Then how can you open without a license?" I asked him.

"Leon is going to get it on his name for the six months."

Leon, one of John's younger brothers. He was married about three years to a young widow. She came from mixed blood. Her mother was Polish, father Lithuanian. I saw Bella a few times but not enough to know her character. Bella seemed to be a nice looking woman, only her eyes always looked like if she just got up off her bed or she was just so tired she wanted to go to bed. And John said Benny would help him in the store.

Oh, I knew it! They were always willing to help John, even go in as partners with John, as long as they didn't have to put up any money in it. So when John went out of business they didn't have anything to lose.

And so to start the New Year right we started John's junk shop and it started good because John knew a lot more people in Jersey City than in Maspeth. John visited plumber shops, saloons and hardware stores, and on Saturdays our store was filled up in no time.

On March 4th, 1914, a snow storm came as a blizzard. It knocked all the telegraph poles and electric wires to the ground. I believe that storm lasted twenty-four hours and it took about three days to clean off the streets of the wires. So Ben and I thought that the company didn't need that wire and we were buying it. John was still working in Brooklyn and Leon was trying to get a motorman's job on the public-served trolley cars. Nobody wanted to throw a good job away, so Leon was one of the extra stand-ins in case one stayed home. Leon had to be at the Greenville Car Barn Station every day and Leon's wife was our steady customer from the time we moved into the junk shop, borrowing money. Every day a quarter, fifty cents for Leon's car fare and his lunches.

John took a few days off to look for a place where he could sell his iron, brass and copper. Mornings before he went out to look for a dealer, as I was still spitting, John made a fire for me and brought a pail of coal from the cellar and took the ashes out. Bella was watching John doing that for me. She started complaining that her Leon never wanted to do that for her, so she asked John to do that for her also. Bella called John "Brother Johnny". "Brother Johnny, will you come up to my house and bring me a pail of coal from the cellar?" says Bella. Well John thought that Bella might not feel well so he went.

Leon and Bella were living in John's and Leon's father's house. Leon wasn't at home when John and I were living there at first. When we lived in Brooklyn, Leon was boarding with his sister Mary, but he didn't like it and said what he knew about his sister Mary he could write a book. So he got married and lived in his father's house. John knew where the cellar was, so John brought the coal up. Bella asked John to take her ashes out and make a fire for her. John did and didn't think anything of it, but that went from twice a week then to every day. Bella got in the habit of saying that her fire was stronger and burned hotter than mine.

One day Stella came to my store and said to me, "What's the matter with you? You want Bella to take your John away from you?"

I said, "Just what way? I don't know anything about it!"

Stella said, "The whole neighborhood knows it and you don't know it!"

I said to Stella, "I bet you that even John himself doesn't know what he is doing!"

When John came home I told John how people were talking about him, so when Bella came and asked him to make her fire hot, John refused and she turned to me and said, "Leon's family had better stop talking about me! What do they think Leon married? An old maid? Leon married a young widow!"

I laughed and said, "What's the difference between a twenty-five year old maid or a twenty-five year young widow? You're still five years older than Leon!"

Bella ran out of our house mad.

The next day John was away. I heard somebody calling me. I was in the kitchen. I went to look out the window to see who is was. It was Bella, by the fence. I went out to see what she wanted as she stood on the other side of the fence. All I could see was her head and her fist shaking at me and hollering, "Hey you! If you don't shut your mouth, I'll break your neck for you!"

I said, "Is that all?" I said, "If you have something to tell me, come inside. I've seen dogs fight through the fence. I'm not a dog type."

Bella yelled, "For twelve years you didn't have a baby, now you're going to have one! I hope it will rot in you before it comes out!"

I turned to her and told her, "May God pay you the way you wish me!" and went in and shut the door behind me.

Suddenly a riot, then a voice, again calling me. This voice Stella. Stella hollered, "Tonia, come on out and help me to bring the drunkard where she belongs!"

I went out to the empty lot. There were my two sisters-in-law. One was stretched out on the ground, the other one was lifting her up. I asked, "What has happened to Bella? I thought she went home!"

Stella said, "I want to know the same thing!" Stella said the neighbor's children were playing in the empty lot where Stella's children were playing too. They all saw Bella falling to the ground and they made a riot. Stella's son, Stanley, nine year's old, came after me and said Bella was dead on the lot, but she was as usual, drunk. Stella picked Bella up by her arms and I picked her up by the feet and dragged her over the lot and up to her rooms. After Stella slapped Bella's face a couple of times she woke up. Stella said to me, "Come on, let's get out of here before she recognizes us and uses a broom on us for our good deed!"

Stella came with me and I told her of Bella's wish for me. Stella said, "How does that drunkard know? She is married three years and doesn't show any signs! Maybe she's not worthy to have them!" Stella knew what was the matter with me and she was glad for my sake and she was glad that she would be near me. Stella was a midwife. She always wanted to help women in their hard time, as many of them still didn't believe in having a doctor, but wanted a midwife. Stella didn't know how to write and she didn't have higher education, just reading. She asked doctor Piskorski, who was a Spanish-American War doctor, and he was the Wasielewski's family doctor. The doctor helped her so she passed the midwifery examination.

Stella said, "Bella is not a decent woman or she wouldn't say such a thing to another woman, especially one who never did her any harm."

When John heard of Bella he went to Leon and said, "Leon, if you want any carfare or lunch money you have to come and get it yourself. I am not giving quarters and fifty cents to Bella anymore."

"What quarters? What fifty cents, John? I never asked you for carfare or lunch money! Too bad you didn't tell me of this sooner," Leon said. "I was wondering where she was getting the money for a bottle every day!"

When John found out Leon wasn't getting any of the fifty cents and quarters he stopped giving to Bella. I don't know where she was getting her drink or money for it, but a couple days later Stella got the S.O.S. from one of our neighbors to come and take Bella out of her house. Stella came after me and said, "Come on, we've got a job on our hands!" There was a party, and Bella went there without invitation and got herself full of whiskey, went to the toilet and stretched herself out on the floor in such a position that the lower half of her was inside the toilet and the top of her was outside in the hall. People were walking over her and passing bad remarks and the owner was disgusted and was glad when Stella and I dragged Bella out, and just in time. Leon was coming home.

I said, "Leon, your wife is very sick."

Poor Leon said, "Let her die!"

But Bella didn't die, she was figuring how she could hurt me.

One day a policeman came into our junk shop and asked for

John. John knew the policeman since John, the policeman and Frank Hague were playing ball together and picking cigarette butts off the street. John told me that the policeman said John should expect a visitor from our station in a day or two. Some woman reported to the captain that he was running a junk shop in her husband's name. "That must be your sister-in-law. You have to do something – some kind of alibi in a hurry!"

The next day John took all he could on the truck and brought it to the foundry and sold it. He asked Leon to stay home for two days so he could help with something when the police came.

The Captain came two days later as John's friend had warned him. The Captain looked the place over, looked at the books and the license and asked, "Which of you is Leon Wasielewski? Leon said, I am, and my brother John here is my salesman."

The police went out and didn't arrest anybody.

Bella was watching from the window of her house, mad. She couldn't do anything to John, so she turned on Leon. Bella went to the Public Service and told the office that she wanted to find out how much money Leon was getting a week, because someone told her that Leon was going out with a girl and spending his money, not giving her enough to live on. Public Service paid Leon and laid him off. They felt if his wife didn't trust him, the company wouldn't either. Leon took Bella and moved to Bayonne. We closed up our five month's running business with three dollars lost. John sold the metal to the small foundries on credit. Some still owe us money. Lawyer Butler took fifty dollars to collect the money for us. He told John that some of the foundries closed up, out of business, or moved. Can't find an address. And there was fifty dollars more lost.

Work in the foundry slowed up and John got laid off. Several weeks we drew most of the money from Joe's for business and had only one hundred fifty dollars left. I asked Joe for it and Joe said, "Where am I going to get it?"

I said, "I'm not asking you to lend me money, just pay me back what you borrowed from me. People rent a saloon in one of your houses," I told him. Joe disposed of them and opened a saloon himself and he had no money.

Stella came to me later and said, "Tonia, here is part of the rest of the money Joe owes you. For the rest, don't pay him the rent and you can take groceries for it, but don't tell Joe that I paid you. Let him worry for it. I'm going to be on his neck so he will save the money he owes you so he will have less to drink up, and when he gives you the money you can give it back to me."

Dear Stella, she always had a way out of things. I wish I had her nature! We did as suggested and came out fine.

CHAPTER 22

The Herring

Then came August 25th, 1914. I spit out my herring. Twelve pounds four ounces. I named him Stanley Ludwig. Stanley, after John's father. Ludwig, after King Ludwig III of Bavaria. Thank God Bella's wish didn't come true! My son came strong, healthy and good looking like John. Stella was with me during the birth like a mother and didn't charge me a cent.

I was happy with my little herring and so was my Joe. Joe was over nine years old now. When Joe heard that he had a little brother he took some money out of his bank and ran out on the street where he saw a peddler selling fruit and vegetables. Joe bought two pounds of grapes and brought them in to my bed and said, "Here little brother, this is for you!" Stella and the other visitors laughed and said it was very cute of Joe.

Yes, Joe was a cute boy and I loved him as if he was my own. I loved him twice as much after my baby was born, because then I knew I was meant to be a mother. I was proud to be Joe's mother and tried to show Joe that, but either I didn't know how to raise Joe or it was something from Joe's parents that was in Joe. No matter how I tried, I couldn't keep Joe from having long fingers and everything his fingers reached for stuck to them.

When Joe's mother left Joe with me I didn't know Joe's stomach was poisoned with cigarette butts that he was picking off the floor in the agency house where Joe's mother was last staying and waiting for jobs. That's why she didn't even stay with Joe one week in our house before we found out Joe's trouble. When Joe's mother disappeared the next day I had Joe taken care of by a doctor and it took a week to get Joe to throw up the green poison from his stomach. So you see, Joe did give me trouble right from the day he came to our home, and by taking care of him in his sickness my heart grew more toward him.

As Joe was the only baby in the house he had everything a boy needed. Nothing extravagant, but plenty of clothes and proper food. John built Joe a two story house bank from egg boxes, with toy furniture and carpet in it. The house was three feet high and it had a special safe that money dropped through the chimney slid into. We were putting Joe's allowance into the chimney, and when our friends came to visit us they were dropping in all kinds of coins for Joe. Joe was five years old when John built the bank for him and the money started to drop in.

Joe started to go to school when he was six and started to learn bad things instead of good. He had plenty of money every day. He was buying candy, sodas and all kinds of toys and giving them to the children in school, which I didn't know anything about. I trusted Joe. I didn't suspect anything and no one told me of his actions in school. Joe had plenty friends. He was willing to run errands for people and I didn't mind. I rather thought it was nice of Joe to learn to work, until complaints started to pile up. Joe went to school and lost the money. Joe brought the wrong change. I didn't know if it was Joe's fault or not, and I didn't want Joe to be neither the suspect nor did I want him to fall in the bad habit of losing money or not watching the change when he was trusted. I stopped Joe from doing errands, but that didn't stop Joe from having money and blowing it on his school mates.

One holy day some friends visited us. Upon going home they were arguing. The woman asked the man if he took money out of her pocket. He said, "No, it might have fallen out on the trolley car. Well, it's only a dollar, it might have been pulled out with a handkerchief." People always found an excuse where their money could have gone. No one guessed the right direction.

One day my niece, Stella's daughter, and Stella's cousin, came for a weekend. The girls wanted to go to Coney Island the next day, so they were figuring the money – how much they could spend on a good time. Then they found that money was missing out of Aniela's pocket. "It's only a dollar," they said. It must be the Italian gave them the wrong change from the five dollar bill at the push cart where they bought the bananas and grapes. I began to worry. It had happened too often in my house. But we went to Coney Island - the girls, John, Joe and I. We had a wonderful time and I kept strict count of how much the girls had spent there. I knew how much John had spent. I knew how much money I gave him that day to give the girls a good time.

When the girls were ready to go back home the next day I asked them if they had enough carfare left to go home. Aniela counted hers. She said yes, she had enough. Her Aunt counted hers and said, "That's funny. I was sure I had mine, but I must have lost a dollar." I was afraid to think it, but my suspicions were against my Joe. I didn't say anything to the girls. I returned them the money that they spent at Coney Island and told them the treat was on us and they then went home happy.

I was waiting for the following day when Joe went to school. What would be the news? Miss O'Gara, Joe's teacher, who lived in the same house on the first floor brought the news when she came for lunch. Miss O'Gara said, "Mrs. Wasielewski, Joe is playing a rich man again to the children today, and I don't think Joe is doing any errands for the money he is spending. He had what would be a good week's pay if he was working steady. I don't want to hurt you," Miss O'Gara said, "but you'd better count your money if you have any put aside, because I caught him when he took fifteen cents off my mantel piece. I sent him in to get me a glass of water when I was on the porch. The money was right over the sink and Joe knew it was only father and I that were here and father wasn't home from work so I knew it was Joe that took it."

When Joe got to the door he looked at his teacher. He kind of changed color. Miss O'Gara said, "Joe, you took the fifteen cents from the mantel piece."

Joe blessed himself, crossed his heart and said, "No."

"But Joe," Miss O'Gara said, "I'm teaching you children if you do a wrong thing you have to admit it. How can things be found out if you won't tell the truth? Lies will bring lies on top of lies and nobody will find the truth. If you don't do wrong and people want you to prove it, you bless yourself and cross your heart to prove that you didn't do it. But you took the fifteen cents!"

Joe, blessing himself and crossing his heart again said, "No!"

I said to Miss O'Gara, "Miss O'Gara, I am not a teacher. I didn't ever go to school, but I remember what my mother taught me when I was Joe's age, that no matter how many lies you pile on top of one another you can never cover the truth. Sooner or later truth will come to the top like oil. You pour oil into a bottle, then pour water on top. You can have more water, then oil, but oil will come to the top always." And to Joe I said, "Joe, didn't I teach you the Ten Commandments? Not to use God's name in vain! You steal, you lie, and you are blessing yourself to cover your sins with God's name!"

I paid Miss O'Gara fifteen cents and took Joe up and gave him his lunch. After lunch I took a razor strap in my hand and asked Joe a question. I said, "Joe, I want the right answer from you without using God's name here. Don't I feed you enough? Are you going hungry?" Joe admitted he never was hungry. "Haven't you got enough clothes?" Joe said yes. "Don't I give you money for ice cream and candy every day?" Joe said yes. "Then why did you steal?" Joe started to bless himself. I said, "Did I ever hit you with this strap?" Joe said no. "Then put your hand down and talk. You took Miss O'Gara's money." Joe said yes. "You took money from Aniela's and Stella's pocket." Joe said yes. "You took Mrs. Locke's money." Joe admitted that he took money and from whom he took it. I didn't hit him that day but I gave him a promise of a good beating if it happened any more.

I paid the money to all who lost money in my house and they all were surprised to hear of their loss. They said I didn't have to give them back the money, but I felt better when I returned the lost to them, and from then on I watched Joe closely every morning. I held my door to the hall open until I heard Joe close the door to the street.

One day I didn't feel well. I couldn't get up to fix Joe his breakfast. Joe got up, fixed his own breakfast and served me a cup of coffee in bed and told me not to worry about his lunch. "If you're sick, mama," he said, "I can fix my own lunch too." I let him do it that day. The next day Joe got up early and pleaded with me that I should stay in bed and he would fix his meals for the day, but I felt better and got up to hold the kitchen door for him as usual until he shut the outside door. Joe somehow didn't want me to hold the door open that morning. He kissed me goodbye once and told me to shut the door so I wouldn't get the draft. I told him to hurry to school or he would be late. He kissed me again and said, "Good-bye, mama," and again, "Good-bye, mama." He went to the stairs, turned back and kissed me again. Something was telling me Joe is up to some mischief, but I didn't know just what to do. I stood in that door and coaxed him to hurry to school. "Good-bye" from the second floor, "Good-bye" from the first floor. I was answering his good-byes and then something stuck me suddenly. I slammed the kitchen door quickly and opened it quickly but quietly and bent over the stairs to see what Joe was doing. Joe was still in the hall and I saw him put his hand under the stairs carpet and pull out something and put it in his pocket. He stood up and looked up and saw me standing there watching him. His face changed color and he didn't know what to do or what to say.

I said to him, "Are you still here? You are late to school."

"Good-bye," he said, and out he went.

After he went out I went down, wondering what he pulled from under that carpet. I put my hand there. There was nothing. I stood for a minute, but something told me to stick my hand on the other side. I did. I pulled out seven cents. I tried the next step. Two nickels. Then I went from the first step of the first floor to the last step of the third floor, and every step on both sides of the stairs under the carpet was money. Nickels, dimes, quarters, fifty cents. Something like seventeen dollars and fifty cents total!

Joe came home for lunch. I didn't let on that I knew anything until he came home after school. I said, "Joe, have you got any money?" Joe said no. "What did you pick up from under the carpet on the stairs this morning?"

He said, "I dropped my pencil and picked it up."

"Joe, who put the money all over the stairs? You did."

Joe lifted his hand to bless himself. I took the strap. I said, "Joe, I've been praying to God and I taught you to pray so God would make you a good boy, but God can't make a good boy out of you if you don't want to learn to be good, so this may help you," and I beat him. Not for the money, but to stop him from stealing and telling lies. Then I asked him where he got that much money from.

Joe said, "From my bank papa made."

I went to look the bank over and I saw no damage. I said, "How did you get it out?" Joe showed me. He loosened one of the glass windows in the kitchen. It was big enough to put his hand through, and while we were dropping the money through the chimney he was taking it out through the window. All the money I counted putting in myself and what John put in was over thirty-seven dollars, besides what our friends were putting in every time they came to visit us.

We never put any more money in that bank for Joe and we stopped giving him an allowance for a long time for punishment. I felt sorry for the beating I gave Joe and I was always worried what Joe would grow up to be.

When my Stanley was a few months old and I wanted to go out shopping, Joe asked me to trust him with the baby. At first I was afraid to leave the baby with him. Joe pleaded, "Trust me, mama!" I did. Joe really was good if he wanted to be and he took good care of the baby, as good as I did when it came to feeding the baby and changing diapers. Joe took care of the house when I was out or sick.

Better than John did. But when I trusted him with money, Joe forgot himself in my home or someone else's home.

One Sunday morning I sent Joe to find out for me if Stella was going to church. I wanted to go too. Joe went to Stella's house and did not come home on time to tell me if she was going or not. When he did come it was too late to go. I asked him the reason why he was so late and if Aunt Stella went to church without me, although she never did before. Joe said Auntie was ready to go but she lost a five dollar bill that she was going to give to the priest to have mass. Joe said they all looked around the house and on the lots and the sidewalk from her house to the trolley car and couldn't find it, so Aunt Stella didn't go to the church.

Two days later Joe brought home a pair of new roller skates. I asked him where he got them. Joe told me a boy in school lent them to him. When Stella's children came from school they told Stella Joe had a five dollar bill and bought himself a pair for one dollar and a half. Stella came to me with the witness. Joe saw them coming and his face changed. I knew Joe was in trouble again, so I said to him, "Well, Joe, it looks to me like you know what those boys are going to say when they reach here!"

Joe said, "Yes, it's about the five dollars. I took it mama. I saw Aunt Stella putting it in her prayer book. She left the prayer book on the table and went into the bathroom. I took it from the book. The boys saw me buying the skates today."

"You pleaded with me to trust you, Joe. I trusted you and you went back to your bad habits again! How much did you pay for the skates?"

Joe said, "One dollar fifty."

"Where is the change," I asked him.

"I stuck it in the rain pipe in the back yard," Joe told me.

"Don't you know that if we had rain today the money would have washed away from under the pipe?"

Well, he said he would have picked it out from the pipe before it would rain.

When Stella crossed the empty lot and reached the house I had the five dollars ready for her. Stella said, "How did you know?"

"I've been figuring on Joe," I said. Sunday when he was helping to look for it, and when he came home from school with the new skates I knew where he got the money for them even though he told me that some boy in school lent them to him."

January 1916 we had visitors from Chrome, New Jersey. It was Stella's cousin Stanley Gryczeski, and the other was Mr. Beigert, who was a foreman in Goldsmith Detinning Company, and ran a bakery on the side. Mrs. Beigert kept the bakery. The Beigerts kept one baker who baked the bread, and one delivery man. Our friend, Stella's cousin, was the delivery man. I didn't know what the Goldsmith Detinning words meant. Mr. Beigert told us that there were carloads and carloads of tin cans coming to the place and going through a de-tinning process separating solder from the tin cans and some other mixture that makes up some salt and the cans are flattened into a bundle weighing a couple hundred pounds to a bundle. The company had so much of the stuff bundled up that they intended to mold the tin can bundle into ingots and send them out to the ammunition foundry to make ammunition out of them. So the company was looking for a man that would build them a cupola chimney and start and run a foundry and take care of men workers in that foundry. Mr. Beigert was talking to his wife about it – that the company was going to advertise for a man of that ability and our friend told Mr. Beigert he knew a man who could answer the purpose. Beigert promised our friend Stanley a good job in the de-tinning place if he got him the man, and Stanley brought Beigert to see John.

If John was an educated man he could have made good there, but John wasn't educated. John wasn't even wise and Beigert took him for an easy fool. John and Beigert talked things over. Beigert said to John, "We will guarantee you a steady job at twenty-one dollars a week for three years if you sign a contract that you will stay with us for three years." John signed it for twenty-one dollars a week for three years, then later in 1916 eighteen other foundries were paying their men from thirty-six to forty-eight dollars a week.

Well, John was a hard-working man. He didn't care how much he made as long as he had a steady job and steak came to seventy-five cents to a dollar a pound, butter ninety-five cents a pound and eggs a dollar a dozen. I don't know how John had figured he could support his family, but he went to Chrome, New Jersey to build and run the foundry for the Goldsmith Detinning Company.

John was boarding with the Beigerts while I was left in Jersey City figuring out how I was going to live on the divided twenty-one dollars a week. He was coming home for the weekend and soon he found out that we couldn't make out living and keeping two homes. He looked for a home near his work so we could live together. John found an old house just three miles in three ways to Rahway, to Carteret and to Chrome. It was called East Rahway. Houses were twenty minutes walking distance from one to another. The old house had nine rooms and rented for thirty dollars a month. It would be nice to keep boarders, but John didn't want boarders so we rented one side of the house for fifteen dollars a month.

Stella was worried about me as I didn't feel well for several months from eating pig's feet and sauerkraut. She wanted me to stay in Jersey City for another month, but I couldn't figure a way no how. John was paying Beigerts twelve dollars a week board and coming home weekends spending carfare, and paying rent in Jersey City. I used all the money I had with the business we lost. I had to depend on John's twenty-one dollars a week, so I had to move near John's work. Stella made John get an old woman to take care of me in the lonely house in East Rahway and we paid her twenty dollars a month. I felt miserable. John never figured things right, always leaving things for me to figure out and I wasn't in a condition to do anything.

The day we were moving to Rahway I didn't have enough money to pay the balance on the rent after I paid the moving man. Stella stuck a five dollar bill in my hand upon settling me on the trolley car to Newark. When we got off the trolley car to change for East

Rahway I got sick. I got scared that I wouldn't reach my new place. The old lady was afraid of the same thing and told John he'd better get somebody private to take me there. John went out of the station and got a man with a car. John asked the man if he wanted to take a sick wife to East Rahway, how much would he charge. The man said three dollars. John said all right, but when the man saw me he wanted to back out. He told John he'd better take me to a hospital. I told the man, "Here's five dollars. I have a midwife with me." So we got to our place before the furniture arrived, without accident and we settled ourselves in the old convent-like house.

One week from the day we moved in was May 8th, my birthday, and I received a lovely present. I named her Rosalia Stella. Rosalia was my mother's name. My sister-in-law was Stella.

We lived in the convent-like house three months, when two German families moved in on the other side of the convent where there were five rooms, and they started to act as if they owned the whole place. We didn't have any water on our side of the house. They didn't like it when we went to pump on their side. They didn't let anyone come to visit us. If anyone came with a car they had to leave it on the road and then walk about two hundred feet to the house. We moved.

We left the old convent house to the Germans and moved a little farther where there were Hungarian people named Sabo. There we had a seven room house to ourselves, a nice chicken coup and about half an acre of land around it. I loved the place. Mr. Sabo was a farmer. He cut some of his land near the road for city lots and put up a couple houses. We moved into one.

There was about a quarter of an acre of plowing land, so the next spring I took a spade and turned the ground up for a nice vegetable garden. I did have a swell garden, and the farmers were surprised twice. They saw me digging and raking and planting in the spring and didn't believe that I would have any vegetables, and when the vegetables ripened they exchanged a couple bushels of their pears and peaches for my tomatoes, sweet corn and pumpkin. That garden helped me a lot to make up the shortage of John's small pay.

I raised some five hundred chickens and two pigs. Stanley Gryczeski (now Rosalia's Godfather) brought a goat and eight rabbits for the children. I was happy in that house with my little family.

John was running the foundry for the Goldsmith Detinning Company day and night, when suddenly the American government stepped into Goldsmith Detinning and upset the work there. They fished out all Germans and Austrians and all non-citizens were discharged. Mr. Gaintshimer wasn't allowed to come near his plant. Soldiers were placed at every corner. John was born in Germany but he was Polish and had his first citizen papers. The army took care of the detinning department plant, but John said he didn't know if the government knew that the army was three days late. The material they wanted was gone overnight three days before they arrived. John didn't know how it happened or where it went. He saw trains, and ships were always staying behind the detinning plant. In the three days before the army walked in the plant was empty. All the two and a half years of John's work – the boxes upon boxes of ingots they had been molding – disappeared, and the ships. The army left John to keep up the work in the foundry, but the company was complaining of a shortage of men and material and kept the work going on very slow progress. John wanted to quit, but the company wouldn't let him go. They raised his pay to forty dollars a week. John took Joe to work as an errand boy through his vacation, and the company paid Joe twelve dollars a week. John was hanging on, doing nothing, for six months. He didn't like it because he felt something funny was going on in the place. John's guess was that all the ingots that were made in that foundry were shipped out to Germany to make bullets against the American soldiers, but of course that was only his guess, and he resigned from the job. I wasn't pleased with his resignation because it was the first nice piece of money I saw in my life for the last of his six months hanging around doing nothing.

So I lost my happy little farm. I sold my five hundred chickens, pigs, goat and the rabbits. I gathered myself eight hundred dollars in cash. I asked John to buy a little place – either the one we lived in, for three thousand dollars, or another one the farmer had for twenty-eight hundred dollars. It was a smaller house but had more land around it. John could get another job, either in Elizabeth or somewhere near. But all John thought of is that we had money, so Jersey City was for him. So to Jersey City we moved. We couldn't find decent rooms anywhere. John found somewhere on a side street, a three story, one-family house with kitchen and dining room in the basement, living room and one bedroom on the first floor and two bedrooms on the top floor. The house would have been all right for all grown-up people, but I had Stanley, who was now four, Rosalia, two years old, and a baby, Frank, one year old, besides Joe. That made too much running around to keep the place clean and take care of the children. Joe was now thirteen, but he couldn't help me as much in the city as he did in East Rahway, so we moved out after one month.

Stella was my help again. She found us four nice box rooms on Newark Avenue near Boulevard over a tailor shop. John got a new job. He worked but a week when we all took sick with a flu. 1918 was a year that every family was laid up with it. You couldn't get a doctor when you wanted. You couldn't get help of any kind. Everybody was afraid to go out to the street to visit or help anyone. In my family I took care of John, Stanley and Rosalie. Joe had it mild. He was of help to me with baby Frankie. Rosalie and I came down with it the worst. I put everyone to bed and gave them the medicine for the night. Coming out from John's room I saw a shiny cross lying on the floor. I knew no cross of that kind was in my house. I bent down to pick it up – the cross was gone. "It's me, my Lord," I said. "Thy will be done." I felt dizzy. Everything went blurry before my eyes. I went back to John's room with the last strength and said, "John, if you can get up and do something, take care of the baby. I'm going."

John asked, "Where are you going?"

I told him, "To the place where there is no return."

He said, "Don't go, wait for me!"

I don't know if John knew what he was talking about or if he didn't understand what I was saying. He did come to my room. I smiled at him, dropped on my bed and went stiff. John saw something had gone wrong with me, woke Joe up and sent him to bring Stella.

Stella wasn't home. She was busy day and night helping people. Stella was an angel. She was everywhere with every race and creed. The doctor was afraid she would get the flu and people would lose their angel. He gave her medicine and told her to take one teaspoon every three hours. She took three teaspoons every hour and she wasn't in bed one day. When she heard that I needed her she came in a hurry and thought she was too late. First she opened my teeth with a spoon and poured hot tea with lemon in my mouth, glass after glass. She then went on rubbing me with alcohol with vinegar until my body turned red. Then she wrapped hot water bags, bottles and hot towels and prayed and waited. When I began to sweat, she thanked God that I would live. She worked from two after midnight to five in the morning until she got me up. I asked her why didn't she leave me alone? I didn't feel pain until I woke up. I was aching all over. "Let me die!" I said.

Stella said, "Stop it! Don't you think of dying now! You got your children to look after!"

Then I got scared of something. I was scared that if I died now my face would look crooked, and I started to pray to God to save my life. I pleaded with Stella to rub my body more to get the stiffness out of me. I thank God and my dear Stella that I came out of that horrible flu, but it left something in my feet. I was so dead that I didn't feel the hot bottles that had opened sores. The bottles burned the flesh and it took me several weeks to heal them. Afterwards they were healed, but they were always swelled up and I had to have them bandaged up every day. My Rosalie got over the flu but had to go through an operation on mastoids behind her right ear which left her hard of hearing in that one ear.

1918 passed, the war was over and John got a better job. Frank was nineteen months old when a fourth baby came. I named her after my sister Victoria, but we called her Vicky. The children were growing fast and they were good. I never had any trouble with them. Stella told me she was jealous because they were too good. Stanley and Rosalie were going to school. I wasn't well since Rosalie's birth and I was getting weaker after Vicky's. The doctor had been telling me that I had to go under an operation. I had been delaying it from year to year and didn't want to leave the children alone. I wanted to wait until the children were older, and in the meantime I was peacefully happy. John was too, until John's bother Benny got an idea of peddling shoes like potatoes, on the street.

Of course all of John's brothers were full of ideas and John always fell for them and always came out the loser. Benny said he had no money to start, and he suggested that John put the money in now, buy the shoes and buy a car and take the shoes in the car and go peddling. John knew I had a few hundred dollars I brought from East Rahway. I couldn't say no for the sake of peace in our family, but I said, "Well, here goes my farm money! I don't think I'll ever own my own home on a farm!"

John's brothers always found a way to spend our money for us. So, John bought a car for three hundred dollars, and bought a hundred dollars' worth of shoes from a Jewish man who got them at auction. He got a peddler's license, and John, Benny and the Jewish man went peddling. They sold the hundred dollars' worth of shoes they had with them in the car. Every time they stopped near a shoe store the shoe store owner called a policeman and wanted them arrested. They showed the police they had a peddler's license and the police force didn't know what to do with them. The vegetable and fruit peddlers could do their business in front of the grocery stores, so they could do the shoe selling in front of the shoe stores. They were covered by law. The shoe storekeepers were mad but couldn't do anything to stop them.

Selling was pretty good through the week, but when they figured out the whole profit for the week they found out it didn't come out so good cut in three ways. The Jewish man took his commission and it left very little profit for John and Benny. They tried for another week and took shoes on credit. I saw that Benny was taking his share, but forgetting to pay his half on the buying part, and after five or six weeks Benny gave up the business as I knew he would. Benny hadn't put anything into the business and he didn't lose anything. John was left to pay for the shoes they took on credit.

John had paid for the car so the car was his, but the car was unhandy to carry the shoes in. The shoes got tangled up and John was losing time getting them paired back up again. John was disgusted and he wanted to quit after three months' time. I was mad. I said, "No! You spent half of the money I tried to save! You are going to stay at it! Pay the man for his shoes and go on your own. If the man buys shoes at auction, so can you, and when you sell them you get all the profit."

I didn't get any credit for my advice, but he tried by himself. He got rid of the car and bought a pie wagon at an auction. The pie wagon had shelves in it that were just nice to keep the shoe boxes in the right place so he didn't have to look for them, he just reached off the shelf like in a store. He was peddling the shoes for three years and the cops didn't bother him anymore.

Then the bums and thieves were after him. In the summertime women bought their children out and tried the shoes on and he could do the peddling by himself, but when winter came he had to go inside the houses. By the time he had tried and sold one pair inside the house he lost a couple pairs off the wagon.

The first year John took Joe to help him. Joe watched the wagon while John was selling inside, but after a while John found out shoes were missing. Joe was doing business for himself. John was at a loss. I said to John, "How about if you go canvassing people who know you already? Go, get the orders and sizes and then deliver to them on Saturdays. Stanley will go and watch the wagon." By taking orders from people he got orders for better shoes. Shoes were accumulating so much that we didn't have a place to keep them and we had to take them off the wagon at night and put them on in the morning. Our landlord got mad at us that we were making a shoe store out of our rooms and told us to pay more rent or get out.

John was traveling all the streets and he saw an empty house with a store. The landlord of the house wouldn't rent it by the month. He wanted three month's rent ahead of time. John fit it in one month's time and we found out how badly we were cheated. We got ourselves settled in the store and the first rain that came at night almost drowned us all. Little Vicky, then fifteen months old, woke up first, calling me. "Mama! Frank poured cold water all over me! I'm all wet and cold!"

I woke up and heard something drizzling all over the rooms. I thought, "No, baby Frank is sleeping with Stanley. Wait! I'll see what happened!"

I put my feet on the floor and found water reaching our bed mattress. I turned the light on and the water was coming from the yard like a river. The yard was higher than the rooms and the store. Water was in every room and everything was floating on the top of it – shoes, pots and pans. I grabbed Vicky out of her cradle and pulled the wet clothes off her and wrapped her in blankets in my bed where the water didn't reach the top yet. The poor baby was shivering all over, her teeth chattering. John barricaded a space near the front door with chairs so the shoes and pots and clothes wouldn't float out the door when he opened it, as it was pouring full speed from the yard through the rooms into the street. We got the water out, but our furniture, clothes and the shoes that weren't in boxes were all damaged.

Vicky got sick with bronchitis and a kidney rheumatism. I nearly lost her. I had a doctor coming every day for two weeks to take care of her. John went to the landlord and told him to come and see what had happened. The heartless man told John he couldn't do anything about it. John asked him to return two month's rent and said he had no right to take three month's rent in advance when he knew the house was dangerous to live in. People told us that the house was condemned for some time and nobody wanted it and he was against the law renting it. I called up the housing inspector three times. I called up the Board of Health inspector several times. Everyone was so busy they couldn't come to investigate. In three weeks' time the doctor called up the Board of Health and told them it was impossible to live in that house. Everything stunk with the dampness the water left and it was too dangerous to move the sick baby. The two inspectors, the housing and the health departments came in to investigate that rat hole on the day we were moving out. You can't blame me that I didn't wish the landlord any good luck for his family. I had no money to sue him. I know when you go to court without money you don't win, and when you get money in court you lose. Honest people always get the hard end.

We had a friend who was in the shoe business for several years and he made big money on shoes throughout World War I. He had his shoe store on Grove Street. On the next block near him was a small shoe store kept by a cooperative, but the people couldn't get along there, so they were selling out. The friend told John about the store and John went and bought them out. They had fixtures and shoes – a hundred dollars' worth. I asked the friend if we would be in his way when we opened up a shoe store next to him. He laughed and said, "Ten stores like them wouldn't hurt me! I'm sure of it."

So John went to rent the store. The owner was Mrs. Sullivan. She had one daughter married to Mr. Malone, who then was a secretary to Mayor Hague, and an old maiden daughter and son Joe, who was taking care of the property. John didn't take a lease on that store, which he should have; he just rented it by month.

The first few months our store didn't make much – ten or fifteen dollars a week profit. I thought it was good. John was still taking orders. We had a place to keep the shoes, but we had no place to live. We made a partition with shoe cases in the back that was big enough to put in two beds, two cribs, a table and a couple of chairs. We gave the rest of our furniture on storage to our friend - a big dining room table, a nice kitchen stove, better chairs and pictures. We had a pot belly stove left by the other people. Our friend didn't like John going to take any more orders because John took some of his customers away from him. Of course John didn't know whose customers they were when he went from door to door canvassing.

Our friend's name was Zloty. He, a Ukrainian, and his Polish wife were friends of ours years back when we all were younger and living near each other. When the Zlotys had children they had trouble getting people to stand up as Godparents for their children.

Ukrainians didn't like Mrs. Zloty, Polish people didn't like Mr. Zloty, so between John and his brother Joe (Stella's husband), Stella and me, we stood up for four of Zloty's children, and from then on we thought Zlotys were our friends. But in business friendship often changes. Zloty told us ten stores like ours wouldn't hurt his store. Zloty over-judged his customers. He introduced John to the shoe houses where he was buying shoes in New York; like Clifton and Thayers, Fishers, and Endicott and Johnson shoe houses. The shoe houses credited us thirty to ninety days. Zloty figured that if we kept the same type of shoes his customers wouldn't change stores, they would be buying in his store. But it seemed his customers didn't like Zloty so much that they stuck to him forever, or just out of curiosity, they were coming to buy shoes in our store. Some of them were telling us stories about Zloty being so independent in war time when business was good that he took many women by their sleeves and put them out of his store, saying, "If you don't like my shoes, get out!"

The time when we opened our store things weren't booming so hot with strikes going around in President Harding's time. All the railroads were on strike and people didn't want to pay ten and fifteen dollars a pair for shoes like during the war. They were looking for something cheaper and John was doing pretty fair on the auction-bought shoes. We got some of the good shoes from the shoe houses, but we weren't selling them as fast for a higher price. Some of the shoe houses found out that John was peddling shoes and they were surprised, but they asked John if he would get rid of some of their accumulated stock for them. Clifton and Thayer had a couple hundred of English shoes they couldn't sell to the stores, so John took them on the wagon and sold them like hot cakes in two weeks' time. People were asking one another, "Where did you buy those shoes?" They were coming from Secaucus, Hoboken, and all over, asking for those shoes that the shoe houses couldn't get rid of. We paid the shoe house seventy five cents a pair as they came – small and large sized from size eight to three for boys and girls. We sold them from a dollar fifty to three dollars a pair. The funny part of the shoes was the girls and boys were arguing with their parents and didn't want to wear them because the shoes were high upper shoes that were too high for the boys and not high enough for the girls. But they were such strong built shoes they out lasted any three of the fancy shoes. That was a benefit to parents in hard times.

Our good friend was turning out to be our bad friend. He didn't like that John struck luck with Clifton and Thayers because they always happened to have something on sale that stores couldn't use beside their good shoes we had in the store too. So first our friend started to tell his customers that he owned our store too, that we were working for him. Then he was coming every day to our store and asking me to send my Joe to his store to help his wife while he parked himself on a bench right in front where people passing by could see him, doing nothing in our store. At first I didn't catch on to his scheme, and through that kind of scheming we lost many customers. Those people that didn't like him, seeing him in our store, passed our store and went somewhere else. Then I tired of having him for company in the store. I told him, "Listen, Zloty, if you are going to sit here watching how many of your customers will come to our store, neither you nor I make any business, so if you want to visit us, go in the back where people won't see you and let me do my business. My friend got mad and stopped his daily visits and my business picked up.

One day I was looking for loose shoes in the back shelves and I noticed a couple of boxes of new shoes. I looked at them. Zloty's shoes. I said to Joe, "Joe, what are these doing here? I know they didn't come here themselves!"

Joe said, "Do you think I'm working for him for nothing while he is sitting here spoiling our business?"

I told Joe I wouldn't have them in our store. "You have to bring them back where you got them from."

Joe took them out of our store, but he didn't bring them back to Zloty. Zloty had himself to blame for it.

CHAPTER 23

Surgery

Come November, December and the whole winter, we had a wonderful business going outside and inside. Then I had to undergo an operation. I was a sick woman since my Rosalie was born, and getting worse from year to year. Every doctor I went to told me different things and was curing me from what they thought I had until I couldn't drag myself any longer. I didn't think I would live. I got myself insured for a couple hundred dollars to help the children when I was gone. Of course I didn't tell the insurance man my plans. He passed me without a doctor, as I had one policy already with that company. Two weeks after I received the policy I went to the hospital. Well, I had one man praying for me hard so I wouldn't die. He was afraid to lose his job for passing me on the insurance without a doctor. Thank God I am still living and I didn't want to die and leave my four babies alone in the cold world. I had been delaying from day to day until I fell on my face and couldn't go any further and didn't know where to go.

I had a surprise. A visitor came who I didn't expect to see. Leo's wife Bella. She was somehow changed. She didn't drink anymore and she told me she just came home from a hospital where she was operated on for her appendix and she had a wonderful doctor. Bella said, "Come with me and I'll take you to him."

I went with Bella to Bayonne to see Doctor Sexsmith. I told Dr. Sexsmith my symptoms and how long I had been dragging that way. He said, "In that case, I can't cure you with medicine. I can't see what is in you. If I cut you open then I will know how to cure you when I find out what's in you."

I told him, "If you have to cut me to cure me, go to it." But he wouldn't come to Jersey City hospitals, so I went to Bayonne Hospital and I nearly lost my life there because of one bad nurse. She was supposed to start her nurse's course before the war, and then she got out and got married. After her husband's death she came back to finish her nursing course. Other patients were talking about her and many were complaining that she was a mean nurse. She had a daughter about eight years old. She was a German and I think she must have hated Polish people because she took it out on me. I'm sorry I have forgotten her name, but anyway she wasn't worth remembering. She was supposed to give me a high colonic every four hours on Sunday as I was going to be operated on Monday. She did it twice instead of four times and said I was done clean.

When she went away from me I mentioned to the patient next to me that she didn't do it right. The lady said, "Wait, I'll ask the other nurse, Miss O'Donnol. She is new around here. She came from Canada with her sister to finish their nursing courses and the younger one is an angel."

So when Miss O'Donnol came into our room to say good night, as her hours were off duty, the old lady Mrs. McDonald, told her about the other nurse. Miss O'Donnol turned around and brought the tubes and pails on her off-duty hours and she was surprised what she got out of me. She said to Mrs. McDonald, "My God, if that woman went on the operating table with that she wouldn't have come out alive!"

Monday I went confidently on the operating table and the doctor told me to count. I smiled at him and started to pray, "God bring me back to my babies," I repeated three times and I saw a bell over my head, and on the heart of the bell I saw my words of prayer, and I said, "Yes, God will bring me back to my babies." I didn't know or hear anything anymore. They had me on the table from ten in the morning to one in the afternoon.

I felt myself thrown on my bed by the doctor and nurses. Doctor Sexsmith slapped me across the face and said, "Wake up you lazy thing and tell me who you love!"

I said, "I love Dr. Sexsmith," and they all started to laugh at my answer.

The mean nurse said, "She hasn't come out of the ether and she doesn't know what she is saying."

I said, "Yes, I know!"

Then Miss O'Donnol asked me, "Do you know who I am?"

I said, "Yes, you are my angel nurse, Miss O'Donnol."

They were all surprised, and the doctor was pleased how nice I came out, but my angel nurse was changed to other quarters and to my misery the mean nurse was the nurse in that room.

I felt fine that Monday, but I couldn't pass water. I hadn't passed since before I went on the operating table. I asked the mean nurse if she could do something for me, and she handed me a bedpan. I told her I couldn't pass water and she said I had to. I was dying for a drink of water and was told it was for my own good that I don't drink. I begged them to just wet my lips. The nurse brought me a piece of ice wrapped in gauze and I was wetting my lips with it. I was getting a high fever and they were feeding me with morphine. I told them the morphine was not helping me any and I was in pain because I couldn't pass water. Tuesday, Wednesday, Thursday, and I couldn't make that dope understand what I wanted from her. I was ashamed to ask the doctor what was the matter with me, and I thought it was the nurse's duty to tell the doctor. All she was telling the doctor was that I was a nuisance and that I rave all night and won't let the other patients sleep in peace.

Friday morning I was driven to madness with the pain and I couldn't stand it any longer. I threw the covers off me and was getting out of the bed – my eyes on the window and my mind on ending it all. Mrs. McDonald asked me what I was doing and I told her I was ending my misery. She pleaded with me, "Please don't do it! Tell me what is the matter with you!"

I said, "I haven't passed water since before I was operated on and they won't do anything for me but feed me morphine to keep me quiet. Even the morphine doesn't help my sufferings!"

She said, "Please, wait just another hour or so until the doctor comes, then I am going to tell him myself."

I listened to her like to a mother. Maybe she would help me. At eleven Dr. Sexsmith came. I laid there half dead and didn't care what was going on. The doctor started talking, "Listen, woman, you came out so nice from your operation and you were so nice all day Monday, what's the matter with you now? The whole week the nurses are complaining that you are bothering them and you won't let the other patients sleep. If you are going to act like that they will remove you to a room where you will be left alone!"

I turned my head away from him and started to cry. Then dear Mrs. McDonald said, "Pardon me Dr. Sexsmith. Did the nurses put on the chart for you that this woman didn't pass water since Monday before she went on the operating table? Did they tell you that the woman wanted nothing else from them, but just begs them to take the water from her?"

The doctor's eyes got big and he clamped his mouth and grabbed for the bell and he rang it and he rang it and stamped his foot on the floor and rang it again. The bad nurse came in smiling and wanted to ask him what he wanted, but he didn't look at her, just kept on ringing the bell. She looked at him puzzled. She looked at me and I was crying. She looked at Mrs. McDonald. Mrs. McDonald looked mad. She smelled something wrong so she didn't know what to do. She just stood behind the doctor and he kept on ringing the bell. Another nurse ran in, and another one, and in turn one after the other. Then doctors started to come in, filling the room, and Dr. Sexsmith kept on stamping and ringing until he had every nurse and every doctor and intern and supervisor in that room. They all looked at him. They thought Dr. Sexsmith went insane, but none opened their mouth until Dr. Sexsmith saw them all in that room and turned to them with a mad look, came to my bed, grabbed the blankets off me, exposed me to them all and then he said, "Look all of you, look! What did you do with my patient? Do I bring my patients here to you to get them cured or to have them murdered by you? Complaining that the woman bothers the nurses! What are you here for? Where is her chart? Have you gotten the woman's complaint? What she wants? What troubles her? No! You have here that she troubles nurses, won't let other patients sleep! The other patient knows what the matter with this woman is – you nurses, doctors, don't know it! If anything happens to this woman, this institute will be responsible for it! I don't bring my patients here to be killed! Hurry up! Take her water away from her and make sure from now on you report <u>her</u> troubles to me, not <u>yours</u>!"

When they took the water from me that noon I fell asleep and slept twenty-four hours without a move. They were taking my water away from me every day for three weeks while I was on my back fourteen days without food or water. I lost desire for water – only what I had to take with my medicine.

One day when the doctor came to visit me I smiled at him. He said, "That's the way I want you to do!" and he smiled back at me. I took his hand and kissed it; I was so grateful to him that he made them take care of me better and that the house doctors and supervisor were visiting me every day. I told him it wasn't my fault that I couldn't smile.

He said, "I know that's not going to happen to you anymore, and not to anybody else as long as I'll be director in this hospital. It always has to be one victim before we find things out, but you should have told me about it right the next day!"

We both thanked Mrs. McDonald for her help. But that lousy nurse - she must have been just as lousy in her heart as her mind was lousy. She saw me kiss the doctor's hand and she was telling everybody that I fell in love with Dr. Sexsmith. Sure I loved him - he brought me back to my babies! I was grateful to him for his kind words that I heard very rarely in my life. Dr. Sexsmith was over sixty and had a beautiful wife, whom I met when I got out of the hospital. She was just as gentle as the doctor.

CHAPTER 24

Joe Leaves Home

I came home to my babies after being in the hospital over a month. John brought Frank and Vicky from Brooklyn where my sister Victa was taking care of them for me all the while. Stanley and Rosalie were staying with their father. I was glad to be home with my children, if not for Joe going wild again. Joe turned seventeen years old while I was in the hospital. John was out for orders and delivering shoes and Joe was the whole boss in the store. We trusted to his conscience and when I came back home Joe didn't want to do as he was told. He went out and got himself a job in a garage. The man was paying Joe nine dollars a week and teaching Joe to be a mechanic. I was glad for Joe's sake, but I knew Joe wouldn't stay there very long because when Joe was fourteen years old I signed a contract with the shipyard people for three years for Joe to learn a trade. Joe lasted there three months. I saw him carrying screwdrivers and hammers around him and asked what they were for. He told me that he had to carry them with him because the other men wouldn't give him any tools to work with and he couldn't learn to do things without tools. I told Joe, "Don't bring any tools home. If you get caught with them going out the yard you will be accused that you stole them."

One day Joe came home and told me he got laid off. I thought it was so. Two weeks later I received a letter from the superintendent asking why Joe was not working, and inquiring if he was sick or something. He didn't tell the office anything. I called up the ship yard superintendent and told him what Joe told me. The superintendent said, "Sorry, lady, but we can't trust having a boy here if he plays that kind of trick!" So Joe lost his job.

Well, Joe was a little older. Maybe he would stay on the job he himself got. And it was work. Joe worked in the garage five months and took himself a vacation without me knowing. The garage manager called me one day for Joe. "Joe is not home. Joe disappeared."

Two weeks later Joe was telephoning from Pine Island, New York, telling me he was with Aunt Maryanna, having fun with his cousins and would be home soon. Joe had luck to get jobs but he never stayed with it. He came from Pine Island, got himself another job in a decorative paint shop. The boss, Mr. Kizer, had a son older than Joe. They were painting design flowers on walls like City Hall and other big buildings. Joe got twelve dollars a week and learned to paint. He worked there a few months and disappeared again. When Joe did not show up to work for two weeks, Mr. Kizer's son came to find out if Joe was sick or quit. Joe never told them anything. The young man told me it wouldn't be so bad if Joe had left the key to the office. If something was lost from the office Joe would be in trouble. He said he liked Joe and covered up for him to his father that he lost the key and said he trusted that Joe was not going to disappoint him. I could do nothing but promise the young fellow that I would find Joe and make him return the key.

A few days later Joe came back. He looked the young Kizer up and gave him the key. Joe was hanging around the shoe store for the Christmas holidays and went out sleigh riding one day and knocked an elderly woman down. The woman was taken to St. Francis Hospital with a broken hip and Joe was taken to jail. My landlord, Mr. Sullivan, came to me with the story and asked if I wanted to bail Joe out. I said no. That was all I could take from Joe. Then I went and told Mr. Sullivan what Joe was and how I got him.

I told him I did the city a favor feeding and clothing Joe and now let the city do something for Joe.

John almost sent Joe to reform school in Rahway, New Jersey, when we were living there because we had trouble with him. We had sent Joe to buy milk from Mrs. Sabo. Joe put the money on the table for the milk and picked the bottle of milk up. Somehow the money always stuck to the bottle. We gave Joe lunch and sent him to school. Joe ate his lunch and was going with the peddlers selling vegetables all day. We got a note from the school that Joe wasn't in school for three and four weeks at a time. I was telling Joe we would buy a horse and buggy. Joe went and took a harness from Sabo's stable, brought it and hid it under our chicken coup. I went to chase the chickens in and looked under the chicken coup to see if there were any chickens there. I saw the harness. I right away called Joe and asked him what the harness was doing there.

Joe said, "Well, you said you were going to buy a horse and buggy, so I thought you wouldn't have to buy a harness."

I told him, "Joe, if I can afford a horse and buggy, the harness will come with it! You take that harness and bring it back to Mr. Sabo before he comes after it with the cops!"

Joe took it back. John was going to turn Joe into the authorities, but I begged him not to. I was afraid that people would be saying that we sent him away because he was not our son. I had Joe kneeling down on his knees with me, praying together so God would change his character. When we stopped praying, Joe said, "Mama, what do I do to be good?"

"Joe, just don't touch things that don't belong to you. Just do what you are told and you'll be good!" I told him.

"Is that all?" Joe asked.

"Yes," I told him. "See how little it takes to be a good boy? Will you try it?"

"All right, Mama, I'll try it."

A few weeks or few months later Joe was doing the same old tricks. So now I told Mr. Sullivan that Joe was old enough to take his own consequences. Mr. Sullivan called his brother-in-law, Mr.

Malone, and told Mr. Malone about Joe. Mr. Malone got Joe out of jail. The woman's family sent their lawyer to me, telling me that I'm being sued by the woman for twenty-five thousand dollars. Joe found out that he wasn't our child. He said to me, "But you raised me so you are responsible for me!"

I said, "Joe, if you are that smart, then you should not have done things that I have to be responsible for. Now that you did what you did to me, you may as well start out on your own!"

But Mr. Sullivan told me not to worry about being sued, because as long as Joe was not my son, and not even adopted by me, they couldn't sue me. So everything was dropped against Joe, and Joe said, "If I am not yours, I don't have to stay here!" He left a note that he was joining the army.

Well, as bad as Joe was to me, I loved him as if he was mine. I cried for a couple of days after he was gone. I thought if he had told me that he was going to join the army I would have given him enough underwear, shorts and socks to last him for a while. Now I didn't know where to send to him and had no time to run around from the business and children to look for him or send things to him. I knew the army would teach him responsibilities and make a man out of him.

Two months or so after Joe left, some woman came to me asking if Joseph Wasielewski lived here, and how old was he. I thought the woman may have been sent by the army, and I thought Joe must have put his age down as older than he was, so I told the woman Joe was twenty-one, going on twenty-two. The woman said, "Mrs. Just, next door, told me that Joe is only nineteen years old."

I said, "Well, who is the mother to Joe, Mrs. Just or me?"

The woman said, "That's right, you ought to know."

I was afraid to say anything or ask for Joe so I wouldn't hurt him in any way. The woman left and I was tending my business.

Things were slowing up on John's peddling routes. I noticed John was getting less orders for shoes, or if he sold them he didn't get much of a profit, but I saw what I didn't want to see in John. He was coming home more drunk every day. That was during prohibition time, and in prohibition time people drank more whiskey than any other time because almost every other household was cooking its own. John didn't drink whiskey for over thirteen years. Now he was made a whiskey taster. In every home he went to he was asked to taste it. John was getting somehow weaker and cranky. I made him stop peddling shoes for good. Well, John stopped peddling, but he didn't stop drinking. He started to visit the saloons too often. Then he came down with pleurisy pneumonia. By then we had rooms across the street from our store, over a butcher shop. I was left all alone with the business. One day he was a sick, raving man who was trying to jump out of the window from the bathroom. A woman next door screamed. Seeing him walking to the fire escape, she called to me. I didn't know what to do! Mr. Sullivan told me to put him into a hospital. He told me I would kill myself running up and down to care for him, the children and the store. Mr. Sullivan asked me, "Where are your friends, where are your relatives? I saw them here every Saturday and Sunday. Now when you need help they are not around!"

I was wondering about that myself. Where are they? I need Joe. Well, then I thought, Joe is in the army. But what has happened to Ben and Dora? Last year when they saw that the business was going good they came and asked John to become partners. I didn't want it then. I knew they wouldn't last long and might put us in some trouble, but as usual John had his last word. John told Ben if he wanted to become a partner he had to put in at least one thousand dollars. We had more stock than a thousand dollars' worth, so Ben blindly gave John a thousand dollars without a witness, and they were coming every Saturday and Sunday to help us in the store for a couple months. Then they backed out again. I told them then that they were not going to get their money in a hurry as we put it into the stock. They would have to wait until we saved enough to pay them. Well, Ben and Dora seemed to trust us, but they went to Leon and told Leon about that and Leon put enough saltpeter in Ben and Dora to create diarrhea. Leon scared them that if John ever died I would never give them that thousand dollars, and when John got

239

sick with pneumonia, Ben and Dora got sick of fright and none of them showed up to help me when I needed help. Mr. Sullivan was kind enough to watch the store for me when I was up with John. Frank was in kindergarten. I asked his teacher to take Vicky in so that Frank could watch her. The teacher was kind and did it for me, and so I had John, and the store, with Mr. Sullivan's help. I kept it on until John got back to health, but he never was himself anymore. He complained of headache and dizzy spells. I told him a couple of times to stop drinking whiskey.

"You didn't have headaches when you didn't drink, John!"

John got mad at me and said, "The more you want me to stop it the more I will drink!"

"Well", I said, "If you feel that way, drink and see where it will get you!"

The shoe business wasn't so busy in summer. John got himself into the foundry again. After six months of Joe's disappearing he showed up. "Aren't you in the army?" I asked Joe.

He said, "No, didn't Aunt Dora tell you I was working on Public Service Trolley car as a conductor? Aunt Dora saw me on the Jackson Avenue trolley many times."

"Why aren't you working today?" I asked Joe.

He said, "The Public Service put new boxes for people to drop the nickel in by the motorman and are laying off the conductors. I was a new man so they laid me off first." But Joe said, "If you would help me so I can buy myself a uniform then I would get a conductor's job in New York."

Me, like the good mother I wanted to be, I gave him money for the whole outfit, even the hat and money belt.

CHAPTER 25

Rheumatism

Joe disappeared. I had neglected myself taking care of John and everything was rundown and I was failing in my health. My God! Year after year, always something new! If not one thing it's another. Just from bad to worse. I got a rheumatism inflammation of the joints, lying down in bed right before the Christmas holy days – one month, two months. Whoever had the dreadful disease knows how painful it is. Dr. Holloway who took care of Vicky was taking care of me, but after two months he told me to change to another doctor. I said, "Doc, you were good to my baby, be good to me. I trust you."

He said, "I gave you every medicine known for that sickness and none helped you. Change to another doctor." Tears were coming from his eyes when he said that. He grabbed for his hat and slammed the door, and from behind the door yet he called, "Get another doctor."

I was swelling more and more. I couldn't move hand nor foot. I couldn't lift a spoon to my mouth to feed myself. A nurse from the Metropolitan Life Insurance Company was coming to wash me and change me. I was lying like a bale of hay wrapped up in cotton. After Dr. Holloway gave me up I told John to call Dr. Piskorski, who was all the Wasielewski's family doctor in past years. But I got worse after his medicine, so I didn't call him anymore.

An old lady who lived in Sullivan's building came to visit me. She said, "I heard you have no doctor. If you want me to send you one I will call him for you. He is a very good doctor. His brother is the highest doctor in St. Francis Hospital."

"All right", I told her. "I'll try him."

The next day a big, husky man came up slowly walking. Whistling to himself. He took his gloves, his high hat and his overcoat off in slow motion, then got himself a chair and sat down by my bed. Then he opened his mouth and asked me, "Well, how long have you been lying here?"

I told him it was three months.

"Hmmm," he said, "That's too long. And how often do you want me to come to see you?"

That got me mad. I was in pain, but that madness picked me up. I sat up. I said, "Listen, doctor, if you think you can cure me, don't go home! Stay here! I'll pay you for it. But if you just came here to find out how often I want you to come to see me, and take three dollars, don't come anymore!"

He got insulted, took his coat and hat and went out. I told myself I didn't want any more of that kind of good doctors.

Then two ladies from a Baptist Church came to visit me. I told them the story of the good doctor. They said if I wanted them to interfere in my affairs, they knew a doctor that cured a lot of people from this sickness.

I said, "Please, send him in. If he helped others in this, maybe he will help me."

"All right." They told me they would call him up as soon as they got home. They did. Seven o'clock in the evening Dr. Finke came. A tall, slim fellow, but he started with a slow motion like the good Dr. Mahoney.

Then he asked me the questions. "How long have you been in bed?"

I told him over three months.

Dr. Finke said, "Hmmm," but he didn't ask me how often I wanted him to come to see me. He said, "That's too long. Let's see. Today is Thursday, seven o'clock. You will be on your feet Saturday."

Well, I thought to myself, another joker. I said to him, "MAYBE!"

And he said, "Well, we will see. I won't be here to see you until Saturday, at the same hour. Get this medicine as soon as you can and take four powders a day with plenty of water."

The drug store was next door to us, so I sent Stanley to get the medicine. I took it as the doctor told me; one right away and four Friday. Saturday at eleven, before noon, I got up off my bed and came to the kitchen, all swelling gone. I was very weak, but I was up. Thank God! It was a miracle to me.

Dr. Finke came at seven and he said, "Well, were you up today?"

I said to him, crying with gladness, "I can't tell a lie, doctor. I did get up at eleven this morning!"

He said, "MAYBE." That "MAYBE" he remembered years after, when I had him for our family doctor. I apologized. I told him I was disappointed with other doctors and didn't believe him.

Dr. Finke said, "Tomorrow is Sunday. You can stay in bed yet, but Monday you get up and don't have to be sick anymore, but take care of yourself here after. Get your teeth pulled out."

I asked him about his magic cure, and he said it was just that he took a special course on how to treat rheumatism. God bless him for that!

So on Monday I went to the store as good as ever.

Oh, yes, my Joe came back, after he spent the conductor's outfit money on traveling. He got himself a job as a shoe salesman in the first department store on Newark Avenue, for the Christmas holy days. After the holy days' rush he was laid off and had no place to go. He came home when I was sick. He came up and said, "I heard that you were sick, Mama, so I came to see you."

"It's very nice of you that you did, Joe," I told him. "You didn't come last winter when Papa was sick." I asked him how he was getting along amongst strangers.

He said, "All right."

I said, "Well, if you're getting along all right amongst strangers, stay there, but if you can't get along, come back."

Joe took both my hands and kissed them and said, "Mom, I'll be good now."

"All right," I told him. "Go take care of the store and show me that you really mean it."

Joe did, and I wouldn't be a good mother if I said he didn't do it right. He kept the books in order as I did – how many shoes we bought, how much we sold every day and how much profit we made. I was satisfied with his work and I told Joe that he could be good if he wanted to be.

It was near Easter time when I went to take care of the store again. After Easter the business went slow on us. John went to work for the Fagon Foundry. As a foreman, John had the authority to pick his own men and pay them a good price as they had to fill in a rush job for the city. They were making the new signal lamp posts. Too bad it lasted only six months, then the foundry moved out to Hoboken somewhere. But John liked Jersey City so much he wouldn't move anywhere else.

While John worked there I said to Joe, "You were a good boy this winter helping me in the store. I want to help you now. Papa is taking men to work and paying them thirty-five dollars a week. That's a good chance for you to make and save some for yourself. I will charge you for food, not for board, and as you have plenty shoes and clothes for a while you can save a few hundred dollars for your future."

I took a bank book out in Joe's name and was putting his weekly paychecks in it for him. When Joe had over two hundred and fifty dollars in his book he asked me for it. He said he would take care of it himself.

I said, "All right, it's yours, take care of it."

Joe got mad at John for scolding him for something, and John transferred Joe under another foreman. The other foreman didn't like Joe, and Joe quit.

I was picking up Joe's shorts and hankies for the laundry and

I came across his bank book. All I found in it was $5.00. Joe came home before John and I showed him his bank book and asked him what he did with his money. Joe had no answer for what he did with it. He only said, "I thought you were going to help me?"

"Help you?" I said. "Isn't over two hundred fifty dollars a help? Isn't the good job you got now and all that money a help to you?"

Joe said, "Anyway, I quit the job and I am going for another."

I told Joe, "Go, and never expect to be taken back anymore!"

Joe went out and I didn't hear of him for three years. I went out of business that year. First it was my good friend Zloty who was trying hard to put me out of business last summer, then the business slowed down. Work was going from bad to worse. People asked for cheaper shoes. I tried to hold the customers and let down on my good shoes, selling them cheaper. Mrs. Zloty approached me and once told me that I had no right to do that. I should keep the same price as always.

I told her I didn't pick a price for them, they should not pick a price for me as to how much I was supposed to sell my shoes for. I said, "The Jewish shoe store owner across the street sells his shoes as he pleases, why don't you go and tell him to raise his price to keep up with us?"

She got mad at me. Then Mr. Zloty came to our store to give me good advice. He said, "Why sell the shoes cheaper? Go to the Priest, give the Priest $25 or so for Christmas and Easter holy days, then the Priest will advertise your store from the pulpit. He will say to people, 'Go to Wasielewski's store to buy shoes,' and when the customers come to buy shoes you can pull in twenty-five or fifty cents more on a pair of shoes that will come back to you."

I was listening, and said, "Yes, to give the Priest on the next holy day! Listen, my friend, why should I grease the pig when he's got plenty of fat on him!" I told Zloty, "Workers are coming to buy shoes from me. They trust me that I don't take money off them and give it to someone else. And if I instead raise twenty-five or fifty cents on their shoes, then will they come back again?"

Mr. Zloty got mad at me. Zloty went to the shoe houses and

told the shoe houses to stop giving me credit. The Fisher, Clifton & Thayer and other shoe houses called him a fool. They sent their agents to find out what's the matter. The agent found things in order and did business with us. Only Endicott & Johnson shoe house took Zloty's advice and didn't come to find things out for themselves. They stopped our credit and sued us for their money. The Endicott & Johnson's two lawyers were fighting hard to get all their three hundred dollars, or something like that, all at once. We didn't have a lawyer. We told the judge we owed them the money and can't pay them all at once because we have to pay the other shoe houses who trust us. We will pay them twenty five dollars a month, or let them take their shoes back. The judge thought it was fair. They didn't want to take the shoes, so we paid them off by twenty five dollars a month, and never ordered any more shoes from Endicott & Johnson.

When we paid them off and their agent found out that we were still in the shoe business, he wanted us to take their shoes to sell again. I just opened the door for him and told him to march out before I take a broom to him. Of course I knew it wasn't his fault. He was only the company's agent and making his bread and butter, but I was mad. Our friend Zloty found out that he can't hurt us through the shoe houses, so he went to Priest Kwiatkowski on Monmouth and Seventh Street and sigged the Priest on us. Priest Kwiatkowski advertised us from the pulpit, telling people not to buy shoes in Wasielewski's store because Wasielewski isn't a Catholic, he is a heretic, and so on and so forth. The Priest said to go to Zloty's store, who is a good Catholic. But people were coming and buying pretty good the winter through and even the next May when the Priest and the Sisters in the school gave the children strict orders that if any boy or girl had shoes bought from Wasielewski's store, that child would not be accepted to their First Communion (a nice Christian teaching)! But of course I had seen plenty of Priests who shouldn't be called a Priest. To me, one Priest reminded me of the ones I met before him, in every town, of the one in Europe and the one when we lived in Maspeth and one from Greenpoint and the one on Green Avenue in Brooklyn where several of us women went to confession. Priest Nowak was arguing with us women to pay five dollars for a book or don't come to Confession. The Priest housekeeper or housewife, whichever you may call her, stood behind the Priest and played five fingers to her nose and stuck her tongue at him and showed donkey ears. That was disgusting. Because I had only two dollars with me, he only gave me one card and told me when my husband came he would have to bring three dollars more. I told him my husband won't come to Confession if he has to pay to confess. He asked me if I go to the church on Green Street.

I told him, "No, I go to church in the same block, St. Ann's Church."

He told me I committed the deadly sin by not going to his church. I told him all churches pray to one God and he said, "Then go there to Confession!"

I did. When a new St. Ann's Polish church on Tonnele and St. Paul's Avenue in Jersey City was built, plenty of Wasielewski's money was put in it. John's brother Joe and Stella, John and I bought a window with our names on it. A new Priest came to the church and brought his own organist and they both had one idea. As they expressed themselves in Stella's store, the more you kick the people the more the people will kiss your foot. Stella told them they had better not try to kick around Tonnele Avenue people because these people kick back. Priest Wrzeciono didn't believe it. He went for money so strong that he said the poorest widow with six children can put two dollars in an envelope for the holy days collection and others can put five and ten dollars in the envelope.

Many people didn't respond to his call, so he said from the pulpit, "Don't put loose money in the collection. It won't be counted even if you put in more than a dollar. Put money only in envelopes." He did this so he will know who and how much they were giving. Many didn't believe or care to have their names known. They just gave what they could, without advertising their names. So the Priest made pamphlets and printed all the people's names that gave envelopes and laid them all over the pews.

He told people to take them home and read them and then he

said, "You will find out how many thieves you have in your church! The ones that didn't give envelopes are thieves!"

I knew John would be a thief because John gave loose change whatever he could. He didn't want his name advertised.

But the Priest made a mistake when he overlooked Stella's envelopes because she said twenty-five dollars went into four envelopes from Joe, Stella, their daughter Nellie and from their smaller children, and not one was on the "good list". A couple more women said their envelopes weren't counted, so the other women and Stella went to the Priest demanding what became of the envelopes they put in. The Priest didn't know how to explain things so he called his housekeeper. The housekeeper started to push the women around, called them names and told them to get out!

The women turned around, grabbed the housekeeper by the hair, and told her, "Oh no you don't, we built that church! You came to live on our hard earned money, calling us names and telling us to get out!"

Priest Wrzeciono found out he couldn't kick the people because they kicked back! So I didn't care how much Priest Kwiatkowski was telling his parishes not to buy shoes from my store because they came and bought and many told me to sue the Priest for trying to ruin my business. They wanted to be witnesses against him and they said they could send their children to Public School if that was the kind of teaching the Catholic Priest and Sisters were giving them. Neither Priest Kwiatkowski nor Zloty put me out of business.

I was doing pretty good until the Holland Tunnel people came, and John's stubbornness itself. Joe Sullivan came to the store one day and asked me if I had any insurance on my stock. I told him no, John didn't believe in having insurance.

"John is not thinking right," said Sullivan. "You go and get insurance on your stock! John didn't want a lease on the store when I offered him!"

I told Sullivan John got stuck on the first lease and he didn't want any more. Joe Sullivan insisted John was not thinking right with his head. "You've got to know how to make a lease, and with who," Sullivan said. "Some company is going to build the Holland Tunnel. They are buying all the houses around here. We will sell ours to them. If you had a lease for all the years you lived here, you would have to get something for your business. I can't give you no lease now because that would be on false pretenses, as we are selling this within a month or two. After they buy it, they may give you three months to move out or may tell you to get out in thirty days as you're only staying from month to month. And when we move out, nobody will care for the house. If maybe a fire starts somewhere and ruins your stock, you'll be the loser!"

God bless Joe Sullivan! I called up the insurance office and got my stock and my furniture insured. I had close to eight thousand dollars' worth of stock in the store.

Epilogue I

After the Fire

As relayed to Granddaughter, Antonia Golonka

Unfortunately, this is where the story stops. There was no more manuscript, and Antonia Wasielewski left off her life story at this point. However, her oldest daughter, Rosalie, relates the following to her daughter, Antonia Golonka:

It was a good thing that mama got insurance on the stock and furniture in the store. There were vagrants and homeless people living in the basement of the building, and while cooking or lighting a fire for whatever reason, the fire and smoke spread upwards through the building. Firemen arriving at the scene pulled shelves and shoes off the walls and put the fire out. Insurance investigation paid for part of the stock, and some of the shoes that were salvaged later were sold at auction. As luck would have it, the insurance policy was to have expired later that week.

Rosalie told that she was probably about eight years old at that time, brother Stanley was ten, brother Frank about six and baby sister Vicky would have been four. Because of the fire, the family went to live with mama's sister, Victoria (Victa) in Pine Island. Aunt

Vicky Blazeski and her husband owned a large onion farm, and the children earned a little money by weeding in the onion patches.

Later mama and pop Wasielewski bought a house on Prescott Street in Jersey City, and from there eventually moved out to the country in Barton, New York, where grandpa died of a long-term foundry lung disease.

EPILOGUE II

A Granddaughter's Remembrance

(by Antonia S. Golonka)

From what I can remember being told as I was growing up, Antonia Wasielewski (my grandmother) and her husband John sold their property in New Jersey around 1945, after the close of World War II and bought a 227-acre farm in Barton, New York, on land contract. Although in New York state, it had apparently been a tobacco farm in years gone by. John was increasingly ill, and they moved with their four children out to the country for a quieter life. There were often times when they struggled to make the monthly payments and came close to losing the property on many occasions. The owner of the property had bought and sold it more than once on land contract, and apparently thought the foreigners would not be able to keep up payments and he would have it to sell again.

Stanley, the oldest son, his wife and family lived downstairs in the large, two-story frame farmhouse, and Rosalie, Antonia, John and me (Antonia, named for my grandmother) now one year old, lived upstairs. My father was a merchant marine and was away at sea most of my younger years, which was probably good, since he was a long-time alcoholic and very abusive.

After a while, Stanley and his family moved out of the farmhouse to a house in the countryside of nearby Waverly, New York. My mother, grandmother, grandfather and now my sister Betty lived in the large farmhouse. My grandfather John died in March 1950 when I was about six years old, from a foundry-related lung disease – probably today it would be called black-lung disease. I believe my mother called it "silicosis". Grandma was a widow for forty years and from what we know, never considered marrying again.

My grandmother was a wonderful influence in my growing years. My mother was not well and life with my father, now home from the merchant marine, was a living nightmare most of the time with too much time on his hands and too little money in his pockets.

Our house had no electricity, running water or indoor plumbing for years, although my father had grandiose ideas about everything. My grandmother, being a simple, hardworking, honest woman, had a hard time with him and his lifestyle of bragging and boasting, with no pot to put it in, and what he did have through marriage, he claimed as his own.

Grandma's son Stanley became an ordained minister and had a little chapel on Talmadge Hill in nearby Waverly. Grandma came to embrace the Protestant beliefs and became a born-again Christian – something that gave her the spirit and power to withstand anything that came her way, whether it was poverty or illness.

I remember Grandma never had much, but she always worked the gardens and helped raise us granddaughters, now numbering three, with the birth of my youngest sister Vicki. My mother had to work in a sewing factory sweatshop (as well as on the farm) to support the family and help keep body and soul together so my father could live in the style he wanted to become accustomed to with his on-again, off-again work ethic. Grandma was the stand-in for mom.

Grandma, from time to time, moved in with one or another of her family – children and grandchildren alike, and helped raise several of her extended family by patiently babysitting in return for her room and board, while the parents worked. A better baby sitter and more dependable and loving one you could not find.

I don't know anyone who didn't have a kind word to say about Grandma. She was a very strong willed woman and a real loving disciplinarian. I recall when we girls were misbehaving, she would warn us, and then tell us what would happen to us if we didn't correct our behavior. As typical children, we usually didn't, and she would discipline us in one of her several unique ways. Because she always wore the old fashioned black "granny" shoes that laced, with the huge, thick heels, she always had a ready weapon. She would take her shoe off and it would come flying our way. Her aim was usually very good, and the thud of shoe against our arm or leg gave us no choice but to shape up. The alternate weapon was one of her rubber galoshes which worked just as well!

Another favorite of Grandma's child-minding techniques was to grab one of us by the hair if we would not pay attention to her. Of course we would try to pull away and holler, "Grandma, ouch, you're pulling my hair!" to which she would respond, "No, I'm not pulling, you're pulling, I'm just holding! Hold still and it won't hurt!"

Just thinking about it brings a smile to my face! She was so wise to us! There were times when we thought we outsmarted her. She would tell us to do something, and disobedient as we often were, we would be about to feel her wrath and we would run quickly and go outside thinking she would get over it when we returned. She would shake her fist from the door and say,

"Honey, I'm not going to run after you! You'll come home!"

We would play outside as children do, and the time would go by and we would forget all about Grandma's unfinished business and head back indoors. No sooner would we be inside the door but a hand would reach out and grab us as that voice said, "I told you I'm not going to run after you! You'll come home! And now you're going to get what I was going to give you before you ran out!" And we would get the well-deserved punishment – usually an overshoe or rubber smacking us on the behind a few well-placed times.

But Grandma as I remember, was always loving, even in her discipline, and fair. She didn't seem to get angry, and her eyes would look at you out of their slanted corners while her head was down, watching her crocheting stitches, when you were bad. One of her favorite admonitions was, "I love you honey, but you gotta listen!" I heard that so many times it reverberated in my sleep.

And Grandma had a voice that was strong and powerful. The kind of lungs that could call cattle in from the fields. She could have been an opera singer with those lungs and would sing all day long, morning and night. Many times, we had to interrupt her to talk to her. If we strayed from the yard we would hear her from what seemed miles away, calling "TONIA! BETUKNA! VIKCHA!" and we knew it was no use to try to say we didn't hear her.

Although she did not respect father, she tried to respect his orders and I believe it was mostly to protect us from the repercussions of any disobedience.

Grandma told us many stories about growing up in Europe. Life was unbearably hard as she describes going out in the snow to tend sheep with feet wrapped in rags because she didn't have boots. How she escaped frozen feet and gangrene from the wet frozen rags is a mercy of God. As I have typed this manuscript these stories have come back to me like reruns of horror movies seen years ago. Her young life was hard, and she seemed to know that ours was not easy either, with the father we had, our mother not well for what seemed like years, and our meager existence on the farm with no modern or social amenities. There was also lots of hard work put upon us by our father which Grandma tried to sneak in and help with so we would be spared the beating that would have surely resulted in any shirking of responsibilities he ordered. But Grandma tried to give us hope for the future and a sound work ethic and strong religious upbringing.

I recall she was a woman of disciplined routine. Up before the crack of dawn, she would be on her knees beside her bed saying her morning prayers. Next she would find her quiet time reading her Bible. By this time it was almost sunrise and she would do her exercises, wash, dress and have her small breakfast of pumpernickel bread and hot tea with honey, or whatever she could find to get her started. Usually grandma was the cook while my mother was working, and grandma would have dinner made and simmering on the side of the old Andes coal and wood stove by ten o'clock in the morning, where it would stay simmering until supper time. The Board of Health would have cringed that it sat out all day, but I don't recall it ever harming us a bit.

Wash day was a certain day, Monday, I think. She would have the laundry washed and hanging out on the lines in the yard before 10:00 am, and tell us stories about the contests Polish housewives would have to see whose laundry was flapping in the breeze first. Laundry back then did not get tossed into a mechanical washer with a roller wringer. It was all hand washed, and wrung out by stooping housewives of any age. Mopping the floors was another scheduled task – Friday, just before the weekend. In between the house and the garden and whatever else needed doing was done, methodically and in disciplined order, just like the rest of grandma's life. I don't think the word procrastination was invented yet. At least my grandmother had never heard of it. As soon as something needed to be done, you did it. You did not put it off until later, you did it now! If my mother mentioned that she was going to make an apple pie, the next day my grandmother would have the apples peeled in the morning, sitting in water and lemon juice, waiting for mother to come home from work to make the pie. When she was awake, Grandma just had a motion about her – a kind of inertia. She moved all the time. Not very quickly, but constantly. And she could get things done. When she wasn't working she was praying or crocheting or rocking or walking or just swaying from side to side. Grandma was perpetual motion.

It was funny to read that she felt she was tall for her age. Grandma was never tall. She measured maybe about five feet two inches, and for most of my childhood remembrance was about one hundred sixty-five pounds. A nice plump granny, not the '90's kind that wear size ten with bleached blonde hair who ride bicycles for exercise. She was plump and wore a stiff corset to hold it all in. She told me many times that once she was very fat and weighed two hundred twenty or thirty pounds. I recall because as a child I thought it was so horrible to imagine her that big. She said that was when she lived in Jersey City. She couldn't walk a block without losing her breath.

She was so miserable and finally got herself to a doctor who was way before his time. He told her for one whole year he wanted her to eat no meat, drink no milk, no cheese, no coffee, no sugar, and limit breads to one slice. She was to eat just vegetables and fruits and eat them raw whenever she could. She said in that year she lost down from two hundred twenty or thirty pounds to one hundred sixty five and stayed on that plan and stayed at that weight the rest of her life.

I remember watching grandma dress in the morning when I would come lay on her bed. It was strange that she didn't care that I observed, but even though she was usually keenly modest, this was the exception. She had so many things to put on while dressing! She had ulcerated sores on the sides of her ankles for many years from poor circulation and damage from veins, no doubt. She had to dress her ankles with salve and put gauze and bandages around them. Then she wrapped the dressings with the stretchy Ace bandages, around and around her legs from the ankles up to the knees. On top of the Ace bandages went the cotton stockings. Very utilitarian heavy duty and very practical. Then she put on her brassiere (not a bra - you couldn't call what grandma wore a bra, it was a full-force brassiere). Then she put on her corset which kind of connected to the brassiere and held it all together. I think it also assisted in giving her the ramrod-rigid posture she was so well known for! A torture chamber of stays and bones and loops and hooks and strings to twist this way and that way and tie it all up. Next she would pull on big baggy bloomers over that corset, and top it all off with a full-length cotton slip before putting on a house dress. I only saw grandma in pants once in my life, and they were what women today would call a split skirt, long, down to her ankles. Grandma didn't wear pants, grandpas wore pants. Her shoes, as I have mentioned, were the old fashioned, generic, black, lace up type with sturdy, chunky heels. She wore these all the time, except when she first got out of bed, and then she wore slippers. Grandma didn't walk bare foot in the house or anywhere else.

Her hair was very long, very thin and dark black with silver threads throughout. She parted the hair down the middle and crisscrossed it around in back and then brought it up on top of her head and twisted tortoise-looking combs in it before topping it off with a spider-web kind of hair net to keep it in place. Until she was very old, grandma's hair was quite black. It never turned the snowy white that so many other grandmas did, it grayed to a silvery salt and pepper for as long as I recall.

And grandma was naturally double-jointed. She amazed me because she could do a complete split sitting on the floor, and I always envied her and felt so clumsy because I never could, even as a young child. It comes back to memory the day someone challenged her, and down she went on the floor to demonstrate. She was an elderly lady even at that time, but still was amazingly supple. In the garden while weeding or picking vegetables she never bent her knees. She would stand and bend from the hips, keeping her knees straight, and work in that position for the longest time. When she stood, she stood tall and very erect – the credit to her corset, I am sure.

But she always chided us children if we slouched. "Stand straight, honey, are you ashamed of your name?" she would challenge as she slapped us up on the back. She didn't want no slouchers for grandchildren, and we were made aware of that all too often. Come to think of it, she also wanted us to be flexible as she would bid us, "Bend down, sister!" when we were looking for something, but not really getting into it. Her idea seemed to be, if you were standing, stand straight and tall, and if you were bending, for goodness sake, BEND!

All the illnesses grandma had through the years didn't kill her. At one point my mother told me grandma had strangulated intestines. Apparently that meant from being so heavy at one time and having the extra fat around her stomach, her intestines somehow became infected and twisted and she nearly died from gangrene poisoning her system. Somehow God in His mercy saved her from even that misery in the mid-1900s. Later in life she had breast cancer, with a radical mastectomy and radiation and the whole routine on one breast. I remember as a 20-something driving her to the hospital for the radiation treatments a couple times a week for several weeks. She never complained. But she survived. She always survived. There was nothing that got in the way of grandma making the most of her life. She had nothing to begin with and existed on next to nothing, but as she always told us, she had everything. She had her God, a place to sleep, food to eat, a warm place to stay, and friends and family. She was happy, and she was the original Pollyanna! She was glad for everything, and she made us understand that was what life was all about – being happy with what you have – not what you lack. Certainly a lost art now-a-days in this time of plenty.

And grandma was the staunch supporter when we were afraid. Her bedroom was off-limits for my father. It was written right into the land contract agreement that my mother had with grandma when they agreed mom would buy the property from her. She had "life-rights" to her bedroom for as long as she wanted to be there, and my father couldn't kick her out – couldn't even argue the point, although I do remember there were times it seemed like he was sure trying to. Grandma's room was a safe haven. When dad would come home roaring drunk and looking for someone to vent his fury on, we three girls (but especially we two older ones) I and my younger sister Betty, would sneak into grandma's room and whisper to her if we could stay there. She knew what we were afraid of – father. She would put her finger up to her mouth and say,

"Shhhhh! Quiet, get into bed and lay still." We would curl up and just lay there under the feather comforter, listening to the commotion in the rest of the house as father caused as much trouble as he could with mom.

Grandma didn't think much of alcohol and tobacco and we learned early that they were both tools of the devil. Tobacco was to be shunned at all costs and alcohol was to be used medicinally for purposes that needed that sort of thing. I can still see her reaching into her old stand-alone tall clothes wardrobe for the bottle of whiskey she kept for years, and putting a couple tablespoons into hot tea for us when we had cramps or a bad chest cold. She didn't think it should be used for fun and foolishness like my father used it, but it did have a purpose. She also made us understand that father was not to be made aware that she kept the whiskey in her closet or he would finish it off and there would be trouble.

Summers grandma worked hard all day in the gardens. We often had as many as four. One would be just for growing potatoes and one for strawberries and asparagus. Then there was an all-purpose vegetable garden, and the fourth would have sugar beets for our pigs, and there was always room for my mother's gladiolus. Grandma loved working in the garden, or at least I always thought she did. She would work for hours and wipe the sweat off her face with her white hanky that she kept tucked between her bosoms. Then she would drink water from a Mason canning jar and go back working again. In the winter she was shoveling snow and bringing in wood for the stoves and I can still see her chopping a few pieces when there was need. We changed to coal for convenience sake, but when money ran out, it was back to wood.

Being the oldest, I helped with the canning and food preparation during summer vacation, and sometimes really resented it. I was a pre-teen and tended to be a bit sassy when this resentment reared its ugly head. My tongue got the best of me when I was helping grandma put fruit in jars preparing for the pressure cooker one hot summer day. I don't recall what I said, but my smart mouth was all grandma needed to decide that she had to put a stop to this disobedience and disrespect before it became a life of its own. She demanded to know what I said, and I repeated it. Grandma reached down so quickly I didn't realize what was happening. She grabbed me, pushed me face down on the kitchen floor, then put her knee on my back and whaled my bottom for me! Later when mom came home, she relayed the incident to mom. Mother was horrified and insisted that I get down on my knees and apologize to grandma and never forget that she was standing in for mother and must be obeyed. I learned a very humiliating but necessary lesson I will never forget!

Unfortunately, my father was not the planner my grandmother was. He would waste his summers sleeping on the couch in the living room during the hot days and carousing around at night. When winter came and there was no wood to keep the house warm he would be forced to cut wood outside in the snow and make us girls go out in the cold with our sleds to haul it back in so we wouldn't freeze. The fire often went out in the house during the winter and the memories of those times still leave me cold, in more ways than one. Grandma didn't like that at all – said Steve was lazy and good for nothing. He should have had all that done in the summer and been able to have all the family stay inside. She said if he wanted to sleep, he should sleep in the winter, but no, he did it the lazy man's way. She was right, but there was no reasoning with my father. He was the man of the house and he was boss.

Grandma didn't think a lot of men in general, what with her father running out on her mother when her mother was sick, and leaving the children at the worst possible time. And her husband John didn't turn out to be what she thought a man really should be, and her daughters' husbands were certainly not the best examples she could give. She often warned us girls about men and told us what to watch out for. Far better we should give ourselves to God and let him pick out the man for us if He should feel we needed one. She demonstrated that fact over and over by examples of men in the family who were no good and how much suffering they caused the women and children. Better they should be alone than to put up with that, and besides, men only wanted a woman for "one thing" she advised. It was years later when I understood the "one thing", but it was well known that grandma was not pleased with the institution of marriage the way she observed it in reality.

For years grandma sang in Uncle Stan's church choir. Her powerful voice booming above the rest. Sometimes you could hear her falling a half beat behind, but the rest of the choir lovingly put up with the church matriarch for many decades until finally the church choir director, my uncle's wife, and grandma's daughter-in-law gently retired her. She had just gotten to the place where she couldn't hear and couldn't keep up with the rest. Grandma took it graciously, but somehow I felt if given her way she would still be there, ancient, but voice booming above the rest, making a "joyful noise" Sunday after Sunday, until the Lord carried her home to Glory.

Grandma loved riding in a car. She never could learn how to drive one – nor a farm tractor, for that matter – on a level field. Mom told me when we were just little children, she tried to get grandma to help her with the haying by having grandma sit on the tractor and just let it roll down the hay field and slightly turn the steering wheel every once in a while so the rest of us could gather the hay with the pitch forks and toss it up on the wagon. Grandma was eager to help, but had no sense of direction. She turned the tractor wheel the wrong way and headed toward the creek, but couldn't figure out how to correct the steering. This, mind you, was on a huge, flat eleven acre field that you couldn't go wrong allowing a ten year old to drive in. She tried, but to no avail. She ended up raking the hay together with the rest of us so we didn't lose both her and the tractor.

But that didn't stop grandma from loving to ride and travel. Any time a relative needed someone to mind the children while they were in a store buying groceries or shopping for whatever, they would call grandma and ask if she wanted to go for a ride. She would be ready and waiting hours before the appointed time. She didn't mind sitting in the car with the children, teaching them how to get along as she watched the people go by in the world outside the car.

Grandma was so stubborn, but usually in a good way. I remember when she was in her eighties, living with her son Stanley, the pastor of the chapel. She heard that the church goers, mostly family members, were planning to build or extend into the shrubbery area around the church, so when her son and family were not around, she took it upon herself to "help". She got an axe and hatchet and began to hack down bushes and weed trees. When her son and family returned they were so concerned that at her advanced age she would have a heart attack, or that even neighbors driving by would think they put the old lady out to work for her room and board. This was very amusing to the rest of us, but not to the son and family she was currently living with. We knew grandma, and we knew that was grandma!

After my younger sister Betty and I married and left home, my father, who bedeviled the family for about twenty-three years, decided to return to the merchant marine as he had always threatened, and left my mother and youngest sister, Vicki. About this time he had been running his own barber shop in Owego, New York and had conscripted my mother as his partner – in work only, not in pay. When he left, it devastated her. She had just gone through treatment for breast cancer and a radical mastectomy and had managed to pull herself back to work at the barber shop. Now he wanted his old life back. He had finagled most everything he wanted for the farm by whining how he had to have a bigger tractor, bigger this and more powerful that, in order to keep up with the farm work. She sold off pieces of the two hundred twenty seven acre property to keep him supplied with bigger and better, and now that all but the last twenty some acres were left, he also left to resume his life with his dreams upon the open seas.

Mother was in her mid-fifties at this time, and totally lost. She too had dreams, but they were unfulfilled, always put on hold to satisfy her husband's wants and needs. Grandma was living at the farm and agreed that mom should go back to her first pre-marriage love – nursing. She enrolled in nursing school at Jersey City Medical Center, sold the bulk of the remaining property to one of her brother Stanley's sons and left grandma in Barton.

The grandson moved into the old farmhouse with his family and grandma lived with them for a while and then moved back on the hill with her son Stanley. She was near the church she loved and was able to help out wherever there was a need, cleaning the church or peeling potatoes, grandma was a worker.

Grandma did well for years. Mom worked at Jersey City Medical Center ten years, and when she returned to the Barton area, grandma was beginning to be more than her son and daughter-in-law could manage along with her daughter-in-law's elderly disabled brother. Grandma was relocated to a "self-care" assisted facility, and a few years later to the Tioga Nursing Home. She needed constant supervision and couldn't be left alone for fear of her falling or other misfortunes.

In the nursing home, mom visited grandma daily, bringing her needed items, taking her clothes home to launder and assisting with daily needs and personal care. Mom didn't feel that the staff had the time to devote to the residents, and since she was a retired nurse, she knew what was needed. Some days grandma recognized her daughter and some days she was very confused and didn't know what was going on. She could be found sitting in her chair, hands clasped, crying and looking out the window, praying, "Why can't I go? I don't want to live anymore. I want to see my Jesus, please let me go."

Grandma had an aneurism in her stomach, and it comes to mind that may have been what happened one day when she began bleeding internally. My mother who was the closest to her during her life was not ready for grandma to go. She couldn't bear the thought, and she told the doctors to give grandma blood. My youngest sister who was a nurse tried to dissuade the blood because grandma was close to 100 at that time and dementia had taken over her thoughts. But mom insisted, and four units of blood were given before my youngest sister convinced mom that it was unnecessary suffering, and mom was keeping grandma here for herself, not for grandma, and it was not a kindness in her suffering. Mom finally relented, and the blood transfusions were stopped. Unbelievably, grandma stopped bleeding and lived a while longer. Her persistent plea was resumed, and her prayer was to leave this world and go home to be with her Jesus.

March 18, 1990, grandma finally went to Paradise to be with her Lord. She left behind four children, twelve grandchildren, twenty-nine great-grandchildren and sixteen great-great-grandchildren. Her son Joe, whom she raised as an unofficial adopted child died in the 60's. Her two sisters lived to their mid-nineties and predeceased her. She was herself amazed to live to such an advanced age. She often remarked that she didn't know why God kept her so long. She slipped from this world to the next, leaving her "misery" that she said always followed her through her life to go to a far better place. But for all the misery she endured, she learned to compensate with humor, hard work, discipline, positive thinking, everlasting optimism and a steadfast faith in God.

Antonia Wasielewski, my namesake, grandma, left us and the world a better place. I only pray that as I grow older, her wisdom and clever quotes from the Bible at just the right moment would follow me the rest of my life. She taught me when I wouldn't listen, and she taught me when I pretended not to hear, but her persistent example and faith in God were her armor and sword in her lifetime. From the ravages of her country, Poland, in the early 1900s as the Russians were taking over the country, to America, her beloved new home when she was 15 years old. Through sorrows, hard work and tribulations, she painstakingly lived all her life. She was a feisty, yet loving example of what a Christ-follower should be. Grandma endured, From Pain to Paradise, May 1886 – March 1990. She was two months shy of 104 years old.

ABOUT THE AUTHOR:

Not sure how to write an "About the Author", for *"From Pain to Paradise – My Life"*, since Antonia S. Golonka did not author the book, her Polish immigrant grandmother did. And after grandma's demise, and the assistance of grandma's daughter, Rosalie Golonka, the broken English of the once unreadable story was translated into an actual manuscript. This is where granddaughter Antonia emerged into the picture. To spare you the duplicate explanation, and further unnecessary typing, please flip to the *"Acknowledgement"* at the beginning of this book for more details.

Having begun awkwardly, we continue awkwardly, to state Editor/Author Antonia S. Golonka, was born in Jersey City, New Jersey, March 9, 1944, moved to Barton, New York before the age of two and lived in the country during her growing years. She chose "Toni", for a nickname in grade school. In the small, hick rural area she called home, high school farm boys often wore manure-clad work boots to school. There the girls were named Mary, Alice, Linda, Carol, but no "Antonia". The child of European immigrants, she knew well she didn't fit in, and the nickname "Toni", was a downpayment for acceptance in the predominately country area where she lived.

Throughout school Toni wanted to excel in something that expressed herself, to show she accomplished something not expected of an immigrant's child. After dabbling in music, it took on the form of writing poetry and short stories by her middle teens, although secretly at first. But they were filed away for "later". Creativity also bloomed into creations in fabric as she designed and sewed originals for herself while still in high school. This was a double blessing since her family was without the necessary means to purchase ready-made outfits to wear as the other girls wore.

Fast forward 50-60 years and after several full-time jobs in the administrative/secretarial field and church life, her creative side was dusted off. Now in retirement, the moth-eaten imaginations of a fertile mind found themselves necessary to the survival of the immigrant's offspring. The grandmother who instilled the love and faith in her life also taught not to waste the blessings God gives us, including talents and abilities. The mom who demonstrated the same teachings by beginning a new career as a nurse in her mid-50s, encouraged God-given talents and abilities. Now never too late, as a legacy to both, the book unfolds, to reveal grandma's miseries from hard European life to America, and provides the core of the oft-revised and edited new foundling book, *From Pain to Paradise – My Life*.

Printed in the United States
by Baker & Taylor Publisher Services